CW00660563

JOHN STEPHEN

JOHN STEPHEN
The King of Carnaby Street

JEREMY REED

HAUS PUBLISHING
LONDON

Copyright © Jeremy Reed 2010

First published in Great Britain in 2010 by
Haus Publishing, 70 Cadogan Place, London SW1X 9AH
www.hauspublishing.com

The moral rights of the author have been asserted

A CIP catalogue record for this book is available from the British Library

ISBN 978-1-906598-31-0

Typeset in Garamond by MacGuru Ltd
info@macguru.org.uk

Printed in England by CPI William Clowes, Beccles NR34 7TL

Illustrations courtesy of Bill Franks and the John Stephen Collection at the Victoria
& Albert Museum. Mike McGrath and Topham Picturepoint.

CONTENTS

For Bill Franks, whose time, generosity and inexhaustible memories of Carnaby Street made this book possible. And to the memory of his lifetime partner John Stephen, who created the entire sixties look.

1

TALKING ABOUT MY GENERATION

When the eighteen-year old John Stephen got off the Glasgow train at Euston in 1952, and stood for a time adjusting to the segueing congestion of passengers arriving and departing from the station's main concourse, he had £13 in a burgundy leather wallet and nowhere to go. His outstanding good looks, thin, 5ft 7in, dark hair raked back into the permanently deconstructed quiff made popular by newly acclaimed and sensationally cool youth icons like James Dean, Tony Curtis and Elvis Presley, foggy blue eyes and a refined facial aesthetic pointing to acute sensitivity, were a distinct bonus given that John Stephen had arrived in London with the singular purpose of transforming the way men looked through designs he was already sketching in notebooks and on the backs of envelopes.

Intensely vulnerable, shy, gay at a time when his sexuality was criminalised, and already given to hints of the bipolar disorder that was to become a dominant feature in his life, the young John Stephen, dressed in a grey flannel suit, white shirt and skinny dark silk tie, as the prescient look, arrived in a London still flattened to a residually grey plateau by post-war austerity, and enveloped in its own microclimate of carbon polluting smog. In fact, the entire city reeked of carbon emissions, a toxic in-your-face soup through which cars and taxis with their headlights on at noon nosed along the Euston Road towards King's Cross and the ubiquitously energised City's square mile. Cars with the names of Austin A35, Ford Anglia, Hillman Minx, Sunbeam Talbot, Wolseley 4–44, Standard Vanguard, or a flash two-tone Bentley R-Type, or Jowett-Jupiter, mostly spray-painted black, maroon, bottle-green or navy blue, featured strongly in Stephen's repertoire of obsessions, the various models serving as templates for the ambitious cars he would come to own in the 1960s, including his trademark Silver Cloud Rolls Royce and a showy chrome-plated, plum-coloured Cadillac, the car he habitually parked outside His Clothes in his self-created fashion emporium – Carnaby Street.

Life had been hard for the youth standing on the edgy concourse, alone in the anonymous crowds, driven by the ambition to realise his creative vision through imaginative flair and unremittingly hard work. Born on 28 August, 1934, at 19 Cromdale Street, Govan, Glasgow, one of nine children, his father Frank Henderson Stephen ran a corner shop in Copland Street, near the foggy industrially-littered dock area of the Clyde, called The Handy Store, open fifteen hours a day, for what was a subsistence level of income, with most customers buying their small utilitarian purchases on credit. John's repressive, deeply conservative, but supportive father, who was widowed with two children, Frank and Margaret, had remarried on 6 April 1928, and through his second wife, Emily Mulholland Marshall, given issue to seven additional children, Emily, Jean, Ina, John, Tommy, Alex and Rae. In his formative years, dominated by the ethos of gossip and the communal dialogue of neighbourhood customers in the family shop, John had bonded most closely with his younger brother Tommy; but there was a dodgy aberrant underside to their relationship, and it centred round an older man called Georgie, also a tenant, who rented a room in the back of their house. Georgie, a retired toilet attendant, was unnaturally devoted to Tommy, and would take him out each day as a child, with John's mother insisting he accompany them. According to John's youngest sister Rae, Georgie who adulated Tommy to the point of taking him to school each day, and returning during breaks with a vacuum flask and sandwiches, treated John on the contrary with deliberate perversity, only allowing Tommy to share the secrets of the legendary treasure box he kept in his room, and acting mean with John, as the intruder on the private world he shared with his brother. Tommy quickly grew to be embarrassed amongst his schoolmates by Georgie's evident infatuation, but more than that, Georgie who had been a public toilet attendant insisted on regularly taking Tommy and John on a lugubrious itinerary of the Glasgow toilets to meet ex-colleagues who worked in them, where they would have tea in the disinfectant-reeking lowlight of the attendant's office.

Innocent or not, the practice of being in toilets that were at the time principal meeting places for cottaging gays, left an indelible mark on the impressionable young John Stephen, and may have contributed in part as a latent psychological marker to his inveterate same-sex attractions. Although

John's mother, whose recurrent breakdowns punctuated his youth as an osmotic pointer to the repeated manic episodes he would experience as an adult, endorsed these outings, John's relationship to Georgie remains unclear, and formed part of the underside to his psyche, about which he was always reluctant to speak, preferring to consolidate his energies in action and unremittingly hard work. John was also made to feel guilty by his parents for his sister Rae's predisposition to bronchitis each winter, his culpability resting in the fact that he had taken Rae out in her pram for a walk one soupy November afternoon, with polluted fog smoking in from the Clyde, and not returned with her until after dark. When Rae quickly developed a serious bronchial condition, the irregular incident was quickly isolated by their parents as the motivating cause, and continually reframed with John as the irremediable culprit who had triggered her yearly recurring and intensely debilitating illness. Rae also remembers the prankster aspect of John's personality, and how as an adolescent he would engage in domestic tricks like removing the light fitting covers, so his unsuspecting brothers or sisters would get a zingy electric shock when feeling for the switch.

John Stephen, like most boys of his Glaswegian generation, had left off his education at the age of fifteen, terminating his time at Bellahouston Academy, and briefly working as an engineering draughtsman, before taking routine employment as a menswear sales assistant at the Glasgow Co-operative department store. It was while working there that he became acutely aware of the limitations of men's fashion, both in the restricted palette of colours available, and of the formlessness of the largely unstructured jackets and voluminously roomy trousers men wore as part of their unquestioning resolve to look inconspicuous at all times. People who are thin tend to think thin, and one of Stephen's earliest perceptions on the retail floor was to note the shapelessness of men's clothes, the lack of fine detail in their cut, and the absence of sex appeal in their lack of body contour.

On his immediate arrival in London on a smogged-out, burnt orange September day, and before taking a cheap room in Camden Town's rundown Parkway, Stephen made a round of the more fashionable menswear windows in the West End, testing his template of thin against the excess of material used in standard men's designs. A decade later, in a *Sunday Times* interview, he commented modestly on his earliest perceptions, and how 'it seemed to me that too much material was being used in most men's clothes. Trousers had so much room in the seat that they were quite shapeless. Shirt manufacturers had no idea about tapering to the waist, and swimwear lacked any style.'

Having secured accommodation in a room he rented for £3 a week, John

Stephen took a job at Moss Bros in Covent Garden, learning to cut in the military department, as well as gaining experience as a salesman on the floor. He was paid £6 a week, a sum that had to accommodate rent, food, bus fares and a chain-smoking habit that consumed two packs of Woodbines or Players cigarettes a day. The nervous compulsion to feed his intensity with nicotine hits had begun as a teenager with cigarettes procured from his father's shop, and was to graduate later to an equal dependency on cigars, something that in his case was to lead putatively to recurrent cancer of the neck.

Living now in the capital that was soon to become the explosive epicentre of a youth culture revolution, the young John Stephen found himself in the formal environment of Moss Bros, 27–29 King Street, Covent Garden, a store founded in 1851 by Moses Moses, and a place synonymous with quality suit hire for evening wear, as well as selling a range of suits, shirts and jackets, and employing staff able to advise on sartorial matters and questions of etiquette. It was a store little concerned with invention, but rather founded on the very principles of correctness that the young John Stephen was conspiring to blow apart. But even at conservative Moss Bros, during the time of John Stephen's employment, a quiet revolution was happening, its subtle intimations largely wasted on the otiose clothes establishment. According to one of the prototypically inventive Mods, Paul Stagg, 'Upstairs in Moss Bros there was a room where you could buy second-hand overcoats. Great big double-breasted overcoats and we would get them to take the shoulder pads out, so that they had this natural Italian shoulder, which was a softer look, rather than that English look. Take the shoulder pads out and shorten the sleeves and you would have the look as best you could.'

While Moss Bros provided John Stephen with the basics in training, this was also a period of increasing resentment and frustration in his life, and twice brought before the manager for being late, Stephen had to explain that his salary didn't adequately provide for both cigarettes and bus fare, and that some days he was forced to walk to work, so that he could buy cigarettes. His salary was raised to £7 a week on account of his assiduous sales acumen, but he understandably felt constrained and inhibited by the formal wear on sale, and the complete absence of modern clothes for a youth beginning to revolt against the reticent styles of the older generation. As the archetypal rebel with an inexhaustible creative vision, John Stephen had started to sniff the undercurrents of the cataclysmic social upheaval triggered by youth that would accelerate with unstoppable momentum as the decade progressed. That he was to be the leading proponent in shaping a new expression of masculinity through his flamboyant and often outrageous designs was already

John Stephen, the youngest owner of a Rolls in Britain in 1962, loved flash cars as an extension of style. He got this Silver Cloud before the Beatles had theirs.

intrinsically apparent to Stephen, as he bussed his way through the turbulent, traffic-segueing West End each morning, looking for signs in the crowd, en route to still another routinely un-stimulating working day in the shag-piled, sniffy and unapologetically formal environs of Moss Bros.

But change was in the air, no matter how tentative, rather like a carjacker nicking the cellulose gloss of a polished wing before slashing it; and the change was indomitably fuelled by youth and the emergence in the 1950s of the Teddy boy as the direct offshoot of rock 'n' roll. Teddy boys represented the first face of a distinctly subversive British youth culture in revolt against the inherited values of social convention. Teds meant business and hung out in gangs on street corners, initially in London's East End, and carried coshes, bicycle chains, razors and flick-knives in the pockets of their long Edwardian jackets. Their energies were fired-up by rock music, dance halls, American movies, urban vandalism and random outbreaks of racial tension. But more than anything, they were distinguished by their clothes. Teds dressed to shock, and in doing so parodied their essentially working class origins by wearing an Edwardian style drape jacket with velvet trim, a high-necked loose 'Mr B' collar on a white shirt, a bootlace tie known as a Slim Jim, skinny drainpipe trousers and suede Gibson shoes with thick crepe soles. Their hair was blown back into a gelled cliffhanger quiff influenced by the likes of Gene Vincent, Marlon Brando and Elvis Presley, and given names like 'the bop,' 'the tevee,' 'the panama,' or 'the back sweep and crest.' Teddy boys tended to drink hard, and like their successors the Mods were intensely narcissistic, constantly checking their appearance and restructuring their hair with a steel comb. Unlike Mods, they were essentially homophobic, engaged in serious gang rivalry and were antagonistically racist, their gangs largely targeting the West Indian population of immigrants who had come to Britain in the early fifties and settled initially in the Notting Hill Gate area of London. Teddy boys as the unrefined template of the Mods were nonetheless sufficiently conspicuous as to make both a consumerist statement and to attract sensational media attention for their highly distinctive fashion, and for acts of marauding violence that included murdering a youth on Clapham Common in 1954, and trashing a West End cinema at the premiere of the Bill Haley film *Rock Around The Clock*. Noting the insurgent youth culture, and its collective temerity, *The Annual Saturday Book*, as a register of the times, recorded in 1956 the view that 'London's now nothing but flash coffee bars, with teddies and little bits of girls in jeans.'

For John Stephen, working on the sedate green-carpeted floor at Moss Bros, the Teddy boys were an affirmation that youth, or at least a disaffected splinter-group, were looking to separate themselves from received notions of convention, not only through anti-social behaviour, but through a clearly identifiable dress code. Teddy boys were the indirect beginning of a liberated youth that used clothes as a means of identifying with pop icons, in the very way that John Stephen was to instigate the perfect symbiotic union of the two in the explosively pop-orientated 1960s. Their emphasis too was on the male as the fashion leader, with Teddy girls, who elected to wear toreador pants and circle skirts, low cut tops and spike heels, relegated to the background. But for the first time amongst emergent youth social unrest was linked to a chain of dominants, namely, clothes, music, attitude, gangs, drugs, alcohol and motorbikes. One of the advantages of the drape coat was its abundance of pockets in which bottles and weapons could be concealed, and that made of good quality wool it kept the wearer warm when hanging out on disreputable low-lit street corners in London's Shepherd's Bush or Ladbroke Grove.

But gay men most usually have a fashion radar that their straight counterparts lack, and John Stephen like other young men in his buried subculture of criminalised friends had through his connections received news of a groundbreaking boutique with an overtly gay slant that had opened at 5 Newburgh Street, off Foubert's Place in Soho, with the promising name of Vince, or more specifically Vince Man's Shop.

Arguably London's first male boutique, Vince was established by Bill Green, a physique photographer with a tiny studio in Manchester Street, Marylebone, who specialised in photographing anabolic steroid musclemen or beefcake. Vince was situated in an alley called Newburgh Street, and given its owner's propensities, conveniently only minutes away from the notorious Marshall Street Public Baths, a popular cruising area in the 1950s for gay men who worked out. Soho's reputation as the epicentre of gay life in London rested not only on its centres of male prostitution, the infamous, polarispeaking meat rack at Piccadilly Circus, and pick-up zones like Leicester Square, but also on recognised gay establishments like the Golden Lion in Dean Street, The Mousetrap in Swallow Street and the Black Cat in Old Compton Street. Beginning his career as a photographer who shot models wearing provocative bikini-style posing briefs, Green in the absence of readily available garments had begun to have his own line of provocatively minimal briefs made up, and through the popularity of his magazine photographs to issue mail order catalogues of his unmistakably homoerotic designs. Vince briefs and swimwear were sold by mail order through small advertisements in magazines like *Weekend* or *Titbits*, or retailed at Geo Grosse, the big motorcycle dealers and sports shop in the Marylebone Road. And in the effort to expand beyond the exclusive gay niche he had established in Soho, and understandably found limiting, Green ensured his clothes were seen outside London, and stocked in shops like Bobby's in Bournemouth, and at Filk'n Casuals in Brighton. John Stephen had naturally heard of Vince through the gay network, and was quick to window-shop there, recognising in the garments on display the sort of colours, fabrics and styles he had intended all along to introduce into his own eventual line of men's fashion. Bill Green's lead had come from holidays taken in Italy and France, where he had noticed 'the younger people were wearing black jeans and black shirts and I thought this hadn't been seen in Britain, everyone was so busy wearing blue jeans imported from America. So I got black jeans and black shirts and similar things made in this country, and they went like a bomb in those days. And I started designing stuff myself. People said the clothes were so outrageous that they would only appeal and sell to the eccentric Chelsea set or theatrical way-out types.'

Green's success lay in part in realising that his essentially gay clientele required tight-fitting clothes that gave erotic contour to the erogenous zones. Italian trousers, in the hands of the likes of Bill Green, underwent three distinctive alterations to imitate the close fit of blue jeans: pleats were removed, horizontal pockets were introduced and cuffs largely vanished. An early client, Peter Burton, who recalled the beginnings of Carnaby Street in his book *Parallel Lives*, and who ran the pioneer gay club Le Duce in D'Arblay Street, at the apogee of Mod culture in the mid-sixties, recalls, 'because Beryl's {Vince's} you remember, was the shop where you got the chino, and it was the whole look that was in part to do with the American military. You know, chino being American soldier's wear.' Green chose unusual fabrics like velvet, silk and bed-ticking for hipster trousers and was the first to introduce pre-faded denims into the repertoire of men's fashion. The shop's window display promoted snug cire briefs and shocking pink hipsters, at a time when pink for men was strictly synonymous with gay taste, while the rails inside were flush with white polo-neck jumpers, Italian-style knitwear and colourful matelot tops, as well as a range of hipsters specially manufactured for Green, with the flagrantly scandalous tailoring detail of a minimal five-inch rise from the crotch to the waist. A contemporary shopper at the time observed, of an arrival at Vince Man's Shop, 'The only other person we saw was a tall, well-dressed young Negro who bought a pair of the coloured denim hipster trousers. The Negro was obviously homosexual and I realized that homosexuals had been buying that stuff for years. They were the only people with the nerve to wear it ...'

Green's small colourful shop, run with temerity and flair (resident neigh-bours would actually lodge complaints about his risqué window displays), soon became a buzz word to men in search of liberating individual clothes. Green's flamboyant stock and originality were the modernist spearhead at a time when only Jons in Soho, and the over-fussy Dale Cavana in Belgravia, offered any sort of alternative wear for attention-seeking men. According to the antiques dealer and inveterate fashionista Christopher Gibbs, 'Vince's was faggy, theatrical, cock-a-snook at the folks who went there. There were always enough of them to keep the show on the road. Dale Cavana was more Noel Coward, fancy bits of tailoring for people who wanted to startle the evening. I think they would do anything you asked.' That Vince's had quickly achieved consolidated gay notoriety for its body-beautiful camp designs was the measure of George Melly's axiomatic joke at the time: 'I went into Vince's to buy a new tie and they measured my inside leg.' But for Melly and other Soho sharp dressers Vince's was an indispensable pioneering outlet, and its shape-shifting owner Bill Green was one of the earliest progenitors in intro-ducing gay fashion to a wider mainstream market that included straight men willing to experiment by wearing colourful French and Italian styled casual clothes that stood out in the crowd. Colin MacInnes in his prototypical Mod novel *Absolute Beginners*, one of the first novels to take urban youth culture as its theme, and to observe contemporary clothes with a minutely fetishistic eye for detail, describes his fashionable character, Fabulous Hoplite, as 'wearing a pair of skin-tight, rubber-glove thin, almost transparent cotton slacks, white nylon-stretch and black wafer-sole casuals, and a sort of maternity jacket, I can only call it coloured blue', undoubtedly drawing on Vince's stock as the source of his description.

Although awareness of the shop's existence spread largely by word of mouth in the gay underworld, Green also expanded his trade by adver-tising in magazines such as *Film and Filming*, and through issuing regular Vince leisure wear catalogues that were often subscribed to on account of the provocatively dressed and significantly worked-out models, that at the time included the young Sean Connery, who brought physique to his line. Green's early mandate on selling stylishly Italian-influenced clothes to a younger generation anticipating radical changes in how men looked, quickly paid off, and earned him wholesale contracts with Marshall and Snelgrove and with Macy's in New York, lucrative deals that allowed him to upscale and move into larger premises on Foubert's Place, just that much closer to Regent Street for passing trade. Trading under the name Vince Man's Shop, situated on the corner of Soho at 15 Newburgh Street, and at Foubert's Place, and

providing opening hours of Monday, Tuesday, Wednesday, Friday 9–5.30pm, and Thursdays 9 to 7pm and Saturdays 9 to 3pm, Vince Leisure Wear was also available through the stockist James Grose Ltd, 379 Euston Road, London N.W.1. In the 1957 catalogue for which Sean Connery modelled leisure wear, posed sitting outside at a café table, the aspiring actor was photographed behind dark shades, with his black gelled hair combed back into a fashionable quiff, wearing a Capri shirt, item No 622, in navy and white horizontally striped denim, priced at 47/6d, and also wearing pre-shrunk crotch-provocative jeans in 'faded' blue denim with two front and two hip pockets and legs tapered to 16in as French style No 306 in the itemised catalogue. The new 24-page illustrated catalogue for which Sean Connery had been conscripted as a model was available on request by phoning Ger 3730, and promoted Vince as leading specialists in swim and beach wear, shirts, slender line slacks, jeans, jackets and sweaters, all in exclusive continental styles for men. Green's subversive slant on homoerotic lines regularly invited controversy on account of his window displays, and on one occasion having over-padded a pair of black minimal cire briefs with tissue paper he was confronted by an elderly woman neighbour who threatened to call the police on account of the outrageously offending item. 'Go ahead and do what you like madam,' was his irrefutable response, 'I need all the publicity I can get.' Vince's trade however, was given a massive Boeing lift-off by the saturation of American shows and musicals that ostentatiously lit up the West End theatre repertoire throughout the residually grey cultural tone of the uniform fifties. It was the emergence in these shows of the butch chorus boy with a worked-out physique, rather than a draggy, effete, limp-wristed queen, that highlighted the evolving gay prototype as muscle rather than gelatine. According to Richard Channing, ' there was even one show, *Wish You Were Here*, where the cast dived in and out of a swimming pool set up on the stage, and because bikini underwear was coming in all the boys wanted the tightest of tight trunks. And where could they get them but Vince's?' Martin Stone, a journalist at the time, before becoming an ace virtuoso slide-guitar player with the Mod-venerated the Action, remembers buying a red and white gingham *Bill Green,* check tab-collared shirt at Vince's, an Italian import, as a risqué fashion first, *beefcake* but recalls refraining from entering the shop initially, on account of its repu- *photographer,* tation as a gay flagship for a strictly homosexual milieu. *and owner*

Graham Hughes, however, as an acutely fashion-conscious youth in the *of Vince shot* 1950s, credits neither Vince nor John Stephen as being the first precursors *models posing* of the look, but instead points to an outlet called Courtney Reeds, near *in his self-* Leicester Square, as the place where it all started. 'They had underwear and *designed briefs.*

sold knickers, girl's knickers that were actually sexy, before anywhere else even thought of displaying them. It was considered gay or camp because this was 1958. You could get a little catalogue, and it was as close to being able to buy a porn book as you could get ... It was the only shop before Carnaby Street or the King's Road that promoted the Mod look.'

And as a sign of the changing times the newly emergent bohemian women in London looked for their influences to their more liberated and stylish European counterparts, adopting the gamine look, with its simple black jersies and short, almost boyish hairdos associated with film actresses like Audrey Hepburn (*Sabrina* and *Funny Face*) and Jean Seberg (*Bonjour Tristesse* and *A Bout de Souffle*), as well as the groundbreaking sensational French novelist Françoise Sagan, who was celebrated not only for her books but for the variety of her sexual partners and for driving fast sports cars in short skirts and bare feet as the style-chasing example of the free life.

John Stephen's early reconnaissance of fashionable London menswear shops, existing during his time of employment at Moss Bros, and often made during his lunch hour breaks, naturally led him out of curiosity to Dale Cavana's gay-orientated boutique in Kinnerton Street, Knightsbridge, which like Vince specialised in tight-fitting leisure wear with a camp emphasis, and was according to the omnivorous fashion chronicler Nik Cohn, ' a most camp establishment with its windows full of skin-tight trousers, lacy briefs and cards saying "For You Monsieur."' But while the initial North West London Jewish Mods started going to Vince to buy white jeans and black polo neck jumpers to emulate the Left Bank Paris look, the clothes at Dale Cavana were exclusive and high-end items that provided John Stephen with the valuable insight that if new trends in clothes were to be made available to youth, then it was essential they should above all be affordable.

Part of Stephen's professionally cued itinerary of shops also took him to Austin's on Shaftesbury Avenue, founded in 1946 by Louis Austin, a former sax player, a shop that specialised in importing American Ivy League styles and button-down seersucker shirts. To the rapaciously clothes-hunting teenage Andrew Loog Oldham, who would go on to manage and produce the Rolling Stones, Austin's on his clothes shopping forays into the West End, 'was a feast of reversible houndstooth and herringbone, staggered vent jackets, worn with broadcloth button-down, pin-through and tab-collared shirts.' Dougie Millings, the early tailor to the Beatles, was the cutter at Austin's during the 1950s, and established a reputation there as an intransigent, defiantly single-minded individual, whose popularity with customers overrode that of his diffident cigar-chewing employer Louis Austin. In retrospect Millings recalled, 'I got on with Louis quite well, but he was a short man, and very bossy. He'd come in and say, 'I don't want any bloody smoking in the shop,' but he'd be smoking a cigar, blowing it into my face. He had a terrible habit of calling me Millings. I used to think, Christ, this is worse than being in the army. There were four of us, all cramped together. The other three had been there twenty years and were frightened of this little man.'

Unlike Vince, clients went to Austin's not for individually stand-out fashion, but for impeccably cool tailoring. Austin's imported declarative Brooks Brothers shirts with generous roll collars, and famously tapered American Arrow shirts in ice blue and candy pink, as well as Bermuda and Madras leisure wear jackets. The American Ivy League Brooks Brothers look favoured by Louis Austin was a classic design: jackets had no more than two or three buttons, natural rounded shoulders and a conspicuous back vent. The trousers sat high on the hips, but pleats were optional. The shirts were structured with a soft roll collar that was buttoned down, as a characteristically significant detail. The success of Austin's as an imperative Haymarket outlet to 1950s fashionistas faced with a severe limitation of menswear outlets was such that its owner Louis Austin could afford to live full-time in a suite at the exclusively upmarket Savoy Hotel.

John Stephen spent his lunch breaks, often returning there obsessively after work, doing constructive research in the windows of both Austin's and Cecil Gee, the other energetic male fashion emporium, also situated on Shaftesbury Avenue, a fashion-forward shop renowned for Italian-cut custom-made suits and a range of colourful knitwear and shirts that appealed to the Soho jazz modernists of the 1950s. Cecil Gee's range of products, while being more affordable than Austin's, still seemed unaccountably expensive to the impecunious young Glaswegian, dressed in his one suit, and dabbing his reflection self-consciously in the windows at styles he had come to assimilate, while always adjusting them in his head to his own innovative designs. His ambition was bigger than what he saw, and his potential to realise it simmered on hold. Lack of money – and he was determined to go it alone – was severely restrictive to his material vision, so too his newness to London, and the innate shyness that kept him from making resourceful social contacts within the fashion milieu. He was aware that his good looks were noted by other men in the Piccadilly confines, but that most were frozen into alienation by their same-sex attraction in a society ruthlessly hostile to gay people. Eye contact was as far as he got, but inwardly he was driven to succeed, and carry his vision forward no matter the resistance.

Unlike John Stephen, whose sympathies directly meshed with the youth generation he was to dress, the Lithuanian-born Cecil Gee was not so much a clothes enthusiast as a speculative entrepreneur who sighted a gap in the market for unusual leisure wear and hit it with impacting market precision. Thirty years older than John Stephen, Cecil Gee was born in Vilnius, Lithuania, in 1902, and came to London in 1914, the middle child in a family of three, whose father was a self-made, energetically prosperous jeweller. Cecil Gee began life working for the family business, but due to internal conflicts quit his father's employment and initially worked as a window dresser in the East End. Putting to effect the fashion experience he had gained in this pursuit he borrowed money from his family and in 1929 opened his first premises on Commercial Road, Whitechapel, in London's East End. In the mid-1930s, Cecil Gee moved to Charing Cross Road and set up a three-floor menswear store at 106, 108, 110, creating a new trend by selling off the rail suits, jackets and trousers, dispensing with the convention of made-to-measure suits as standard tailoring. By the early 1950s Cecil Gee expanded his West End concern by acquiring more premises, this time on Shaftesbury Avenue, and began to dress the black musicians who were a regular feature in the Rupert Street Soho jazz clubs in the Ivy League style. Cecil Gee hung images of musicians on his shop walls, in the way that John Stephen was to feature blow-ups of pop stars in his Carnaby Street boutique interiors, and Gee was the first clothes retailer to install a Gaggia coffee machine in his shop on Shaftesbury Avenue, as a hint that shopping could be a form of recreation. His rails brimmed with imported American, Scandinavian and Italian clothes, as well as stocking his own designs made up by an Italian tailor called Giorgio, who specialised in making mafia-styled double-breasted chalk-striped gangster suits, sharp-cut affairs with livid paisley or vermilion satin linings to the jackets.

While Cecil Gee altogether lacked John Stephen's rebelliousness in wanting to give youth a separate identity through their choice of dress, his shop windows nonetheless added electrifying colour to the West End, in contrast to his almost uniformly monochrome contemporaries. In the mid-1950s Gee had started going on business holidays to Italy with the window dresser, Ivan Topper, and returning with Italian clothing including black silk knit ties and purple and orange mohair sweaters as examples of rogue colour introduced into the otherwise subdued palette of available men's knitwear.

But the enterprising, brilliantly entrepreneurial Gee was already too far removed from youth, both by his age and affluent lifestyle, to pick up directly on the growing intransigence of a generation looking to individuate through a growing obsession with clothes, music, and in the case of the Mods, illegal

Mr Handsome. John Stephen believed in dissolving his and hers into unisex.

pills. Cecil Gee, despite his sensitivity to the need for individual expression in men's clothes, remained dichotomised in his business interests, also offering a traditionally classic style through his purchase in 1954 of the Savoy Tailors Guild, and under this formally conservative logo offering a refined, upmarket approach to customers through selective Mayfair outlets.

To the teenage John Stephen, who in addition to his daytime job at Moss Bros was working at night as a waiter in a Fortes coffee bar in Piccadilly to help finance the £300 he needed to set up in business, Cecil Gee's shop on Shaftesbury Avenue was not only an inspiration, but also, no matter its introduction of Italian colour into monochrome British menswear, still represented the backward rather than the forward edge to the present. Not only were the clothes expensive, and out of his price range, but the majority were imported from France and Italy. John Stephen realised early on that by having similar clothes made up in the seething network of workshops that constellated Soho in the 1950s, he could considerably lower prices as well as experiment with limited runs of the sort of innovative clothes he intended to filter into the youth market. '"Why doesn't someone in this country make clothes like this?" I overheard people say again and again. Suddenly I knew I would make really modern clothes for young men with a British label,' he recalled in 1965. 'I had found a vacuum in the market and that was the first step towards success.'

The intense radiating vision that John Stephen had brought with him to London now glowed with the energies of a temporarily constrained, but unstoppable ambition. Post-war London was a city in need of rehabilitation, and youth, he sensed, were the key to unlocking the city's potential. For young Mods, who still hadn't laid claim to a collective identity, suits had to be made or modified by tailors of the day like Sam Arkus in the West End, Lou Rose in the East End, and the legendary Bilgorri of Bishopsgate, who famously styled early Mod enthusiasts. As the Mods looked to American jazz musicians like Chet Baker, Miles Davis and Stan Kenton for style tips, so trouser legs began to narrow in accordance with the Ivy League look and casual wear grew slowly to be an acceptable option to the ubiquitous formal suit worn on all occasions.

One August day in 1955, while working behind the counter at Moss Bros, John Stephen was approached by a tall, wirily athletic man, clearly attracted not only to his uncommonly good looks, but also to the sparkling personality he brought to an otherwise sedate establishment. Bill Green of Vince intuitively recognised that John Stephen was manifestly out of place in the stultifying correct atmosphere of his workplace, and offered him a job on the spot working as an assistant at the rapidly flourishing Vince. John Stephen was already sufficiently in the know to be aware that Bill Green, despite ghettoizing himself into a largely polarised gay market, was for all his quirkiness the man of the moment in terms of upbeat fashion and erotic swimwear. For the up-and-coming John Stephen, the boutique situated in Newburgh Street, one block east of and parallel to Carnaby Street, was to prove the starting point to measure the needs of a progressively defiant youth against the fashion available to its demands. Already the body-beautiful obsessed photographer Bill Green had started to attract a more varied clientele of pop stars, young actors, Piccadilly rent boys and the Chelsea Arts Club bohemians to his clutch of adventurous customers; and the shop was fast earning a reputation as the coolest menswear outlet of its kind. John Stephen had nothing to lose, other than the security of his job at Moss Bros, and sensing that his future lay more in the direction of Soho than Covent Garden, he decided to accept. Soho at the time was a zone best known for its restaurants and jazz clubs, its square mile run by Italians, Greeks, Jews, Maltese, Budapest street rats, and was infamous on account of its red light district, with tight-skirted spike-heeled girls openly selling sex in its maze of alleys. Soho had in the 1950s become a capital within a capital, a microcosm or cosmopolitan ecosphere where marijuana was smoked in clubs with names like the Cozy Hatch and the Fullado, and where black American servicemen had introduced amphetamine or speed as a revved-up recreational drug into the cool nightlife on Archer Street, next to the nearby Windmill Theatre, that boasted a nocturnal showcase of seamed nylon legs and strippy dancing girls. There was also Club 11 on Windmill Street, where the jazz musicians Ronnie Scott and John Dankworth took a rehearsal room and began creating improvised bebop sounds that ubiquitously permeated a neighbourhood of sleazy lowlife underground basements, regularly monitored by the police for illicit drug dealing. And Carnaby Street, the alley Stephen would within years transform into London's major fashion hoopla, was at the time the site of a single bakery, an established tobacconist Inderwick's, the landmark Morell's hardware store, a harness shop with a life-size wooden horse in the window, Rene the florist's, Como Snacks, a coffee bar, a rundown greasy spoon, a Lyons Tea Shop, and most notably the Central Electricity Board that took up almost half one side of the street, as well as home to the innumerable workshops that fed the nearby garment industry district north of Oxford Circus.

As an attractive young assistant, likely to prove popular with the Vince clientele, John Stephen was offered a salary of £12 a week, as an incentive to have him leave the security of his job at Moss Bros. Bill Green, whose shock tactics of filling the window with his trademark leather posing pouches had attracted both neighbourhood threats as to the indecency of his window displays, as well as customer appreciation for his notoriety, was in the process of going places. To Colin Woodhead who dealt with the shop as an advertising executive, 'Vince's was at the top end of Carnaby Street, with the leather posing pouches, butcher-boy caps in leather, the works, it catered to an extremely unconventional crowd.' And John Pearse, who was to be a lead player in the shaping of 1960s fashion, remembers that, 'if you had an Equity card, you got discount at Vince's. It attracted a lot of out of work actors buying polo-necks. The shop itself smelled of Aqua da Silva and was definitely exotica. I bought white polo-necks there and these edgy hipsters, which were around four pounds, quite expensive at the time.'

Vince's predominantly camp, gender-antagonistic line and the need to subvert to attract publicity won Bill Green a dubious reputation and a diverse clientele that included Peter Sellers, George Melly, Pablo Picasso, who bought a pair of suede trousers from the shop, the King of Denmark, and the young actor Sean Connery, who modelled for the Vince catalogues, having been a Mr Scotland finalist in 1950. But these were early days, and the shop, located in an unattractive backwater behind Regent Street, was too marginalised and too branded by an overriding gay signature to be rehabilitated to the poppy modernistic mainstream that were to become John Stephen's customers. Vince's customers were predominantly labelled queer, and as a downside the precinct also attracted gay-bashers who hung out in the alleys looking for unsuspecting targets for their misplaced homophobic aggression. Carlo Manzi, an early London Mod remembers, 'the first time I went down there, a mate of mine said, "You guys want to go down Carnaby Street, but watch it! It's full of poofs. It's where they go to get their clothes."' Gay men, who chose to express their identity through clothes at the time John Stephen started working for Vince, socially networked in the cluster of small streets around Piccadilly Circus, often meeting in the area under the County Fire Office Arches on the Regent Street side that was protected from the elements. And already there were signs of a distinctly ghettoized but rapid proliferation of gay clubs opening up in the capital, like Leon Maybank's the Calabash in Fulham, the Festival Club off St Martin's Lane, to which members had their own private key, the Rockingham Club, and central to Soho the A&B, which stood for Arts and Battledress, and which attracted unorthodox professionals and glitzy celebrities.

John Stephen in interview was almost uniformly reluctant to talk about the time he spent working at Vince, and tended to downplay the experience and little acknowledge the profound formative influence Green had on shaping his early and daringly original tastes in fashion. Although Andreas Spyropolous, a small shirt manufacturer from North London, who opened the boutique Donis in Carnaby Street in 1957, claimed dubiously to have been the London progenitor of hipsters, Bill Green was indubitably the initial proponent of denim for men, and the first to market pre-shrunk, pre-bleached clothes, a risque line that proved so popular that he was to supply Harrods with his trademark homoerotic signature. At Vince's, John Stephen remembered in 1965, 'the clothes were made upstairs and as soon as they came into the shop they sold. I was just standing there taking money. Suddenly I thought, if this guy can do it, so can I ...' What Bill Green couldn't have realised at the time was John Stephen's inordinate ambition, and that he had in fact admitted to his employment someone whose imaginative flair and remorseless work cycle would over the next five years dramatically supersede Vince and all contemporary rivals in his ambitious thrust to dress youth on a commercially epic scale. But the transition from working for Bill Green for almost a year to setting up in business himself, just round the corner in Beak Street, wasn't a direct one. John Stephen's infectious charisma as an assistant at Vince won the attention of Nicholas Perry, another pioneering individual who was in the process of creating a men's boutique in Blandford Street, Marylebone, having already opened in Pembridge Road, Notting Hill Gate. Perry, sensing his extraordinary talent, put John Stephen in as the teenage spirit to set up the shop, an experience that provided Stephen with the opportunity to order in unusually colourful Italian and French knitwear, as well as import blue Levi jeans to be shrunk-fit from the States. In fact, both the Levi's and striped denim trousers with which Stephen stocked the shop, were so successful that within weeks they were selling in their hundreds. John Stephen was only at the Nicholas Perry boutique for a few months, but the experience reinforced his conviction that imported clothes remained exclusive on account of their price, and that only by establishing a viable British counterpart and producing his own could he succeed in his attempt to democratize fashion.

It was shortly after quitting at Nicholas Perry in 1956, to set up by himself, as well as terminating his night-time job as a waiter at Fortes, at the Piccadilly Circus branch, that John Stephen met Bill Franks, the man who was to become his lifelong partner, as well as his chief business associate, at a party in Marylebone. The attraction was immediate, and Bill Franks remembers that John Stephen was already dressed with characteristic dandified panache in a sharp suit, shirt and tie and mirror-polished oxford brogues. Bill Franks who was born in City Road, London, on 25 August 1937, and brought up in Burnt Oak Edgware, where he attended the Edgware Secondary Modern until leaving school at the age of fifteen, had worked variously in an Edgware factory producing women's underwear, and as an apprentice cutter and trimmer at a car manufacturer Thrupp & Maberly, part of the Rootes Group, in Cricklewood, where he had learnt to cut leather for car upholstery. Compulsorily conscripted into the army at eighteen to serve in the Medical Corps stationed at Fleet in Aldershot, he had been given a dishonourable discharge on account of professing his homosexuality. Examined by a psychiatrist, he was discharged as unfit for service, came back to London, and took a job as a theatre technician at Queen Charlotte's Hospital on the Goldhawk Road, for £8 a week. He was working at Queen Charlotte's at the time he met John Stephen, and within six weeks the two decided to live together in a small room in Bayswater. By pooling their joint savings, the two were able to raise the money to fulfil John Stephen's dominant ambition of starting out in fashion, by renting an undeveloped single room, one floor up, in Soho's Beak Street, an unfashionable address, but one located in the next street to Bill Green's Vince, and propitiously right in the heart of the Soho tailoring workshops.

2

UP ABOVE THE WORLD

When John Stephen and Bill Franks moved into an unheated, run-down single room on a second-floor at 19 Beak Street, Soho, in early 1956, and set up business there under the name John Stephen, the neighbourhood couldn't have been less conducive to passing trade. The unlit street, unrelieved by colour, was cheap rent and little else with John Stephen paying £3 a week for a space that included the use of the untenanted basement as a workroom. Painting the walls burnt orange and cream, adding a few fabrics as drapes, and covering tomato boxes with purple felt to make the limited space appear marginally more attractive, the two moved in optimistic that the world would discover them in time, no matter their initial lack of capital. For John Stephen, who was prepared to work unremittingly hard, the process of running an independent business without any form of backing was a challenge demanding extraordinary capacities of self-conviction and youthful resilience. To maintain an independent concern he had to buy the fabric, design the clothes, make them, press them and attempt to sell them, often having to make the sale in order to pay for the fabric. He was faced too with a resistant ethos in which men ubiquitously excluded all bright colour and individual detail from their dress, the endemic sobriety of British menswear in the uniformly reactionary 1950s proving an insurmountable obstacle at first to his evolution as a designer. Additionally too, he was in the bad end of Soho, an exclusion-zone that went irredeemably dead as the horse-latitudes in the uneventful afternoons. Soho's attraction in the 1950s was as a fugitive nocturnal village, a subterranean underground of dives and cellar clubs, quite

The Mod pioneer Bill Green relocated to Foubert's Place in 1961.

distinct from its daytime world of tailors, tobacconists, newsagents, restaurants, fabric and millinery retailers that supplied the Soho rag trade. He was however, in terms of having garments made, ideally placed to avail himself of the small fabric shops and workshops rooted in the complex of alleys behind the great shopping thoroughfares of Bond Street, Oxford Street and Regent Street, a nucleus of concealed industry that acted as the interface between craft and the more public terrain of the dress shop and the department store. In fact much of the rag trade had relocated to the Carnaby Street area of West London after the extensive devastation of the city's East End as the major disaster area of Luftwaffe bombing during the war.

A concern as small as John Stephen's newly founded business, Bill Green's Vince or Nathan Spiegal's Paul's, the first boutique to open on Carnaby Street, couldn't have been maintained without the immediate proximity of local facilities that allowed them to run up single or extremely limited numbers of a garment, usually on credit. Up above the world in Beak Street, John Stephen fixed up a length of blackboard with screw-on legs in the middle of the room, made up a few shirts and pairs of trousers and bikini briefs and began advertising 'Exclusive Menswear.' It was that simple and defiantly independent; a random chance generated in a city in which most small businesses acting without advice proved to be the fall guys to bankers, landlords or acquisitively ebullient bailiffs. John Stephen's only business credential, other than reckless ambition, was coming from a shop-owning family who had somehow survived on a tenuous level. When he made his first sale it was a patterned silk tie costing 13s 6d, or 75 pence, as a measure that his clothes could be noticed no matter how small his beginnings. Resolutely undeterred by lack of foot traffic, John Stephen adventurously designed hipster trousers in flame-red, lavender, pink and burnt-orange cotton denim, as well as grey and dark blue wool, and displayed denim button-down and tab-collar shirts in peacock blue, foggy grey and lipstick pink, choices so at variance with mainstream fashion that they appeared tropically hybrid to anyone but emergent Mods and gay men wanting to party. The young Cliff Richard proved to be an early customer, and gave kudos to the shop by wearing one of John Stephen's mink-coloured mohair jumpers on stage at the nearby London Palladium. But custom was discouragingly slow, and the financial situation often critical, with the obscure second-floor shop attracting as little as eight or ten customers a week, in a capital that still proved obdurately resistant to change. While still at 19 Beak Street, John Stephen's early forays into advertising in the summer of 1957 followed Vince in the use of crude black and white drawings of musclemen or casually dressed James Dean look-alikes, to intimate that a fashion marker had been established in a little known back street, euphemistically glossed as Regent Street, and that its moniker was gay postulating as straight – butch doing beach. For the informed gay man Stephen advertised an unusual horizontally striped woven denim shirt with a front breast pocket in red and white and blue and white, to be matched with beach blue pre-shrunk denim jeans, with hip pockets, wide belt loops and a low-rise zip fly. Not that stock came in any numbers. 'In those early days we could only afford to have one of each style, which was on show in the most popular size,' Bill Franks recollected, with mail order purchases having to be made up on demand. Bill Franks attributes their persistence in the face of neglect to the fact that they were young enough at the time to recover from the possibility of failure, and therefore all the more determined to succeed, despite having no backing and no street level shop-front. Chain-smoking, hands fidgety with anxiety, and massively resourceful with ideas for which the shop couldn't pay, John Stephen had to wait his time until the newly emergent youth intersected with his vision.

London in 1957 wasn't as yet the up-tempo capital of popocracy it would become in the great flameout of the sixties, and for John Stephen and Bill Franks the basics of survival were called into question each week. The supercilious fashion press, with their accent on regulated couture, weren't interested in off-the-map rogue outlets like Vince and John Stephen with their subversion of macho currency, and expected their quirky signature to quickly fade or remain confined to limited gay interest. Chris Stamp, the East End entrepreneur who was to move into pop management at the time, remembered, 'We thought Carnaby Street when it began was for poofs, it was nonsense. We liked to look slightly androgynous, but that was so geezers would think we were easy to take, then we'd kick 'em.' The risk involved in dressing in clothes considered extracurricular to masculine protocol was expressed by Carlo Manzi in the negative reception he experienced at home, on buying a shocking for the time, pink shirt. 'I bought a pink shirt from a shop called Gay Lord. It had a giraffe collar and a tab front. I put it in the wash. The next day I went to get it and I couldn't find it. I said to my mum, "Where's that pink shirt?" She said, "I've torn it up. It's a duster now." I couldn't believe it. I said, "Why?" She said, "Because everyone will think you're a poof." She said, "I'll give you the money to buy a new shirt, but please, don't buy pink."'

But unlike Bill Green, whose primary concern was physique and not clothes, or the sartorially chic Cecil Gee, who changed his shirt twice a day, Stephen had a mission that was compounded into youthful genes, not only to change the way men looked for ever, but to make clothes and the

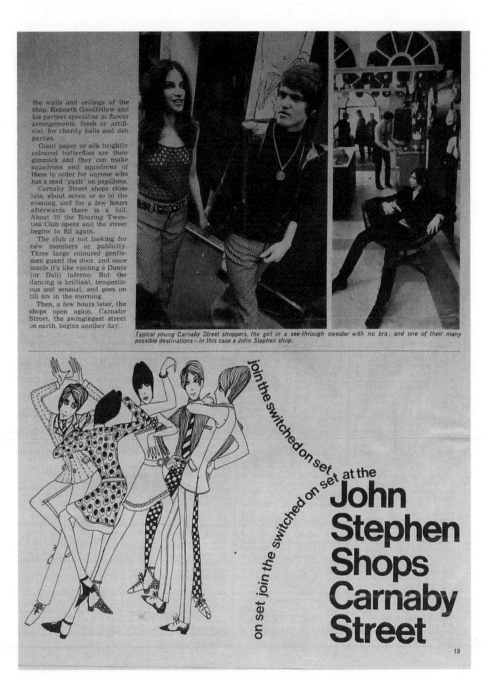

the walls and ceilings of the shop. Kenneth Goodfellow and his partner specialise in flower arrangements, fresh or artificial, for charity balls and deb parties.

Giant paper or silk brightly coloured butterflies are their gimmick and they can make squadrons and squadrons of them to order for anyone who has a mad "pash" on papillons.

Carnaby Street shops close late, about seven or so in the evening, and for a few hours afterwards there is a lull. About 10 the Roaring Twenties Club opens and the street begins to fill again.

The club is not looking for new members or publicity. Three large coloured gentlemen guard the door, and once inside it's like visiting a Dante (or Dali) inferno. But the dancing is brilliant, tempestuous and sensual, and goes on till six in the morning.

Then, a few hours later, the shops open again. Carnaby Street, the swingingest street on earth, begins another day.

Typical young Carnaby Street shoppers, the girl in a see-through sweater with no bra; and one of their many possible destinations — in this case a John Stephen shop.

join the switched on set

on set join the switched on set at the

John Stephen Shops Carnaby Street

19

John Stephen's name was inseparable from Carnaby Street, and his art director Myles Antony responsible for interior design, window displays and logos.

compatible awareness of self-image into a necessary lifestyle. Nobody before or afterwards was to provide the individual with such a rapid update of detail-obsessed fashion, to the extent that styles were deleted every week, in part to keep a distance on rivals, and in part as the expression of a creative imagination driven to burn-out by the compulsion to keep on reinventing image. It's a given that all originals, including John Stephen, are subject to being critically undermined by their more limited contemporaries, and Tommy Roberts, a regular visitor to John Stephen's initial concerns in Beak Street and Carnaby Street and who was to open the pop-art fashion shop Mr Freedom in 1968, got his assessment of the early John Stephen facilities at the Man's Shop in Carnaby Street radically wrong. According to Roberts, 'there was no changing room, so you'd try the trousers on in the corner then come back in an hour and they'd have been taken up. But there was no designing. Carnaby never produced a designer.' Bill Franks is adamant that no John Stephen shop was ever without a changing room, and that Stephen was indubitably the originator of the look and putatively the only extempore designer of his generation who worked the needs of youth into his ingenious repertoire of street-cred designs.

Basically, the Mod subculture to which John Stephen was to provide an indelible look began with a few cliques of East London teenage boys with family connections to the garment trade in London in 1956, the year that Stephen opened his first proper shop at No 5 Carnaby Street, with a small workroom in the back. The tiny boutique given the name John Stephen remained his retail outlet until December 1959, when he relocated to 49/51 Carnaby Street, a shop built for him by his landlords on a converted bomb-site that came to be known as John Stephen The Man's Shop, with a lease of 21 years and a fixed rental of £1,200 per annum. Originally the term Mods was used to describe fans of modern jazz music, although the term was quickly diffused beyond musical tastes to designate a lifestyle associated with European clothes, scooters, French Nouvelle Vague films, musical tastes that graduated to American R&B and soul, Jamaican ska and British beat music, but above all with an acute concern to be obsessively and self-regardingly individual, and to cultivate an image radically distinct from the collective by an epicurean devotion to minute details of dress. Mods as hedonists were the products of a culture of constant change, and were largely protean shape-shifters in search of new sensations, outwardly exhibiting cool, and often emotionally indifferent to the girls who entered the peripheries of their male circle, choosing to dance alone and to treat society with a diffident, defiantly superior attitude.

Mods were Mod-friendly only to their own, and uniformly disinterested in most other aspects of society, their essentially narcissistic, self-referential culture always on the point of imploding into immediate extinction. Like John Stephen, who lived fast and burnt himself out by the end of the sixties, the Mods inhabited a parallel speed trajectory that blazed an urban glory trail across a decade so lacking in precedent, and so without continuity, that its isolation, almost as a future space-time reversed into the present, gave rise to the whole myth of the Swinging Sixties as an epoch magicked into existence by drugs, music, clothes and visionary idealism: a time elusive and evanescent as a UFO sighting, and communicable to nobody who failed to experience its euphoric, accelerated happenings.

Mods were in Paolo Hewitt's celebrated phrase, 'little masterpieces' of invention, often working class kids who transformed themselves into the key players of their generation as the purveyors of a look almost singularly derived from John Stephen's early Carnaby Street creations. If the Mods began by having to construct their own clothes through alterations done by tailors, it was because they lacked a designer with the imagination to accommodate their needs. Bill Green's clothes were too outright camp to have wide popular appeal to Mods, and Cecil Gee too exclusive to be affordable, leaving John Stephen as he gathered experience and momentum to access the fastidiously precise clothes requirements of a youth generation committed to imposing its particular and highly innovative look on conventional society. Not that Mods were confined only to the expressive cultivation of image through clothes, music and pills – there was also an intellectual basis to their urban ideology, and one derived from reading the French existentialists popular at the time, the philosophic works and novels of Sartre and Camus, and by association the seminal writings of the openly gay ex-convict Jean Genet. David May, who was in the front-line of the Mod attack, makes the legitimate claim that. 'Mods were always intellectual. There was a large gay element in it. On Saturday afternoons we'd go to get our hair done in the women's hairdressers ... We didn't fight rockers, we were far more interested in some guy's incredible shoes, or his leather coat. But underneath this, one did read Camus. *The Outsider* explained a lot by way of alienation. A sort of Jean Genet criminal lowlife was also important to our ideals. We empathised with outlaw figures, people who went out and stole and so on. And until the drug squad appeared in 1967 there was this period, for me from the age of fourteen to eighteen, when the police didn't impinge at all. We lived in this whole other world: getting stoned and hoping to get laid ...'

During the transitional period of the late 1950s, when they were still trying to make a name for themselves, John Stephen and Bill Franks, with very little money, but fired-up by indefatigable enthusiasm to succeed lived variously in rooms in Holland Park, Nightingale Lane, Clapham, and on the Fulham Palace Road, frugally, basically, but always stylishly, with John Stephen maintaining his dandified appearance as the outward presentation of success to the unsuspecting. In this respect, Stephen, while having no direct affiliation with Mod ideology, nonetheless subscribed to their ethic of placing clothes first, as a very conscious identity, and as a way of dissolving associations with class or background. Mods often came from working class origins, but kept their suits, jackets and trousers clean under wraps, and spent hours pressing their clothes before going out in defiance of their small postered bedroom in the family's council flat in Acton or Waltham-stow, and, protected by a fur-trimmed parka, burnt into the West End on a Vespa or Lambretta to show off a ruthlessly scrutinised identity to other attentive teenage fashionistas waiting to be seen in or around Carnaby Street. Clothes, or more specifically John Stephen's clothes, were a form of emancipation to this youth, and a means of expressing themselves singularly through a liberating reinvented identity. Mods were so cool they created the notion of classlessness in Britain for the first time, and were the more disturbing to their contemporaries for being without an overt political programme, their ideology if it existed at all being rooted in aesthetics, pop and the increasingly prevalent look. Mods were pillheads, wired to the moment by speed, the accelerated rush of the drug finding its sonic counterpart in black R&B and soul music, and its mechanised equivalent in the fuel-injector of a hotted-up, gizmo-stacked scooter, projected across town in a series of rapid-fire staccato bursts through gridlocked traffic. Mods were like John Stephen, incapable of standing still and so terrified of growing old they lived by accentuating their involvement in the moment, extending time by staying up all night and recklessly partying into the Soho dawn. When it came to drugs, John Stephen was their opposite, his naturally hyped-up neurochemistry demanding a regime of prescribed downers to stabilise behavioural irregularities like disturbed sleep and his violently oscillating mood-swings. John Stephen was so metabolically hot in his younger years that his dynamic belonged more to a NASA space project than the natural biorhythms of the human body: his speed of initiating ideas and seeing them executed in the cutting room being nothing less than optimal attack: manic blow-out.

In the first years of opening the John Stephen shop in Beak Street, Stephen and Franks, too poor at the time to own a car, zipped across town on a lipstick red Vespa, with Bill Franks riding pillion. In need of cash, the two made personal deliveries of a garment if called for, and memorable to Franks are the flame-red Vespa-powered regular visits to Tooting to supply the forward-looking Mrs Ada Harris, as their first real patron, with customised hipsters and shirts made to specifications for sale in her Wimbledon Arcade shops. Any customer at the time was one to remember, and amongst the curious drawn to their tiny, improvised, burnt-orange walled shop, Franks recalls the mercurial phenomenon of a conventional pinstripe city-type, who underwent a total transformation within the shop, placed his own clothes in a John Stephen carrier, and went out wearing bottle-green hipsters and a peacock blue denim shirt as a radical remake of image, a spectacular flash-forward from outmoded inherited values to the new, as though in discarding his suit, he had rejected his past in favour of the unconditional present.

All clothes on display in the Beak Street shop were made to standard size: shirts were a tapered, slim-bodied 14½in collar, and trousers 28in waist, and jackets 36in chest, a skinny aesthetic that was to remain consistent amongst youth right through the 1960s. Obesity wasn't an issue with the new generation and Mods despised fat as antipathetic to their wired, cut back to the bone look. For the small, limited clientele, motivated by curiosity, who actually made it up the stairs to the second floor at 19 Beak Street, there was the reward of discovering innovate black see-through Aertex T-shirts on sale, matelot vests, a range of McCaul polo-shirts in unusual colours, rather than in the usual five basic colours, hipsters in wool and denim, a variety of bikini briefs and leather posing pouches, and as a money-spinner, and subject to availability, the much-coveted blue Levi jeans imported from the United States. John Stephen was one of the first London retailers to bring pre-shrunk Levi's into the country, despite lacking a licence, and to sell them for what was then the outrageous price of £45, advising customers to shrink them in the bath to achieve a tighter, sexier fit.

The inventor of denim jeans, Levi Strauss, was motivated by the Californian gold rush in the mid-19th century to manufacture durable working pants from a twilled cotton cloth from France called serge de Nimes, and in 1873, Levi Strauss & Company began manufacturing the characteristic pocket stitch design. Levi Strauss and a Nevada tailor David Jacobs co-patented the process of putting rivets in pants for strength, and on 20 May 1873, they received US patent No. 139,121, a date now considered the official birthday of blue jeans. By the 1950s Levi's blue jeans, originally branded work wear clothes, were made fashionable once pop and film stars like James Dean, Marlon Brando, Marilyn Monroe and Elvis Presley began to team the fabric with winning leather jackets, elevating the profile of jeans to hip leisure wear.

Pre-shrunk jeans were not introduced until the 1960s, so breaking in Levi's usually involved jumping into a hot bath and allowing them to dry-on for a personal contoured fit.

Something of the devotional care early Mods attached to Levi's is remembered by Ken Brown in his recollection of the period. 'The care you took with your Levi's was unbelievable. When you washed your jeans you didn't just put them in a washing machine, you used to place them on the draining board and scrub each knee and likewise the fly so you would get the ring coming through the buttons. The knees and crotch had to be white. That, believe it or not, was the look.'

Jeans, as John Stephen presciently sensed, were a lucrative teenage winner, a movie star image accessory with a potentially unlimited market, and by obtaining a short-term licence to import Levi's, over and above their many copyists like Wrangler and Lee, he secured himself valuable income for the limited numbers he was permitted to import. Their arrival Franks remembers was sporadic, limited, and almost straight in and out of the shop on availability. But business for John Stephen remained painfully slow, his customers comprising a cocktail of tentatively emergent Mods, gay hustlers from the Marshall Street Public Baths, actors and occasional pop stars looking to add significant colour to their stage clothes. The 1950s were the times of the scruffily dressed Beatniks, and on a literary level, one of the sharpest observers of his time, in noting the transition in fashionable image from beatnik to mod, trad to new, was the cult novelist Colin MacInnes. MacInnes' excavation of London's and in particular Soho's subcultures shares themes in common with Jean Genet's novels, in absorbing a world of gays, pimps, dealers, rent and disaffected lowlife into the richly textured London milieu he made so distinctly into the resources of his fiction. There's a passage in his seminal novel *Absolute Beginners* that perfectly describes the edge on which John Stephen as a designer was living in the late 1950s, with Mods starting to go public in the presentation of a new masculinity that fused components of stereotypical gay fashion with an edgy streetwise attitude that made the wearing of a suit and tie into something uptight. MacInnes perfectly gets the times. 'If you know the contemporary scene, you could tell them apart at once, just like you could a soldier or sailor, with their separate uniforms. Take first the Misery kid and his trad. drag. Long, brushless hair, white stiff-starched collar (rather grubby), striped shirt, tie of all one colour (red today, but it could have been royal-blue or navy), short jacket but an old one (somebody's riding tweed, most likely), very, very, tight, tight trousers with white stripe, no sox, short boots. Now observe the Dean in the modernist number's version. College-boy smooth crop hair with burned-in parting, neat white Italian rounded-collared shirt, short Roman jacket very tailored (two little vents, three buttons), no turn-up narrow trousers with 17-inch bottoms absolute maximum, pointed-toe shoes, and a white mac lying folded by his side, compared with Misery's sausage-rolled umbrella.'

The difference between Misery and Dean in MacInnes' awareness of London street-cred fashion in the transitional decade from beatnik to modernism is crucial to the tension-point on which youth and John Stephen as a designer pivoted at the time. In expectation of better times Stephen had graduated from driving a flame-red Vespa to the ownership of a first car – a roomy midnight-blue Humber Supersnipe estate. It was to be Stephen's first indulgence in fulfilling a habitual passion for smart cars that perfectly accommodated the film star looks of their sharp-suited owner, who at first drove recklessly without a licence, and later on as dangerously with one, having at the time amazed his partner Bill Franks by passing his driving test first time.

While still at 19 Beak Street, John Stephen acquired the services of Malcolm Bhola, a black cutter with an inimitably sharp eye for detail, who was at the time working for Bedlow in Newburgh Street, making up casual clothing for the trade, as well as private customers like the anorexically-waisted teenage Mick Jagger, who brought in his own designs for custom-ised hipsters in anticipation of his sizzling androgynous sex-appeal as a performer. Malcolm Bhola, whose cutting expertise was linked directly to the empathy he felt for John Stephen's designs, as well as the speed with which he could execute a pattern, was to prove seminal to John Stephen's accelerated expansion in business. Uncomplaining, genial, loyal, and as hard-working as his employer, Bhola's twelve-hour working day, extending to six days a week, was to make him into the invisible drive-unit behind the Carnaby Street explosion throughout the entire duration of the John Stephen emporium there. A quietly spoken, affable and eminently self-effacing individual from British Ghana, Malcolm Bhola remains one of the great uncelebrated heroes of 1960s fashion, who helped co-pilot John Stephen's abundantly rapid-fire invention of ideas into the reality of form. Malcolm was not only indispen-sable as a cutter, but gifted with the ability to withstand stress, and during the time of his twenty-year span at Beak Street and Carnaby Street, never stopped even for a lunchbreak or considered taking a day off for illness. His work ethic was absolutely essential to the hyperactive John Stephen's habit of enthusiastically selecting fabrics from the little shops in Soho and wanting to see the results of his purchases instantly transformed into samples, which Malcolm was obligingly on hand to do.

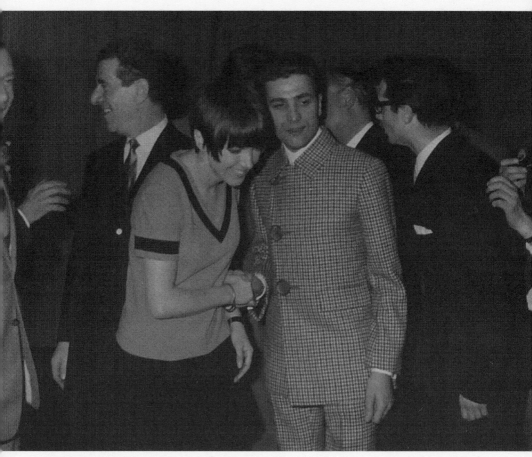

John Stephen and Mary Quant share a fashion moment in Italy. If Quant created the 60s look for women, then John Stephen did it for men.

Meanwhile, almost contemporaneous with John Stephen, Mary Quant and her husband Alexander Plunkett Green, together with their lawyer partner Archie McNair, had opened her first Bazaar boutique at 138a Kings Road Chelsea in November 1955, her revolutionary designs and tantalisingly flirtatious mini-skirts cut to 7–8 inches above the knee and worn with brightly-coloured patterned tights creating the origins of what was called the 'Chelsea Look.' The shop was such a contagious and immediate fashion hit amongst the Chelsea set that the initial stock was sold out within the first week. Making use of size zero leggy mannequins as display, often dressed in purple or platinum wigs, the shop attracted attention for its sheer uncompromising risk, and its sales assistants included George Melly's wife Diana, as well as Kiki Byrne, who went on to pioneer her Glass & Black shops on the King's Road, famous for its line of simple black shift dresses. One could argue that Mary Quant did for women what John Stephen singularly instigated for men, and that was to help liberate a younger generation through breaking the inexorably constrained fashion mould and expressing their unashamed sexuality through clothes. Like John Stephen, Quant rejected the indomitable concept of haute couture with its preconceived seasonal collections, producing as many as twenty-eight unscheduled collections in her first three years, and like Stephen designing clothes that were classless, androgynous, bold and defiantly original. Like John Stephen, and the two formed a warm, sympathetically supportive friendship, Quant was essentially a maverick designer who lacked formal training, having had a typical art school background at London's Goldsmith's College. After briefly taking a job with a couture milliner, where she would sometimes spend an exhaustive three days stitching a hat for one customer, Quant out of deep-seated frustration with the fashion *status quo* decided to go it alone, and in the mid-fifties, at the same time as John Stephen was configuring his first revolutionary designs for men in Soho, opened her own design house and retail boutique in consistently arty Chelsea. With no business plan, but a desire to make inspired clothes democratically affordable, Quant, like Stephen, set about disrupting the *status quo* with shock-tactics based on her own designs: mini-skirts, knee-high, white, patent plastic, lace-up boots and tight skinny ribs sweaters in stripes and ostentatious checks. Like John Stephen in his innovative outlet, the newly opened The Man's Shop in Carnaby Street, Quant was dissatisfied with the price range of European clothes available to her through import for Bazaar, and decided that the shop, if it was to attract the attention of lively foot traffic, should be stocked with her own aggressively simple designs. To consolidate her independence Quant bought a sewing machine and with its simplistic function operated solely from her bedroom, making things like small white plastic collars to brighten a black sweater or dress, and black stretch stockings to be worn with her self-created mini-skirts and Norfolk jackets trimmed with ostentatious fur collars. She initially experimented with balloon-style dresses and by mixing large spots and checks with virtuoso temerity. Better financed than the entrepreneurial John Stephen, in that Bazaar, situated on the ground floor of premises next to the Markham Arms, with Quant's jazz club/restaurant, Alexander's, in the basement, was financed by the triumvirate of Quant, Alexander Plunkett Green and Archie McNair, the shop became an immediate sensation with Chelsea types, and unlike John Stephen situated on an obscure Soho second floor, its windows commanded the attention of the steady stream of moneyed King's Road foot traffic. But like John Stephen, Mary Quant was singularly a phenomenon of her times, prepared to shock to gain media attention and committed like Stephen to making clothes that gunned attention by their sheer inventive dare. 'I've heard of clothes described as dishy, grotty, geary, kinky, mod, *poove* and the rest of it', she wrote unapologetically in her autobiography *Quant on Quant*. 'The clothes I made happened to fit in exactly with the teenage trend, with pop records and espresso bars and jazz clubs.'

Expanding to a larger-scale workroom where she employed a number of machinists, as well as opening a second Bazaar on the Brompton Road, Knightsbridge, Quant, like John Stephen, characterised unrestrained audacity, the rise of the individual against the stranglehold of haute couture, and the ascendancy of credible imagination in touch with the needs of the times, and able to continuously re-invent street fashion as a form of disposable art. It was Quant who popularised faux-Cleopatra style kohl eyeliner, the inimitably sexy Vidal Sassoon bob, ingénue pinafore dresses, shiny plastic raincoats, artily patterned tights, black and skin-tone see-through panties and ace coloured coordinates, as part of her uncompromising repertoire of clothes given an irreversibly modern flavour.

An early Quant and John Stephen aficionado, who worked for a short time as the suitably outrageous Bazaar window dresser, Andrew Loog Oldham, a chameleonic and obsessive fashionista who wore makeup at a time when it was outlawed for men, went on to image-shape and independently manage and produce the Rolling Stones in the seminal period from 1963–67. Oldham in his minutely detailed and euphorically vitaminised autobiography of the period, *Stoned*, remarks that 'The Quant look came to be topped off by the strikingly functional and sexy statement that Vidal Sassoon brought to hair. Iconised by photographers Bailey, Donovan and Duffy, Quant's empire was the one true manifestation of pop in the years between the archetypal rock 'n roll of the mid-50s and its eventual second coming with the Beatles in the mid-60s.'

Oldham's comment excludes the equal importance that John Stephen's flawless taste and polished business savvy provided for menswear in a decade spot-lit by his imaginative creations, his fashioning of the pop image being inseparable from the emergent and highly controversial dynamic of London bands like the Rolling Stones, the Pretty Things, the Kinks and the Yardbirds, all of who were individually dressed by Stephen's flagship boutiques the Man's Shop and His Clothes, as the coolest shops in town. John Stephen's frontline business acumen also led opportunistically to his being the youngest owner of a Rolls Royce in Britain at the time, impulsively acquiring his prestigious Silver Cloud model on hire purchase, in advance of the Beatles, partly as synonymous with his celebrity appeal and partly to subvert a class system that uniformly identified the Rolls Royce generically with aristocratic blue-blood genes.

In 1958, while still resident at No 5 Carnaby Street, John Stephen was advertising himself as 'Leisure-wear King' in a sensitively distributed British physique magazine called *Mod Men*, the censor mark over the genitals of the otherwise nude male model on the magazine cover making it very clear that the journal was directed at a gay readership. John Stephen's pictorial advertisement of an elegantly dressed Mod male, presented the clothes modelled with reassuring confidence as 'A fine sweater-shirt made of new Swiss fabric with raised stripe; single button collar and button cuff, available in light blue, navy blue, royal blue, black, red, lime, tan, and sand, 45 shillings or 7 dollars.' Stephen listed three addresses for the availability of his McCaul leisure wear: 19 Beak Street, 5 Carnaby Street, with the telephone given as Regent 5116, and 2 Wimbledon Arcade, Wimbledon Broadway, London S.W. 19, where a small essentially un-lucrative outlet managed by Bill Franks, was largely supported by purchases made by Ada Harris for her neighbouring Broadway shop, but otherwise succeeded in generating only minimal business from passing trade, and was let go in 1960 as a potentially interesting, but resounding commercial failure. A similar short-lived business venture during the same period was the tiny, eponymously named one-room shop John Stephen opened on the Fulham Road, beneath the cheaply-rented flat he shared with Bill Franks, on the site of what is now the Charing Cross Hospital, stocking a very limited supply of shirts, ties and knitwear that made little impression on the largely disinterested passing foot traffic. Graham Hughes, an energetic teenage fashion aficionado, remembers the shop's incongruous location, and the fact that he was given licence to purchase a shirt there on credit. The place was, according to Hughes, 'the smallest shop you've ever seen in your life. It was originally an estate agent's and was really tiny. It had one shirt in the window, and you could pay on the book. My Mum asked me what I wanted for Christmas, and I said I wanted this particular shirt, and she went down there and gave the assistant half a crown a week, every week for months, until Christmas.'

Just how closely linked men's casual wear was to the homosexual milieu in John Stephen's formative years as a designer and retailer is made apparent by the sources in which he advertised, the fashionable young man in his advertisement, with the gelled, meticulously constructed quiff, sweater-shirt, tight pegged French cotton slacks and suede Chelsea boots being instantly recognisable to readers as a gay stereotype. Beak Street, where Stephen retained a workroom, on the relatively uneventful west edge of Soho, was a world apart from the Regent Street association that Stephen supplied with his relatively unknown Carnaby Street outlet, the only recognisable landmarks in the neighbourhood being Morrell's Stores, selling domestic hardware items, a stationer's called Taylor's where John Stephen bought the pencils and notebooks he used for drawing his designs, the tobacconist's Inderwick's, owned by Frank Welby, whose hand-made and imported brands of cigarettes and speciality meerschaum pipes were to become popular in the sixties amongst John Stephen customers, and a few local shops and cellar restaurants. What Stephen had on his contemporaries, however, even in the resistant market of the late 1950s, and to a degree shared in common with Mary Quant, was the ability to produce clothes faster as well as radically cheaper for a younger market, a quality that unnerved and unsettled the more traditional proponents of men's fashion like Austin Reed, Simpsons of Piccadilly, Harrods, and the enduring Mayfair elegance of designers like Norman Hartnell and Hardy Amies. Stephen was the unaccounted rogue gene in the system who threatened to upend conventional notions not only of menswear but gender, and if he was, in 1958, still predominantly dependent on the attenuated pink pound for income, then his tentative move to a shop front in Carnaby Street was within years to greatly facilitate his ambition of dressing the new wave of classless discriminating youth looking to express themselves through a fashion they could call their own. Prior to Stephen's maintained clothes offensive only gay men who were at the time unanimously legislated against for their sexuality dressed in a way that stood out distinctively from others in the crowd. Something of the insidious police methods of monitoring and persecuting gays indigenous to Soho is recollected by the

John Stephen made his shops into theatre with bold camp flourishes.

maverick uninhibited bisexual record producer Simon Napier Bell, in his autobiography *Black Vinyl White Powder*, who recalls from acute personal experience how 'plain-clothes police hung around in public toilets masturbating, waiting for gays to reveal themselves. If they did, they were beaten up and arrested.'

When in 1956, John Stephen and Bill Franks took a lease on the newly available 5 Carnaby Street, as a small shop rented from St James Property Co for £10 a week, their expectations of increased trade in a downgraded undeveloped Soho back alley were at the time considered small. Vacating all but the basement of their Beak Street premises, kept on as a store and cutting room, Stephen was later to say of the implicit risk incurred by the move, 'If I hadn't had a very understanding landlord that would have been the end of me. But he led me around the corner to Carnaby Street, showed me a shop, and suggested I got to work right away.' No 5 at the time was situated opposite a devastatingly imposing undeveloped bomb-site that John Stephen was to take over when it was redeveloped by St James Property in 1960, and call the reconstructed shop The Man's Shop, as the first of a number of outlets given a specifically gender-signposted name. The move to Carnaby Street necessitated the employment of a machinist, and a highly motivated red-haired young English woman called Miss Ivy Dean was recruited to work in the basement, having served her apprenticeship at Simpsons of Piccadilly, where trainees were only allowed to cut on paper for the first six months of their ruthlessly scrutinised employment. Like Malcolm Bhola, Ivy Dean excelled at working at speed, a facility vital to the fact that alterations to trousers were done downstairs while the customer waited, the necessary adjustments and pressing taking no longer than five to ten minutes on average. With a unit of four comprising himself, Bill Franks, Malcolm Bhola and Ivy Dean, John Stephen as part of his optimistically youthful incentive projected a new air of optimism surrounding the opening of No 5 Carnaby Street. A small loan from Barclays Bank helped facilitate renovations to the tiny shop, which was given a canary yellow front, with orange boxes covered in red felt as its interior features, and decorated additionally with canary-yellow drapes, oak cupboards and a red polished changing room. Always concerned with the fine points of interiors, John Stephen was in part responsible for revolutionising the way menswear shops looked, and like Quant at Bazaar, established the prototypical boutique aesthetic that was to be copied by an entire generation of 1960s fashion retailers. Prior to Myles Antony's appointment as design consultant in 1959, Stephen's windows were dressed by the technically perfect, but unadventurous Warren Scott from Robinson & Cleavers, the Irish linen store in Beak Street, and his white shop carriers with the JS lettering and black motif of a perfectly posed boy made for them in small quantities of up to 500 by Progressive Supplies. If the interior of No 5, and more so that of the Man's Shop, opened in 1959, struck the uneducated public as unapologetically camp in its colour-coding and use of body-beautiful male mannequins and blow-ups to promote minimally cut briefs and hipsters, then the dismissive mainstream reaction, inevitable at the time, was quickly diffused when teenage Mod culture affirmatively hitched their ambiguously straight image to gay styles, and in a weird reversal of subcultures, adopted gay clothes, even simulating same-sex relations by an implacable attitude of cool expressed towards women.

To supplement the shop's income, discreet ads for briefs were placed in the personal columns of papers like *The Standard*, *The Evening News* and *The Star*, and the necessary practice of issuing clandestine illustrated mail order catalogues continued on occasions, although printing costs were affectively prohibitive, and the circulation discontinued as shop custom increased proportionately. With No 5 Carnaby Street stocked with his trademark brightly-coloured hipsters, some of them made in poplin ordered from a Manchester supplier, Burgess and Leadwood, button-down collar cotton and denim shirts customised in blues, pinks, orange and grey, Dutch boy caps and sexy black see-through and leather briefs, John Stephen's exceptional Man's Shop began to attract wider notice; the extraordinary nature of its stand-out clothes largely promoted initially by word of mouth. But to maintain a business that at the time the fashion press wouldn't take seriously on account of its low end Soho address, and netting on average £40 a week, demanded unremitting dedication to hard work, and the increasingly versatile Bill Franks found it necessary to learn how to cut and sew, as well as establish some sort of business system for an otherwise unpiloted independent fuelled by Stephen's intensely creative but largely impractical dynamic.

The break necessary to putting John Stephen's backwater shop more securely on the map came felicitously from a totally unexpected source. A salesman from McCaul's knitwear, faced with a large export cancellation for colourful polo shirts, had met with a unanimously negative response at the large number of West End outlets he had tried to interest in stocking a garment considered too risqué for absorption into the repertoire of conventional menswear. Instantly recognising the potential for selling in the knitwear to his young clientele, in search of new upbeat Italian-styled fashions, John Stephen amazed his partner Bill Franks by impulsively ordering 2,000 of the garment on sale or return, the boxes stacked in the workroom as a high-rise cardboard architecture waiting to be stripped open and tried on the public. To the initially sceptical Bill Franks, the results proved spectacular, with the pastel coloured three-button polo sweaters proving an unprecedented hit from the moment they went on display, and so infectious was the demand that the shop was able to discount the product at three for the price of two. The unanticipated financial success of the venture apart, the shirt's popularity was a clear indicator to John Stephen that there were signs of a potential mass market for men's clothes in unusual colours and unisex styles, if the new generation would only connect.

The McCaul's success was also a signal to John Stephen that he had transcended his niche reputation for selling transgressive clothes largely to theatre people and butch gays cruising Marshall Street, and reached a wider, and encouragingly younger generation anxious to wear the sort of clothes they had seen in French nouvelle vague movies, or previously only associated with exclusive European wear or with a distinctly gay provenance. Ruth B. King in her *Sixties Memories*, interestingly recalls the little shops indigenous to Carnaby Street before its 1960s saturation, including an 'invisible mender,' and that the sartorially infallible John Stephen had something going with a member of staff at Galleries Lafayette on Regent Street, where she worked, and would sporadically dart into the shop in knife-edged pressed suits during lunch-hours.

Although John Stephen lacked all sense of formal business acumen he and Bill Franks were sufficiently forward thinking and necessarily expansive to invest any profits made in leasing other small shops in Carnaby Street as they became available. Now living together at a small flat in Sussex Gardens, Paddington, that was to be their home until moving to a luxury five-room flat in Jermyn Street, Mayfair, in the mid-sixties, they quickly established their hold on the street through The Man's Shop, managed by the stunningly attractive, sexually ambidextrous Pat Simms, a young man who had responded to an advertisement placed in *The Standard* and was working at the time as an electrical salesman. Simms' vibrant personality, ability to simulate camp and sparkling sales efficacy attracted customers like the pop stars Billy Fury and Cliff Richard, with Richard insisting on Simms' personal advice and attention when choosing trousers and knitwear for casual and stage wear, and additionally bringing in his band and dancers to buy clothes for a London Palladium residency. Cliff Richard was an assiduous John Stephen customer between the years 1960–63 and gave some pointer to his ambiguous sexual orientation by going so far as to invite John Stephen to spend a weekend with him in Brighton. Another early customer to the Man's Shop, on a regular basis, was Dusty Springfield's brother Tom, who searched the racks for gloved-on hipsters and the latest colours in giraffe-necked tab-collar shirts.

It was Bill Franks who interviewed and assessed staff applicants, early on establishing the John Stephen criteria necessary for employment. Managers had to possess a charismatic and likeable personality, including the ability to project, – if you can't sell yourself you can't sell the clothes – good looks were a prerequisite, so too was age, with most managers coming in at 17–18. An eloquent enthusiasm for clothes and the ability to wear John Stephen's designs to good effect in the shop were also vital to the post, with some of the managers changing clothes two or three times a day to stay ahead of their customers, as was discretion, in that managers were taught never to approach customers, but to leave them to the pursuit of relaxed browsing, a radical innovation at a time when customers were generally pressurised into buying by officious and over-inquisitive staff. John Stephen gave an entirely new and modern flavour to retail by dissolving the barrier between staff and customers into a fluent interchange of common interests, and by instituting an informal relaxed atmosphere in his shops, in which customers were known by their Christian names, and encouraged to return. 'I'm certain,' Stephen was to comment, 'that much of the success of our boutiques is because we have teenagers working in them who really care about clothes. I think finding enthusiastic staff is half the battle, for their enthusiasm can be infectious enough to make the casual customer really fashion conscious and eager for new ideas.' The personalised service initiated by John Stephen shops went a long way to triggering an unprecedented 20th-century phenomenon in which men rather than women became the inspired leaders of sixties fashion. It was the male Mods who created the sixties look and the girls who followed as rivals consigned to second place. 'Men are worse than women now, they drive us mad,' John Stephen commented at the time. 'They come in every week demanding something new. Even the ones who haven't got money try to be original. They'll sew black patch pockets on a white jacket or something like that.' In George Melly's putatively skewed estimate, 'Mods remained purists and for a time re-established their pre-eminence by quite coolly turning towards overt homosexuality and going to bed with any showbiz queen who was famous and smart enough to reinforce their tottering egos.'

As John Stephen expanded in Carnaby Street, so each of his shops took on its own individual signature, often dictated by the manager's idiosyncratic preferences, but always overseen by John Stephen, who insisted on scrupulous hygiene, helped design the interiors, together with Myles Antony, allowed no food in the shops, but natural to the times permitted staff and customers to

The name John Stephen was soon displayed on several shops along Carnaby Street.

smoke, Stephen himself often being seen with his features fogged out by a blue spiral cumulus cloud of cigar smoke. Stephen's obsession with scrutinising his shops for cleanliness extended to searching even the tops of picture frames for an incriminating patina of dust. Pictures of current pop stars, newspaper clippings of interest to Mods, blown-up photos of regular customers wearing the store's best fashions, and the use of iconic album sleeves in display all created an in-store ethos that helped facilitate the commitment of a new generation to identifying clothes with the pop zeitgeist that celebrated the look as the direct expression of their music.

The significant furthering of John Stephen's inexorable hold on Carnaby Street occurred in 1960, when the bomb-site opposite No 5 Carnaby Street was redeveloped by St James Property Company, with Stephen deciding spontaneously to take the L-shaped shop put up by the prospectors as 49–51 Carnaby Street, a space that became the legendary The Man's Shop, at a rent of £1,200 a year on a 21-year lease. Typically acting on impulse, irrespective of his financial state, Stephen with characteristic temerity accelerated without collateral, a policy he would continue to do throughout the 1960s, at times almost bankrupting his organisation due to his unstoppably expansive momentum. Stephen's usual working day began typically at 7.30am, and continued through to 7pm, seven days a week; his addiction to the endorphin boosts triggered by obsessive work linked to a tirelessly resourceful creative dynamic that in terms of sheer unrivalled prolific invention totally outstripped all his incurably plagiaristic contemporaries in sixties' men's fashion.

With three shops in Carnaby Street, John Stephen was starting to make something of a cult name, to those in the know, although business by way of foot traffic continued to be frustratingly slow. Additional support for the shop came from the advocacy of Gordon Deighton, who as a features writer for the influential fashion journal *Man About Town* was instrumental in drawing attention to Stephen's provocatively unusual designs. An early visitor to the street at the time, Lloyd Johnson, recalls, that 'Before him [Stephen] Carnaby Street was just a backwater; the only thing there was the tobacconist's. When he opened a shop there, the scooter boys started discovering him. It was a great shop. There was a guy called Mac who worked in that first John Stephen shop on Carnaby Street. He used to smoke B&H with a Dupont lighter, and he'd always offer you a cigarette when you came in. I can remember going in there in 1960 and Mac had on a leopardskin waistcoat. In a funny way it was a throwback to the rockers and in another a prediction of what would happen in 1966. That was incredible. If somebody wore suede shoes or a pink shirt or white roll neck then, they were considered a bit off, but what was happening with John Stephen was completely different.' Buying a pink shirt at the time or a pair of white skinny pre-shrunk jeans was viewed as a gay trademark, an aberration that was unanimously seen as an overt acknowledgement of same-sex orientation. 'I remember one particular Friday lunchtime,' Lloyd Johnson continues, 'you got paid in cash in those days, when a friend went with me to Austin's on Shaftesbury Avenue, and we both bought pink tab-collared shirts. My mate took his back and got a white one because people were calling him a poof. But I thought bollocks I'm not returning mine, so I wore it on Monday morning on the train to work. I was sweating, so many people were looking at me. I wore it with a blue knitted tie, a blue suit and Annello and Davide boots, and looked the business.'

Another vitally important addition to the creation of the inimitable John Stephen look was the employment of Myles Antony in 1960, as window dresser and design consultant to all his shops. The Dublin-born Antony, who had studied art under the noted Irish painter, Fergus O'Ryan, had originally met John Stephen in a concealed gay café on two floors, called La Rouge et Noire, in Foubert's Place, off Carnaby Street, a two-time place, that acted straight in the day to customers and gay at night. Living with his hairdresser boyfriend, Paul, in a flat in Nottingham Street, off the Marylebone High Street, and working full-time for the department store Whiteley's in London's Queensway as a window dresser, Myles' aesthetically refined good looks complemented Stephen's own dark version of lounge lizard masculinity, and on first meeting an immediate creative chemistry was established between the two bright young things, each nurturing a defiant penchant for unapologetic camp as the ostentatious spearhead for fashion display. Myles Antony had personally discovered Stephen's newly opened The Man's Shop in 1960, on the occasion of his twenty-first birthday, when his boyfriend had bought him a strikingly unorthodox shirt with a black base with deep turquoise and purple stripes as a one-off from the alluringly individual and extremely limited stock on display. Antony had already patronised Bill Green's Vince, as an outlet for gay men, but The Man's Shop proved an altogether more stimulating attraction, the originality and inventiveness of the clothes standing out to Myles as altogether far livelier in their uninhibited style and modern colours than the imported and often precious leisurewear available round the corner at Vince.

John Stephen's cutting-edge clothes, distinguished by the originality of their colour and fabric, had come to Antony's attention again, while working at Whiteleys, through the nearby His Clothes at Queensway, and by going into the shop and learning that they were looking for a window dresser in line with Stephen's forward-presenting vision. Advised to arrange an appointment with John Stephen himself in Carnaby Street, Antony was astonished on arrival to be interviewed by the unforgettably attractive young man he had met originally at the Rouge et Noir, been to bed with, and never entirely forgotten. Invited to do a trial window for 49/51 Carnaby Street, and taking time out from his job at Whiteley's, Myles responded to the challenge by drawing and painting two designs of the Greek god Apollo, one in turquoise and green, the other in pink and red, displayed prominently in two painted arches, charging an optimal £15 for his ambitiously-placed design. Stephen and Franks were sufficiently impressed by the display's vivid use of camp artistry and boldly accented colour to ask Antony back to their Jermyn Street apartment, to discuss details of permanent employment to dress the windows of their three shops, and where to consolidate trust, the cheerfully domestic Bill Franks cooked sausages and mash for Myles, while Stephen adventitiously discussed terms of employment with the fine arts trained design consultant who was to prove crucial to the expansion of the John Stephen shops throughout the entire sixties decade. The job was secured for £15 a week, as a considerable improvement on the basic £11 Antony had received at Whiteley's, with Antony additionally insisting on not working on Saturdays. He was also, and more importantly, given complete artistic freedom by John Stephen, an astutely liberal delegator who overviewed, but never curtailed, or attempted to moderate Antony's often flagrantly controversial homoerotic windows. Myles Antony remembers the pronounced nervous shake to John Stephen's hands as indicative of the high level of anxiety that was one of his dominant characteristics, so too a detachment from the sensual, and an apparent objectivity towards the flagrantly homoerotic aspects of his designs, that Myles associated with the repressed nature of his upbringing. It wasn't that Stephen was disinterested in sex, it was more that he was forced by the times to live in denial of his sexuality. Something of the alternative nature of the street, and the relative marginalised wasteland it represented in 1960 in terms of foot traffic, is evoked by Myles Antony's recollection of the excitement he felt and generated to staff whenever the impossible happened, and somebody was sighted entering the street, with all the apprehension that it could be a prospective customer. It was Myles Antony who was responsible for designing the interior of the newly leased and seminal His Clothes; the exterior of the repurposed shop appearing curved, as the building didn't lend itself to a vertical façade. Taking his seminal ideas from the contemporary movie *Cleopatra*, and downscaling them to budget, Antony created a suspended ceiling for the shop with coloured overhead lighting, the Perspex panels lit from the inside, designed three arches for a delicate Gothic-style tracery effect, and had three walls pained white and one a slab of imperial purple with the designated colour mixed by John Oliver at Notting Hill Gate. Each of the innovative shop's three fitting rooms was set into the concentrated purple wall, and there was a grey and white tessellated tiled floor, the ensemble in its entirety presenting an illusory fantasy world accessible to the individually-motivated customer for the duration of time spent in the shop. One particularly engaging early Myles Antony display at His Clothes utilised home-designed props, including copper paper sculpture masks, sprayed polystyrene blocks to simulate the effect of crumbling ruins and cut-out tiles in gold on the copper floor, all made in Antony's resident Carnaby Street design studio. To emergent teenage Mods from the likes of London's Shepherd's Bush or Walthamstow, Myles Antony's unparalleled interior for His Clothes was like an illusory film-set into which they stepped as incongruously fascinated participants. As committed to the look as John Stephen, Myles Antony, who was as Stephen expanded into the sixties' furore of torrential commerce appointed a director, worked with corresponding dedication and flamboyant panache to introduce gay politics, purely on a level of camp, into the art of window dressing, and into the continuously inventive colour-moment that the John Stephen sixties' look represented.

John Stephen, for all his disinterest in practical affairs and the mundane aspects of running a business, was sufficiently hard-headed and adaptive to realise the ingredients necessary to sustain a continuously expansive independent concern. A few years down the line, in an interview with Rosalie Shann for *Reveille*, he outlined a few basic beliefs that had proved instrumental to his unprecedented success in men's fashion. 'I believe,' he told Shann, 'there are three things necessary if you want to reach the top from the bottom rung of the ladder. First, you must give the public what they want, if possible just at the time they're beginning to realise that they want it. Second, you must work, not just eight hours a day but on and on. Third, you must plough back. In other words when you make your first £100, don't go mad and rush out and buy a car. Continue using public transport and put that £100 right back into the business.'

It was by employing instinctually simplistic and largely self-taught principles as a basis for expansion that John Stephen was able within years of setting up in a dodgy lowlife red-light district of Soho to transform his individual bi-sexual look into sassy uninhibited pop cool. It was inevitable too, that Soho as London's cosmopolitan village, was geographically to become the core of the youthful revolution that started to gain consolidated core

*The pop singer
Eden Kane
models one of
John's striped
jumpers. The
female model
wears a man's
suit. It's 1963.*

momentum in the late fifties. It wasn't only the cheap rental of shops that had attracted John Stephen there at a time when the district was unconditionally dead, but also the unconscious realisation that the new generation's fashion needs were best complemented in his mind by Soho's formative network of clubs and cafes, than anywhere else in the city. From the uninhibited lipstick-slashed girls for sale in zippy pencil skirts, seamed stockings and spiked heels, clustered in the complex of lugubrious alleys behind Wardour Street they had made into their own, to the newly opened record and clothes shops, the rave jazz cellars, the cafes as meeting points in which a quirky and eclectic bohemianism prevailed over social status or sexual orientation, and the increased availability of street drugs, youth were drawn to Soho as the basis of change and demonstrative youthful rebellion. Cellars like the Last Chance, the Kilt, La Poubelle, the Coffee Pot, the Limbo and the Roaring Twenties were all subterranean meeting places packed with teenagers, pimps, rent boys and lowlife characters, all picking up on the exhilarating beginnings of a new liberated epoch. Again, it was Colin MacInnes, in his seminal novel *Absolute Beginners*, who gave expression to the dominant youth incentive of the time, who in turn undeniably helped John Stephen inaugurate his particular line of sexually ambiguous clothes. 'In this Soho,' MacInnes writes, 'the headquarters of the adult mafia, you could everywhere see the signs of the un-silent teenage revolution. The disc shops with those lovely sleeves set in their windows, the most original things to come out in our lifetime, and the kids inside them purchasing guitars, or spending fortunes on the songs of the Top Twenty. The shirt-stores and bra-stores with cine-star photos in the windows, selling all the exclusive teenage drag I've been describing. The hair-style salons where they inflict blow-wave torture on the kids for hours on end. The cosmetic shops – making girls of seventeen, fifteen, even thirteen look like pale rinsed-out sophisticates. Scooters and bubble-cars driven madly down the road by kids, who a few years ago, were pushing toy ones on the pavement. And everywhere you go the narrow coffee bars and darkened cellars with the kids packed tight, just whispering like bees inside the hive waiting for a glorious queen bee to appear.'

MacInnes' localised Soho, was also John Stephen's, and the kids who located to Soho's hedonistic and increasingly sexually ambivalent ethos were in time to make his shops into the liveliest and most congested that London's menswear had ever known. It was also fitting, given the devolution of class instigated by a newly disaffected youth, that John Stephen, as the least socially privileged of the new wave of London menswear designers, should feature as their chosen spearhead. Interestingly none of Stephen's early competitors like the entrepreneurial Bill Green of Vince, or the more socially privileged trio of Cecil Gee, Louis Austin or John Michael, the owner of Sportique in Old Compton Street, ever came near to rivalling him for sheer inventiveness, audacity, pop glamour, uncompromising experimentation, and for bringing the entire guest list of the sixties' meteoric superstars, from the Beatles to the Rolling Stones and Jimi Hendrix to his self-created centre of fashion gravity, Carnaby Street, London W1. With the landmark Shakespeare's Head pub, originally owned in 1736 by Thomas and John Shakespeare, who were distant relatives of the poet, dominating the Liberty entrance to the street, and the poet's life-size bust looking down unsuspectingly on pedestrians from a second-floor window, no other contemporary London street had ever attracted so diverse a mixture of youthful energies so singularly concentrated into the pursuit of clothes.

John Stephen, even before the precipitant Mod invasion, with its fanaticism for the look, was starting naturally to expand within financial limitations as the 1960s got under way. In 1961, the magazine *Style For Men* reported on the opening of the eponymous John Stephen outlet in Regent Street, branding it the first and altogether unexpected men's boutique in Regent Street. The shop was opened by the pop singer Eden Kane, a.k.a. Richard Starsteld, whose May 1961 No 1 smash released on the blue Decca label was *Well I Ask You*, followed by another Top Ten success *Get Lost*, in September of the same year. Kane's stunningly attractive looks, together with his preference for customised Italian-cut suits made him the perfect sartorial advertisement for John Stephen's incursion into the traditionally conservative and ubiquitously high end territory of Regent Street. The association with Eden Kane reinforced John Stephen's by now mandatory status as the designer who dressed pop stars, and the shop's innovative profile squeezed reluctant praise from a sceptical reviewer. 'The new boutique is sparsely equipped, but it has two essentials – varied and interesting merchandise – and thanks to some publicity a promising market. John Stephen's practical approach suggests some useful propositions to other retailers. Public relations come high on the priority list.' Myles Anthony remembers John Stephen being so emotionally overwrought by having improbably secured an outlet on Regent Street that he sat out on the steps distracted and in tears, refusing to join the fizzy shop party.

That John Stephen too had set about subversively reversing received notions of gender through his clothes, was made obvious when the *Daily Sketch* drew attention on 18 September 1961, to the fact that John Stephen used girls to model men's clothes. A photograph showed model Suzie

Kendall wearing a red and white striped sweater, leather jerkin and twill trousers, while Virginia Lyons modelled dogs-tooth trousers and a peacock-blue denim shirt. As a clear pointer to the gay subtext implied by the unisex nature of John Stephen's clothes, the journalist concluded by commenting that at His Clothes 'even men's ties have a new use as hair ribbons.'

Even though John Stephen continued to be perceived by the mainstream as a rogue gene infiltrating the system, a transient style-bandit who would quickly burn out, he had nonetheless come to stay, and the neatly-lettered black-on-white John Stephen label, printed to order at Witherington House, suddenly tagged a garment with street credibility amongst young style-completists at the time. Not only was John Stephen local to the Sohoites, but his clothes were eminently affordable, as well as providing extravagant colour moments to the cognoscenti. He had already provided the Beatles with round-collared suit jackets, the Rolling Stones with dark blue leather waistcoats worn for their early Marquee and TV performances, as well as dressing Cliff Richard, Billy Fury, Long John Baldry, Heinz, Eden Kane and Johnny Kidd and the Pirates, as a few of his early celebrity customers. As the 1960s got under way, so John Stephen was to become the chief exponent of Mod fashion, the designer who created the distinct look adopted by teenage Mods, and whose signature was to extend to eleven shops in Carnaby Street alone, as well as branches in the other mainline arteries of fashion, the King's Road, Old Compton Street and South Kensington. This shy, unaffected individual, whose genius lay in the application of detail to style, and the ability to think fast forward, was to create the London look, and in doing so to give Mods an individualistic, fiercely competitive identity. For the first time in their short evolution, the Mod fashion leaders, or Faces, found themselves outpaced by the accelerated ideas of a designer whose stratospheric imagination knew no check on the taboos it was bound to break, and in the unstoppable drive of its creative ingenuity. And Stephen had begun, against all probabilities, to find a market in the new emergent youth culture who called themselves Mods, and who were predominantly the subject of Gillian Freeman's 1961 cult novel about gay relations and lifestyle, *The Leather Boys*. Arguing her case for a feminine obsession with clothes, observed more often by men than women, Freeman describes the rites of passage made by a typical fashion-conscious young Mod of the times. 'He began to change. It took him a long time because he liked to look really smart ... He always took great care of his shoes, which he had hand-made and which cost him a lot of money. Tonight he was wearing a suit but sometimes he wore a narrow-shouldered jacket, with plum-coloured stripes, and sometimes a leather jacket with saddle stitching. He tied his tie carefully in front of the little mirror and then bent his knees so he could see to do his hair.' And he was of course, from the detailed description, wearing John Stephen's clothes.

3

THE LOOK

Legend has it, and the myth-making remains obscure in its exact origins, that at first there were only twenty Mods in London, a group that included the seminal names of Peter Meaden, arguably the first London Mod, who was at the outset of their career to manage The Who, under the name the High Faces, Peter Sugar, Michael Simmonds, Patrick Uden and Marc Feld, soon to become Marc Bolan, as some of its diffidently trendy progenitors. Three of these names, Marc Feld, Michael Simmonds and Peter Sugar, were to feature in the September 1962 issue of *Man About Town* in a feature addressing fashion called 'The Young Take the Wheel.' Town called them 'Faces Without Shadows', a triumvirate of fashion obsessives living ahead of their time. Lacking money to spend in Vince and John Stephen's His Clothes, the three had devised ways of altering retail clothes into customised, and of living continuously and ostentatiously ahead of fashion expectations. Marc Feld had little distinctive musical originality at the time, and was a largely inept folkie derivative of Bob Dylan, his only ambition being to be recognised on the street for his dandified look. 'You got to be different from the other kids,' Feld insisted. 'I mean you got to be two steps ahead. The stuff that half the haddocks you see around are wearing I was wearing years ago. A kid in my class came up to me in his new suit, an Italian box it was. He says, "Just look at the length of your jacket," he says. "You're not with it." he says. "I was wearing that style two years ago," I said. Of course they don't like that.' This coterie, with their lack of any political programme, were committed to an aesthetic revolution that placed the look or a very specific dress-code as seminal to their lifestyle. Essentially solitary, narcissistic individuals, Mods gave style attitude. As a movement they cultivated elegant, often self-designed clothing, talking, dancing, black R&B and soul music, drugs in the form of speed, and an almost feminine mode of transportation – an individually fetishised Italian scooter, rather than the throttle power and black leathers of the archetypal 1950s biker boy looking dangerously mean. And nowhere was the early union of art school chic to Mod attitude better exemplified than in the early posters advertising the punkishly anarchic, Pete Meaden-managed The High Numbers. Clean white artwork reversed out of solid black, with optimal lower case sans-serif lettering down the right-hand side, complemented by a bleached image of Roger Daltrey in profile, worked as a poster motif to provide the band with a suitably confrontational image that was strikingly arts school modern, before their change of name to the more economic sounding The Who. The process though, was continued as a graphic, in sharp black and white, under The Who moniker, utilising six letters, with one distinct embellishment, an arrow which originally pointed upwards out of the 'o,' and was then moved to extend the vertical thrust of the central 'h,' a graphic representation of the band's one central image: Pete Townshend's windmilling right arm in its apex, before crashing down on a rudimentary chord.

Mods were literally, as a symptom of their times, clothes obsessed, and before opportunistically discovering John Stephen's eventful chain of small boutiques in Carnaby Street were largely reliant on jobbing East End Jewish tailors to give them the look they had improvised. The most famous of these was Bilgorri's of Bishopsgate, where Mods had tonic suits made up to individual patterns incorporating two small lapels, three pockets all with flaps, four buttons on the front, the top one only fastened, two vents, and sharp narrow trousers. Suits were almost uniformly worn with pastel-coloured Brooks Brothers button-down collar shirts and basket-weave shoes from Raoul, elastic-sided Chelsea boots purchased from Anello & Davide on Charing Cross Road, or the 'fine poynts' variation launched by an East London concern called Denson, who were on the back of John Stephen's initial success to bench-make a boot called Carnaby Street. John Stephen himself regularly purchased black Chelsea boots from Anello & Davide, who were essentially theatrical shoemakers, but their affordably unusual styles, originally made for flamenco dancers, attracted impoverished art students from St Martin's and Mods from all over London to their West End shop as the 1960s gained momentum. Their elasticated boots, popularised by the

The cool gang. John Stephen centre surrounded by Georgie Fame and the Blue Flames all dressed by John.

Beatles and polished a cellulose glossy black, gave additional emphasis to the sharp line of figure-skimming hipsters readily available in John Stephen's noted and proliferating shops.

John Stephen had chosen his location well, given that Mods were to make Soho into their own identifiable recreational territory. Driven by the compulsive need to shape a new ethos for their generation, radically different from the uninspired monochrome dress sense and cultural vapidity of the post-war generation, Mods took readily-available office jobs in order to earn and spend liberally on clothes, music and pills, in the all-night clubs they had made into their signature meeting places. Mods were the first genera- tion of serious clubbers, blocking themselves on pills so as to dance the night away, and as importantly draw attention to themselves through the inimitably pioneering clothes they wore. And according to Andrew Loog Oldham, a ruthlessly committed early sixties' exponent of the look, 'wearing John Stephen's clothes compared with playing guitars or drums as a lad's first serious commitment to banddom.'

Myles Antony, always one of the most perceptive observers of the early Carnaby Street scene, was continually fascinated by the way in which teenage Mods began without precedent to make up on arriving in the street, sitting on their Lambrettas or Vespas, outside the shops, meticulously applying eyeliner and eye-shadow, and using makeup usually loaned them by their girlfriend, with Myles following suit by wearing kohl on his eyes at a time when it was taboo for men to do so. Carnaby Street was suddenly the safe precinct for Mod-adopted androgyny, and the street itself provoked an unusual ambiva- lent gay response in straights, as well as being a renowned cruising area with both factions meeting along a seamless line of fashion invention. For Myles Antony and John Stephen, the world of inherited gender appeared to have been impossibly reversed, with heterosexuals wanting to look stereotypically gay and gays out of inveterate habit downplaying their same-sex attraction by dressing in adapted Mod leisure wear. Carlo Manzi, an early proponent of the look, has suggested quite rightly that Mods were into male appreciation, and that women played a secondary role in their code of ethics. 'If you think about sexuality, well in Modernism you dressed for other blokes. You were far more interested in a guy coming up and saying, "Great suit," than a girl coming up and saying, "Great suit", because the girls didn't look particularly good. Mod girls were never as attractive as Mod boys. They wore clothes that didn't enhance their figures, although you would look at a girl if she looked like she had spent a bit of money.' It's interesting how in Manzi's experiential theory, that the assessment of a woman's clothes were seen as essential to her credibility, and that a failure to adopt the look led to her being dismissed as unworthy of attention, no matter the significant qualities of her personality.

Mods preferred to hang out with each other as an endorsement of cool, and being naturally hedonistic they liked drugs as the push into alternative states. In the edgy Soho precinct between D'Arblay Street and Wardour Street, the cluster of amphetamine clubs, where speed-dealers pushed blues stamped with the manufacturer's name SKF (Smith, Kline and French of Welwyn Garden City), included amongst others La Discotheque, Le Douce, a gay club, the Coffee Pot, the Huntsman, the Limba Club, the Granada and the Take Five. Most famous of all, and with its bright young things unanimously dressed in the latest update of John Stephen's clothes, was the Scene Club, situated in Ham Yard at 41 Great Windmill Street, and managed by Ronan O'Rahilly, as part of the notoriously underworld Nash gang operation in Soho. The pill-head Mods, dressed to kill and with a cutter's eye for the precise detail of an 18- or 22-inch jacket vent or the chisel-point of an olive-green basket-weave shoe, were in part attracted to the club's red-walled interior, with chill-out cushions placed round the edges of the dance floor, and by the resident DJ, the incandescently charismatic speed-freak Guy Stevens. At the time Stevens owned the most comprehensive collection of imported black music in London, taking in thousands of rare soul, gospel, blues and R&B discs, only available as expensive imports, the glossy record sleeve images of the artists wearing cool Ivy League or sharply cut Italian mohair suits, going a long way to influencing the way in which Mods dressed. Speed-dealers, as a ubiquitous part of the Mod recreational scene, operated inside the club, selling Drinamyl pills, largely sourced from the London docks, or as the recycling of repeat prescriptions in five, tens, twenties, fifties and a hundred, the drug maintaining the user's option to stay up all night dancing to the DJ's idiosyncratic R&B grooves. Speed as a recreational drug was a way of life for London Mods, the triangular purple hearts becoming endemic currency amongst clubbers, a subterranean commodity that appealed to users, not only for the euphoric rush of energies it promoted, but perversely as a challenge to the health risks, like burn-out and paranoia, that were significantly coded into the data of abuse. The slogan SPEED KILLS was painted in enormous black letters on one wall of the Marquee, and just inside the entrance to La Discotheque, as a cultishly proclaimed death-rite, with a poster next to the ticket-office at La Discotheque reading: '£50 Reward. The management will pay £50 to any person who can provide concrete evidence direct to the police that any member of the management of The Discotheque Club is responsible for the sale of purple hearts – The Committee.' And Soho as the elected centre of speed dealing, its square mile of accelerated club life constituting a nocturnal Mod microsphere, was also the target for repeated police raids, with thousands of purple hearts regularly littering the floor of the Scene Club or the Marquee like hail with the abrupt arrival of the police. The situation, sensationally fuelled by the media, became so acute that an alarmed government proposed a maximum fine of £200, or six months' imprisonment for those caught in possession of Drinamyl without an authorised prescription, and additionally persuaded the manufacturers Smith Kline and French to dispense with the drug's attractive colour and shape, and to replace the pharmaceutical template with its update Dexedrine, otherwise known to Mods as blues or dexes.

The importance of music to Mod chemistry was something taken up singularly by John Stephen, whose shops were the first to play loud in-store pop music, both as an incentive to attract customers, and as an energy compatible with his youthful clientele, the majority of whom were aged 15–25. According to the fashion critic Nik Cohn, 'To reach the teenage market, Stephen turned His Clothes into something equivalent to rock 'n roll ... Above all, he made his shops like amusement arcades. He had records blaring as loud as they would go, kaleidoscopic window displays, garments hung around the open doorways and spilling out across the pavements, in imitation of St Tropez. For the first time shopping ceased to be a chore. Instead of ducking in and out quickly, kids would go along especially, as a treat, and trail slowly along the parade, fingering the clothes in the doorways, dazzled by colours and deafened by pop ... But this was all embellishment. Underneath, the central equation was that, every time you walked past a John Stephen window, there was something new and loud in it, and when you counted out your money, you found you could afford it.'

Part of essential Mod living, which found another parallel with John Stephen's permanently wired charge, was to fill the moment to maximum input, and speed as a drug accentuates the concentration of living optimally in the present, without care for the continuously projected future. With the sound full-on for Doris Troy's plaintive vocal on *Watcha Gonna Do About It* on a crackly Atlantic yellow-labelled vinyl 45, the male dancer, one of the faces pushing the floor to overspill, demanded attention by his Vidal Sassoon-styled hair, his black velvet tie bought at John Stephen's His Clothes, his elephant cord hipsters, a John Stephen first, bought at The Man's Shop, and by his Jam Gibson black and white contrasting shoes. Dancing alone to the block and bang, his hair with a short half-parting across the centre of the head, with the hair combed in opposite directions, away from the parting, creating a two-tiered look, and lacquered into position, remained immaculate on the dance floor. There was no escaping the femininity of the cut, or the fact that Mods dressed with far greater attention to detail than the panda-eyed, bobbed, mini-skirted girls competing unsuccessfully for their attention on the pill-blocked floor of the Scene Club, with its convoy of wacky, mirror-cascading, customised scooters parked outside in the rainy Piccadilly yard. Doris Troy, Wilson Pickett, Irma Thomas, Martha and the Vandellas, Lee Dorsey, their black voices intensified by molten fault-lines of passion, rode above tough beats, driving horn riffs and the belly-dancer flutter of tambourines, forming a sonic halo around the Mods scattered at the entrance, discussing trouser alterations done by Ivy Dean, or the best colour John Smedley polo, or more pertinently the latest John Stephen gingham shirt to appear in one of his windows, a shirt fashioned from a remnant in an edition of no more than three, and likely to have disappeared entirely by the following shopping Saturday.

John Stephen's designs were by their originality inseparable from the image of emergent British beat merchants like the Rolling Stones, The Who, the Pretty Things and the Small Faces, all London-based bands tolerated by Mods, as their individually high-octane energy music and defiant attitude expressed through their idiosyncratic choice of clothes could be readily metabolised like speed and converted directly into contagiously delirious dance. But at heart Mods favoured black music, including Tamla Motown, as the genre largely personified and celebrated the outlaw as hero, the under-class as avengers, and was in an oblique way a political statement, an ideology somatised by dance, and readily assimilated by the energised dynamic of youth culture. Dancing the night through on French blues or purple hearts was not only an affirmation of being unapologetically young at a particular optimal moment in time, the early 1960s; but by extension an awareness that the present they were encountering could never be recreated in the same way twice. And as part of the narcissism cultivated by their exclusive cult, Mods had developed a dance called the block and bang, with movements devised to allow for the compressed space in crowded clubs, which had intricate, fast-moving, edited steps, that had the participant appear to be dancing in on himself to the exclusion of the floor. And if the energised adrenalin high of Saturday night on the dance floor, inevitably dissolved into the flat grey plateau of Sunday morning, then that was by all accounts another time, another place, light years away from the fadeout of Doris Troy's achingly resonant phrasing, her voice sounding like lived-in velvet to the Mod dancer not ever wanting to let the song or the moment go.

Carnaby
Street

John Stephen
es el inventor de
la moda
Carnaby Street
y está a la cabeza
de un vasto
imperio.
A los veintinueve
años es el dueño de
buena parte
de los
establecimientos
situados en
la célebre
arteria y
de una extensa
cadena con
ramificaciones en
el extranjero.

*John Stephen
1964, and the
best looking
man of his
generation?
Below, the
suspended style
of window
dressing
adopted by
Myles Antony.*

Something of the shape-shifting evanescent qualities of the sixties' look, always in danger of imploding due to self-aggrandisement, was captured in essence by an active participant, Lloyd Johnson, who observed that 'When it was called the Mod look, that was when it started going silly. The look, was in fact, much more Ivy League and preppy. The really heavy side of Mod came out of the East End, with midnight-blue mohair suits and those great coloured shirts in mustard or blue with a black knitted tie from John Michael.' Something of the self-invention needed to create the naturally improvised look early on, when there weren't designers to facilitate the itchy need for clothes, and John Stephen's designs were necessarily consigned to a limited gay subculture, was recollected by Michael Moke, one of the early and pivotal progenitors of Mod. Moke recalls, 'There weren't any books then on style, so we had to take our lead where we could. I went to the south of France and celebrated my eighteenth birthday in St Tropez, then went on to Italy and Spain, all the time learning the look and the way people dressed there. We also went to Nouvelle Vague films and watched the way actors smoked a cigarette, how they buttoned their shirts and jackets and which shoes they wore.'

The diminutively attractive John Stephen, with the drop-dead gorgeous looks of a movie star, and his unstoppable seventeen hours a day work momentum, was more than anyone responsible not only for shaping the Mod look, but for directing men's fashion through its most transitional and innovative decade of the 20th-century. Like his predominantly Mod customers Stephen lived each moment of his life as though it was his last, frantically drawing designs in Soho cafes, personally choosing fabrics for his collections, assisting with the cutting and selling, giving interviews to the media, conducting the overview of his shops, mixing with the customers to learn of their clothes' preferences and drinking hard at night to offset nervous burn-out and periods of total collapse.

Mods were, by their nature, mostly on the move, and the necessary quotient of recreational time needed to compensate for largely routinily uninspired office employment, was the signature written into their speedy lifestyle, with the emphasis placed on looking stylish all the time, a practice exemplified by John Stephen, who as a role-model to the new fashionistas was rarely seen without his trademark exemplarily-cut suit, white shirt and dark tie, some of the clothes being his own, and others the result of expensive Savile Row tailoring.

Mods though, like Stephen in his characteristically industrious work space, were fuelled by a relentlessly dynamic energy. The usual Mod week, subject of course to variation, comprised a uniformly hyperactive itinerary, with Monday evening typically spent at the Scene Club, or the Streatham Locarno, Tuesday at Soho's La Discotheque, Wednesday catching The Who at the Marquee, with Thursday usually reserved for washing hair that had to be blown into shape using a dryer with a hood, while Friday began for select Mods with *Ready Steady Go!* as a highlight, followed by a visit to Soho's the Scene or La Discotheque to buy pills. Saturday was spent unanimously shopping in the daytime at John Stephen's boutiques on Carnaby Street, followed by the recreational pilled-up all-nighter at the Flamingo. Leaving the Flamingo in a gunburst of irate scooter fire at 4am, Mods, after chilling out in the Soho cafes, spent Sunday mornings diligently riffling through thrift for opportune purchases in the East End street markets like Brick Lane and Petticoat Lane. Sunday afternoons were spent hanging out in Harrington jackets, with tartan linings, a Fred Perry polo shirt with its piped collar and three-button fastening, adapted by John Stephen to an altogether broader palette of colours from McCaul's knitwear, straight leg blue Levi's and tassled loafers at the Flamingo, before going on in the evening to the Crawdaddy in Richmond, made famous by the raw, sweaty blues energies of the early sexually ambiguous Rolling Stones. The week would often terminate drinking cappuccinos at L'Auberge coffee bar by Richmond Bridge, or back in the West End frenetically dancing at Tiles, 79 Oxford Street, where the all-black interior was dominated by a DJ in yellow shades as the hypnotic focal point to the low-lit dance-floor. The mobility offered by scooters as a means of economic transport, opened London out for Mods, allowing them to establish a personalised geography of the city's cool spots in which to be seen, although Mod hegemony often remained a local thing, and subject to a particular neighbourhood's variant of accepted lifestyle and dress.

London was for the duration of the 1960s a city liberated by youth as the core booster of its spectacular pop culture. The unprecedented success of the newly emergent arts school inflected rock bands, depended as much on the look, as it did on the appeal of their music, and invariably aspiring bands looking to create a distinct image turned to John Stephen as their undisputed Mod stylist. Stephen's early pop clients included Frederick Heath, best known as Johnny Kidd, who fronted the band Johnny Kidd and the Pirates, and scored hits with R&B movers like *Please Don't Touch*, *Shakin' All Over* and *I'll Never Get Over You*, before his untimely death on 7 October 1966, in a car crash near Bury, Lancashire. An early wearer of matelot vests combined with red, blue and black leather waistcoats, the eccentric Kidd with his black eye patch spent most of his earnings in John

Stephen's Carnaby Street shops. Although John Stephen brought his own inimitable detailed signature to shirt-making, some Mod scooter factions expressed a preference for Ben Sherman button-down collar shirts for their tapered fit, and for the stand-out detail that the originals had red buttons. Founded by the Brighton-born Arthur Bernard Sherman, Ben Sherman were the first company to produce the Oxford button-down shirt with a back pleat, packaged in distinctive black boxes with an orange logo. The shirts proved so popular that pop stars like Dave Berry, Keith Moon and Roger Daltrey of The Who would go to Carnaby Street to buy them on afternoons preceding the evening's filming of *Ready Steady Go!*. But for all their endemic popularity amongst Mods, Ben Sherman shirts lacked the fine detail of John Stephen's creations, and were significant, but basically American-copied in their structure. Buttons featured prominently in Mod sartorial iconography, and Stephen was to use them to innovative effect by arranging them in double and triple groupings on the shirt front. John Stephen and his partner Bill Franks personally selected buttons from Tony Frith's shop in nearby Marlborough Court, appropriately called the Button Queen, which stocked upwards of 20,000 buttons, together with antique tiepins and silver Sicilian tassel buttons for the lapel. John Stephen also experimented by using square and triangular shaped buttons on his denim, paisley, gingham and polka dot shirts, creating styles for men that were through the application of detail the envy of teenage girls, many of who shopped in the early sixties at the upcoming Neatawear, whose windows were visually spectacular. Unusual for the time, the floors, ceilings and back-grounds of Neatawear shops were always turquoise and the models sprayed gold. As one of the first companies to offer innovative styles to young women, they had outlets in Oxford Street, Shaftesbury Avenue and Regent Street, but couldn't compete imaginatively with the unisex attraction that John Stephen's ambivalently-styled men's clothes carried for women.

As an instance of the acutely observed fetishism Mods attached to clothes, something that found its correlative in John Stephen's designs, one of the early Mod coterie, David Clegg recalls how, 'in the early days of the scene I wore a wool worsted bottle green suit. It had three buttons up the front, four buttons on the cuff, slanted pockets, two-inch flap, ticket pocket, pocket on the inside for cigarettes, single vent eighteen inches at the back and flared from the waist. Trousers, fourteen-inch bottoms. I wore desert boots during the day, but at night it was Church's Oxford shoes or brogues. Now your Levi's had to be faded with a patch from the back pocket of an old pair sewn on your knee. And you would wear a Ben Sherman shirt.'

This specific application of detail was the dominant zeitgeist for John Stephen and the proliferating overspill of youth into his shops, like his appositely named Mod Male, a shop patronised by The Who and the Small Faces, whose notoriously manipulative manager Don Arden had his offices situated above Lord John in Carnaby Street, and who rewarded his band members with a subsistence wage of £20 a week, on the understanding he paid their daily proliferating accounts at Lord John and all of John Stephen's individual shops on Carnaby Street. Each part of London had its own Mod zone, with the Shepherd's Bush contingent preferring to dress in three-button tonic Italian suits, button-down collar shirts and black knitted ties, while the prominent East End fashionistas of the likes of Marc Feld and his friends wore period revival or customised clothes that reintroduced the dandy as the paradigm of modern fashion. The liberal expenditure of bands like the Rolling Stones, Pretty Things and the Small Faces on clothes often only worn once, before being discarded, was an undisputed sign to the new generation that youth had created its own lifestyle and wasn't so easily suppressed by the unquestioning dress conformity of a resistant older generation. The Small Faces, 'Face' being a piece of Mod slang for a fashion leader, were essentially a group of East End London teenage Mods, comprising vocalist Steve Marriott, Ronnie Lane, Kenny Jones and Ian McLagan, dressed disarmingly as style leaders like a mercurial temperature change in whatever was new in John Stephen's shops, day by day, week by week. They favoured bold candy-striped cotton Madras blazers pulled from the rails of His Clothes and Mod Male, houndstooth check and tartan hipsters, skinny-rib Shetland knitwear, in all of the amazing 70 colours made exclusively for John Stephen by McCauls, and every variation of shirt style in John Stephen's and Lord John's repertoire of button-down collar gingham, multi-coloured cotton, bold check, denim and poplin shirts with contrasting collars and cuffs. Signed initially to Decca Records, the Small Faces, together with The Who, became a specific London Mod band, scoring high profile hits with singles like *Watcha Gonna Do About It*, *Sha La La La Lee*, and the number one hit *All or Nothing*. The band led by Steve Marriott's gutsy, impassioned, Negroid-inflected voice personified maximum R&B at its poppiest best and in their dress sense were truer to specific aspects of Mod aesthetic than their sensationally pyrotechnic stage rivals The Who. As confrontational wearers of PR hooplas like union jack jackets and pop-art T-shirts, sloganed with red, white and blue RAF roundels, The Who as assumed progenitors of Mod fashion were attributed with downgrading the look by original Faces, and of conceding Mod principles to the fiscal interests of management. Even though Peter Meaden in the role of image-maker to the band boasted, 'I got the suits right, and the T-shirt under that, the boxer boots on, the jeans, the Levi's with the one-inch turn-up so the inner seam just showed from the outside, and Pete's jacket was right on, with the top button just outside ...' their clothes appeared to Faces in the indubitable know to be contrived and adopted without originality. In her memories of the incessantly shape-shifting period in which Mods created street fashion, the stick-thin size zero glamour model Twiggy remembers, 'the Mods changed their style every week. There was one group of boys we thought lovely, they had their hair parted in the middle and wore giraffe-neck shirts and grey suits and desert boots. And within three weeks they'd all cut their hair and wore bright denim and braces. They were endlessly inventive in their fashions; they looked great. They were much more inventive than the girls.'

The Small Faces were of course typically thin, characteristic of the typical 1960s ectomorphic 26in waist shared by so many Mods of the period, and like the Rolling Stones with their similar pre-anorexic figures wore John Stephen's form-fitting clothes to good effect. John Stephen's initial perception right from the start of his commitment to designing body-contoured clothes for men was to remove the shapeless excess of material that buried the sexiness that came from wearing clothes streamlined to the figure. Traditional tailoring had inveterately existed in denial of the hips, pelvis and crotch as focal points of attraction in men, and by designing seminal hipsters with a minimally low rise, and tapering shirts to a skinny contoured fit, and cutting jackets with a standard 36–38in chest width, John Stephen gave men's clothes unprecedented sex appeal by emphasising the erogenous zones as beneficial to both gay and straight guys. If Mary Quant had succeeded in liberating the shapeliness of women's legs by making the mini-skirt endemic to street wear, then John Stephen should be credited through his groundbreaking designs, and there was nothing quite like John Stephen trousers for gloved fit, with emancipating male sexuality, and through the likes of iconic frontsmen like Mick Jagger, whose protruding crotch became part of sixties' ambiguous sexual iconography, in iconoclastically remaking received notions of masculinity.

Another popular addition to Mod accessories in the early sixties was the enduring Dr. Marten Boots, which were first produced commercially on 14 April 1960, giving rise to the vernacularly approved 1460s nickname. Available in black or cherry red leather, they proved great footwear to Mods for scooter riding, and for teaming with crew-neck jumpers and pre-faded blue denim Levi's. As Ian Mclagan, keyboard player to the Small

Faces pointed out, in doing weekly television shows, and performing live sometimes twice a night on the club circuit, no band esteemed as fashion leaders could ever safely wear the same clothes twice. It simply wasn't cool to an audience who looked to the band for fashion tips, and who after the gig rushed out to scan John Stephen's windows for identical clothes, to appear anything less than optimally dressed in fashion firsts. But not all London Mods approved of John Stephen's Carnaby Street morphing of their unique image into the public domain, and some committed Faces viewed his conversion of the look into mass-market hype as exploitation of an ideology and lifestyle that was otherwise frugal and in most cases courageously individualistic. The original Mods who had emerged from the likes of London's Stamford Hill, as a tiny clothes-obsessed sector, dressed in ways that were deliberately unclassifiable, and very often combined market thrift with smart Jewish tailoring for immediate effects. For instance, in 1962, Mark Feld, a.k.a. Marc Bolan, appeared in *Town* magazine as the personification of Mod wearing the amalgamation of a long tailored jacket, a black leather waistcoat, most probably purchased from His Clothes, a pocket handkerchief and a round-collared shirt. The assortment of influences concentrated into a dandified composite typified the elusive and eclectic tastes of early Mods, who in propagating attitude, refused to conform to any categorised genre of commercial hype. In Feld's particular case, it was the dominant influence of his mother, who had up until 1962 worked on a stall in Berwick Street market, who was instrumental in attracting him originally to Soho's notorious square mile with increasing regularity. Feld had in his instinctually gravitational pioneering forays into the West End shopped originally at the likes of Vince and Domino Male, but being tiny in stature, it was really only at John Stephen's His Clothes that he could buy comfortably fitting and wickedly-cut provocative hipsters off the peg. Feld's close friend at the time, Jeff Dexter, a similarly enthused teenage fashionista, remembered that 'the hipster developed in 1962. The scene revolved around several small French influenced clubs like La Poubelle and St Germaine, where the earliest gays dressed in John Stephen and John Michael clothes would regularly go. They had this incredible look and wore these low cut hipster trousers and very tight sailor-type T-shirts, or else very tight Shetland wool jumpers.'

Peter Meaden, often conceived as the singular progenitor of the Mod movement, and one of its dominant self-destructing pill-heads, fuelled by a perpetual stockpile of speed, considered in an interview conducted shortly before his suicide from barbiturate poisoning in 1978 that the ultimate simplistic Mod kit comprised a tonic jacket, blue jeans or variant tonic

Carnaby Street in the early sixties was the epicentre of youth culture for recreational shopping.

trousers in a different colour. But he was above all meticulously precise in describing the exact cut of his choice of clothes. 'Jacket with about seven or eight inch centre-band and it's a starfish quality cloth and cut tight. You wear tight sleeves, tight shoulders, and a comfortable jacket straight enough to be a drape, and small enough to be tight, with just the top button done up, matched with a pair of tonic trousers in a different colour, probably blue or bronze, straight cut and hipsters. You'd have your belly-button showing, with a French crew-neck jersey, and then you'd have a Mod scarf with a single twist in it so it flies out on both sides. A pair of desert boots, and you're set for the weekend. If you got a scooter, you add a pair of dark glasses, maybe a stingy brim hat with an inch-wide brim, an anorak, and then you'd sit on your scooter, and you'd have everything, even your sleeping-bag which is your anorak.'

Meaden's fashion pointillism extends even to the particular of having the belly-button exposed, an innovation for men brought about in part by John Stephen designing skinny knitwear that for the first time exposed the navel as a zone of sexual appeal in men. Mods looked sexy in order to attract girls, but their attitude was one of remaining unattainable, and their exclusively male coterie invited mental homosexuality and gossip as a substitute for intimacy and friendship with girls. While Mods were their own, and not John Stephen's, creation, their sexual ambiguity ideally suited his equally ambivalent clothes, and the two fused in an inseparably symbiotic union for a five- to six-year period of such intense psychosexual transformation that Carnaby Street and Mods became inextricably linked as the undisputed leaders of London's vibrant rapid-fire fashion changes.

The uneasy balance between Stephen and Mods, in itself an unprecedented lucrative partnership, existed too as something maintained by a shared propensity to push psychological and physical boundaries to the limits. Both Stephen and Mods lived on reckless overdrive, and the repeated mental breakdowns that John Stephen was to undergo as the 1960s progressed, requiring extensive periods of rehabilitation in clinics like the Priory, was interfaced by the burn-out of Mod casualties, including Peter Meaden, who used amphetamine as the chemical to project themselves beyond pedestrian living. If John Stephen's manic illness was arguably genetic, and inherited from his mother, then Mods used speed recreationally like gunning the fuel-injector on their customised, fidgety, mirror-tiered scooters. John Stephen's chemically imbalanced and over-accelerated sensibility accounted in part for the seemingly unstoppable work momentum he achieved for much of the 1960s, his abundant creative ideas and escalating ambition to outrival his contemporaries resulting in a similar adrenalin supernova as the one experienced by Mods on high doses of recreational speed. But something of the ideological schism between the two parties, no matter their insuperable mutual dependency, was given voice to by Steve Marriott of the Small Faces, in his analysis of the commercialisation that he perceived as responsible for the death of Mod as an idealist movement. According to Marriott, who was beaten up in the East End of London the first time he went out as a teenager wearing white hipster jeans, 'Mod meant money. It was a way of life gone wrong. It went up its own ass, see. As soon as too much money gets involved, the people who are into it can't be that any more ... Mod never really did cost money at first. You'd buy the cheapest things, but in the style you wanted. The whole thing was to be an individual, and as soon as they started mass-marketing the stuff and up-pricing the hell out of it, then the thing of being an individual was lost. Mod was individual at the time ... There were some set rules, no doubt about it, like the length of trousers, colour of socks, length and style of hair, that kind of thing. But the rest was up to you. Always though with the hair, the trouser length and the shoes, you had to have that right. That was the code that said you were Mod. But then it got out of hand, and like anything, as soon as it was dispersed, it was lost.'

Marriott, who began life as a strict Mod purist or Face, paradoxically became a style icon addicted to Mod consumerism, his role in fronting London's hottest and most authentic R&B band demanding he bought into the John Stephen Carnaby Street style with eclectic diversity, his individual taste setting standards for his fans to follow, with the singer having of necessity to keep one step ahead of his audience. As a sexually prospecting hedonistic teenage band, idolised for their girlie looks, the Small Faces spent most of their considerable earnings – they were paid a £1,000 a gig, often performing twice a night on a burn-out British and European club circuit – on clothes, and avalanches of shirts and trousers being delivered from Lord John, as well as John Stephen's His Clothes and Mod Male to their manager Don Arden's offices at 52–55 Carnaby Street, with bass player Ronnie Lane refusing outright ever to wear the same shirt or jacket twice. If Marriott and Lane developed a preference for a particular shirt, they would order it in every available colour, and John Stephen as an obsessive completist would obligingly make a shirt in as many as forty variant shades of blue, pink or green. Steve Marriott's best friend at the time, Hugh James, recalled, 'Steve and the others would buy enormous amounts of clothes from John Stephen's shops. If he liked a particular shirt he'd buy one in every colour it came in, same for jackets, jumpers etc. After wearing something just once he'd throw

John Stephen created an often inseparable look for men and women without ever losing notions of a new masculinity.

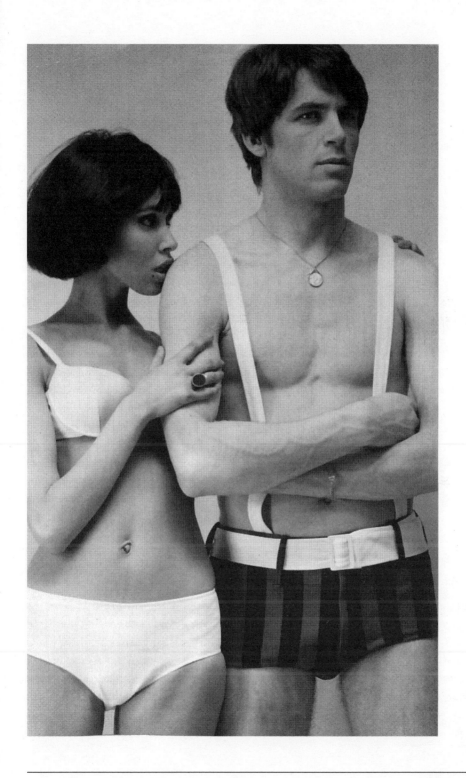

it in a pile in his bedroom and invite me to help myself. I've had literally dozens of shirts and some nice leather jackets from Steve in that way ... Steve never kept specific items of clothing for stage wear. He would go on stage in whatever he was wearing at the time.' And John Stephen's shops offered a range of clothing in colours never before used in men's fashion, tasteful shades like cerise, eau-de-nil, heather, Bordeaux-red, apricot, aquamarine, violet, purple, and endless permutations of blue and green as part of a selectively colour-coded aesthetic.

Early Mods couldn't on their limited earnings afford to have a jacket customised by the likes of Tommy Nutter, Dougie Millings or Peter Golding, or by the redoubtable Mr Green of Billings and Edmonds in Hanover Square, who made sharp bespoke suits with splashy colourful satin linings, and so their attention was drawn to John Stephen as the affordable designer whose clothes matched not only their optimal enthusiasm for the look, but also their pockets. John Stephen's unprecedented success in democratising clothes for young people, was sufficient to have John Crosby, writing for *The Telegraph*'s weekend supplement, comment that, 'on any twilight evening when the day's work is done, Carnaby Street pulses with slender young men in black tight pants that fit on the hips like ski-pants, their tulip-like girlfriends on their arms, peering into the garishly lit windows at the burgundy coloured suede jackets with the slanted, pleated pockets – very hot stuff with the Mods right now. The impact of Carnaby Street is becoming worldwide, Tony Curtis wears Carnaby Street clothes, and so do Peter Sellers and the Beatles.'

John Stephen as part of his initiative had begun designing the collarless jackets popularised by the Beatles as early as 1958, and been left with them unsold, despite their origins having been credited to Paul McCartney's friendship with Astrid Kirchherr, who was at the time on the fringes of the Hamburg art scene, and who was a pioneering advocate of the Chairman Mao-like round collared jacket with black piping and covered buttons for front closure. It was John Stephen who added the velvet collars to the jacket, providing the fine point of detail at which he was so inimitably adept. With fabrics supplied by Burgess and Leadward of Manchester, and making up poplin trousers at £3 a pair, Stephen upscaled his line slowly, week by week, month by month, often to his advantage attending fabric shows in Europe and acquiring sample lengths of material free to make up shirts and trousers in limited editions in advance of the coming season, as an economic means of getting ahead. Any male boutique at the time displaying provocative underwear in its windows came under regular police scrutiny, and Stephen's Carnaby Street shops were visited regularly by the local constabulary from the Beak Street substation who issued cautions, with Stephen's proviso being that the offending items were marketed as fashionable and highly topical swimwear. Obsessed with the idea of shops in general, something inherited in part from his Glaswegian upbringing as a shop-owner's son, and particularly with those of his menswear rivals in the West End, the insomniac John Stephen would often go out on nocturnal window-shopping forays, to check on competitor's displays, refresh his ideas, and come back home fired-up by his snatches of surveillance to work on proliferating new concepts in the early hours. For John Stephen, as much as for Mary Quant, the concept of celebrity was an integral part of the increasing hoopla surrounding their respective popularity as maverick designers to the stars. Quant with her Sassoon black bob, black kohl eye-makeup and unapologetic mini-skirts quickly became the recognisable identity of Bazaar, while John Stephen was regularly the subject of photo-shoots in his resident Carnaby Street, posed outside His Clothes, wearing his own sharply-designed suits, or with the symbol of his material success, a newly-purchased Silver Cloud Rolls Royce, bought on impulse with Franks from a Cricklewood dealer, on a visit to see Frank's parents, used as an ostentatiously strategic prop to enforce his signature look as a glamorous retail hipster, and as the youngest owner of a Rolls Royce in Britain. John Stephen's eminently marketable image, given energetic hype by his PR Mike McGrath, and achieved at huge intrinsic cost, given his naturally introverted character, made his persona amenable to interviews, columns in the dailies, as well as featuring as a pin-up in teenage magazines such as *Fabulous* and *Boyfriend*. Groomed by his publicist Michael McGrath to cultivate the image of a star, every bit as successful as his celebrity clients, John Stephen came to symbolize legendary qualities of virtuoso stardom to a generation looking to reinvent itself through the vocabulary of pop and clothes. Not that Stephen found networking easy, and his publicist recalls that taking him to meet editors for lunch or dinner would often due to social anxiety on Stephen's part, result in him remaining uncomfortably taciturn and wholly withdrawn for the first thirty minutes, after which, and with the liberating effects of alcohol he would start to communicate eloquently about his subject.

What John Stephen shared in common with Mary Quant, apart from their self-made maverick origins, was an absolute emphasis on modernism to the exclusion of period revival in fashion, of the sort favoured by John Michael in his prestigious revivalist line. Mods largely relocated from East End tailoring and opportune street market purchases to Carnaby Street, because like John Stephen in his fashion concerns, they were almost exclusively preoccupied with what was new. The look wasn't seasonal, it was something to be reinvented each time Mods went out, and Stephen dispensed altogether with the concept of arbitrary collections, and instead filled his windows with whatever was his inspiration of the moment. And beginning small, what John Stephen did, like Mary Quant, was to make a boutique, not only into a shop-front, but into a workspace where clothes were made, sold and altered on the premises. The notion of being almost autonomous in fashion was unheard of at the time, and John's sister Rae, remembers how, 'in the very early days of Carnaby Street, John asked me to come to London during a school holiday. I remember him taking me in and out of his shops, and in the basement of one there were people sewing and making clothes, almost like a small factory.' This housing of an industry in a small unit was of course a financial necessity, as well as a means of creating the new spontaneously and without the need to consult with the industry on what the season predicted or routinely dictated. Carnaby Street started out as John Stephen's individual mapping of a look that went London Mod, then finally via his shops in the USA and Europe global in popularity.

John Stephen and Mary Quant through the success of their home indus-tries and provocative strategies of marketing disrupted the entire fashion mainstream by having the individual boutique supersede the place of the chain store. John Stephen, in particular, radically altered the psychological bias of retail by investing the job of shop assistant with *de facto* glamour, rather than generic subservience, and by having his staff dress in clothes similar to those they were selling to customers. This mutually shared obsession for clothes, on the part of seller and wired enthusiast, established an unprec-edented aesthetic rapport between the two, based entirely on the shape-shifting selling power of the look. Mods, like their acclaimed style-guru John Stephen, while being outwardly anti-establishment, nonetheless conformed to an inflexible capitalist work ethic. It was this contradiction in values, the need to earn money from the establishment in order to subvert it, that made Mods so existentially compelling a movement. One of their founder London members, Patrick Uden, expressed in interview what he felt to be the paradox inherent in Mod ideology by pointing precisely to the fundamental incon-sistency in their values. 'The thing about Mods was, they were largely very establishment. They looked the business. They were the first kids to have real jobs and they were proud of it. They wanted Italian suits and shoes as well as American shirts and American underwear. I'm wearing a Brooks Brothers shirt right now, and anyone can tell at a thousand paces it's a Brooks Brothers model, because of the roll on the collar. Now any Mod would know that. They would recognise an American shirt by the double line of stitching around the sleeves. An English shirt made to imitate an American one, notably a Ben Sherman, is not on, okay. It has all to do with exact detail.'

John Stephen's limited edition shirts, all of them significantly different in their stylistic character, and with no two of his shops carrying the same stock, were detailed to the point of appearing acute fetishistic artefacts. His designs were ostensibly one-off personality-shirts that were never likely to be repeated, white shirts with twin-needle charcoal stitching and orange buttons, orange denim shirts with black stitching, and black and white gingham collar and cuffs with three buttons; his repertoire of variations appearing weekly inexhaustible to his committed teenage customers. That his clothes provoked the latent homosexual aspect in what was an all-male coterie was a subtle distinction taken on by Mods who chose to cultivate a popular bisexual image, both as an affront to preconceived notions of gender, as well as a natural marker in the evolution of their self-created mythology. To this faction, John Stephen was the immediate designer of their choice, a stylist whose own buried sexuality and unbounded creative imagination allowed him to transcend social limitations and create clothes that were gay orientated for straights and above all crucially modern. But for diffident Faces who insisted on creating trends rather than following them, Carnaby Street represented a sell-out of their consistently edgy street attitude. As a sign of his increasing ability to diffuse what was called 'drag' into the hetero-sexual mainstream, Stephen, who generally looked to upcoming pop stars as photographic models for his clothes, secured in 1962 the services of the blond British boxing hope Billy Walker for blow-ups used by Myles Anthony in dressing the Carnaby Street windows. Walker, image-wise the epitome of worked-out heterosexuality, but arguably butch, was posed for the photo-shoot with a young model Caroline Neville, dressed in the fashionable striped matelot shirt that John Stephen had made into his own, and a pair of tight-fitting mohair hipsters, as an endorsement of the look. Not only was it revolutionary to have a celebrity boxer, who had become a regular customer, model leisurewear inflected with camp undertones, but as a press triumph for Michael McGrath, it was an explicit statement that John Stephen was in the process of radically dissolving the generic opposition of straight men to the newly-conceived and sexually-ambivalent look. If Bill Green had begun the process in the early fifties by using beefcake for blow-ups and catalogue images, then John Stephen with his more refined and acutely opportunistic publicity-radar had turned to a sports celebrity who also had good looks to generate a sensational hoopla for his shops.

The success of his Billy Walker-themed windows wasn't only in personal

From pop stars to Shepherd's Bush Mods, all fashionistas ended up in a John Stephen shop.

terms a measure of how far John Stephen had outstripped his fashion contemporaries in PR, but also a sign of the rapidly changing times as the sixties started to kick in. On a subtle level, and directed by the androgynous image adopted by pop stars, youth gravitated collectively towards a more flexible notion of masculinity, and while it was to take another five years for John Stephen to introduce tartan mini-kilts for men, shops like His Clothes, The Man's Shop and Domino Male were beginning the work of liberating a generation into a new optimistic awareness of masculinity. Carnaby Street, or Peacock's Alley, as it was commonly known, was under John Stephen's audacious signature already the only place to buy continuously updated and attention-seeking clothes for prescient fashionistas in the early 1960s.

An early and consistent John Stephen customer was the seminal blues singer with Alexis Corner's Blues Incorporated, Long John Baldry, whose influence on the formative London R&B scene was so optimally significant that in July 1962 the Rolling Stones opened for him at the Mod-infested ultra-cool Marquee Club. The 6ft 7in, flatteringly lean gay singer was not only a commanding vocal presence on the club circuit, but a clothes addict, who dressed in sharp grey, silver or blue mohair jackets and trousers, tab-collar shirts and dark knitted ties, mostly acquired from Stephen's His Clothes. Baldry was so drawn to the street that even if he wasn't buying he would drop by regularly to chat to staff and scrutinise whatever was new and compellingly immediate on the rails. And under Kit Lambert's astutely entrepreneurial management The Who were quickly introduced to the Carnaby Street look as a transformation necessary to their dynamic projection as a frontline Mod band. According to Keith Moon, 'the Mod thing was Kit's idea. We were all sent down to a hairdresser, Robert James, and on to Carnaby Street with more money than we'd ever seen in our lives before, like a hundred quid each. This was swinging London. Most of our audience were pill-heads like ourselves. We weren't individually into clothes; we were into music. Kit thought we should identify more with out audience. Coats slashed five inches at the sides. Four wasn't enough. Six was too much. Five was just right. The trousers came three inches below the hip. It was our uniform.'

As an integral part of the look, the John Stephen incentive impacted on his youthful customers through shop interiors that utilized stage design as integral to their essentially camp ethos. The spaces were almost uniformly small, and in the case of His Clothes incorporated a Scandinavian-style blond slatted false ceiling hung next to fine Italianate ironwork arches, while grey and white vinyl tiles hinted at Venetian stone, and velvet or sequinned drapes were used to tasteful effect, creating the effect for the customer of entering into a space dressed precisely to create the shift from reality necessary to induce the altered state complementary to shopping. Buying from a John Stephen shop became a compulsive act for the enamoured customer, senses temporarily saturated by colour and loud music, and with the rush of beta-endorphins in brain chemistry provoking the heady and euphoric sensation of purchase. Individual carriers were designed for each of John Stephen's shops by Myles Anthony, whose natural predilection for camp extravaganza extended with the decade into unabashed brilliant temerity. It was Myles Anthony who was responsible for the sensational blow-ups of nude young men on the changing room doors of Tre Camp that provoked indignant controversy at the time from a morally offended older generation. Celebrity faces came even to decorate coat hangers in John Stephen's Carnaby Street shops, the whole effect being aimed at democratizing clothes through introducing the potential teenage customer to the same fashion racks regularly scrutinised by stars like Mick Jagger or Pete Townshend. John Stephen's alluringly hypnotic interiors successfully suspended the ubiquitous pressures of urban reality for inquisitive fashionistas, with Mod Male boasting gold blinds and gold lettering as a seductive entrée to the tiny immaculately presented shop.

John Stephen shops in the early sixties employed the same tasteful shock tactics as his clothes, in that each was a one-off creation, a diminutive space in which the customer was temporarily on stage in a miniature world of mirrors in which nothing counted but the look. And while delegating authority to his arts consultant Myles Antony, John Stephen took a keen interest in Antony's interior design that employed blow-ups, masks, gothic traceries, Piranesi-excerpted arches and extravagant camp motifs to sensational effect. Mirrored walls were used to prominent effect in all shops to create both the illusion of space in a constricted interior, and to additionally magnify the image of the bright young thing seeing himself for the first time in the newly selected items of his choice. Shirt widths, jacket vents and trouser lengths, and Stephen experimented by placing vents in trousers to secure a better fit to the shoe, were discussed in-store by Faces with the intense seriousness of financiers monitoring the financial index at the Stock Exchange. For advocates of the look, clothes were for the duration of the early sixties all that mattered, and they were a class A addiction. Pete Townshend of The Who recalls the whole Mod-obsessed look as inspired by the manipulation of gender. 'The girls looked like boys and the boys looked a bit like girls: even though they wore suits, they wore make-up. I remember Marc Bolan with full make-up on working as a rent boy to buy clothes, in and around the Scene Club. He was about fifteen.'

A favourite shot of John, the stylist whose acute empathy with his generation had him update the look on a weekly basis.

London Faces at the time were known to each other, and there was rivalry and fighting amongst Mods themselves, who, far from being an integrated fraternity, were often territorially fractious and resentful of each other's status, and outright bitchy about clothes. Their individual strength was attitude, looking good even if you weren't so in reality. Chris Stamp, an early adherent to style, remembers the importance of cool amongst early Mods, and of the significance to the movement of the characteristic Ivy League clothes worn by black musicians on the formative Mod look. 'We sorta liked Gerry Mulligan, Jimmy Smith and John Coltrane; we weren't that into jazz – it was the look. Subconsciously we knew that blacks had no real power in the States, any more than we did, but their clothes made them look in control, not to be messed with.' The aim was always to stand out by invented methods, like the early examples of Peter Meaden and Andrew Loog Oldham, as consummate originators of the look, and to retain sufficient mystique as an individual to dispense with the crowd. 'Certain faces about town led the way,' Ian McLagan remembers. ' There was a dealer we knew in Notting Hill Gate called Denzel and he always looked the business, so much so the *Sunday Times* colour supplement got hold of him and put him on the cover. He had the look. You'd have the look just right, then someone else would arrive in a great shirt. It was one-upmanship. By 1964 you could go down Carnaby Street and pick the stuff off the racks. The Small Faces had accounts in most of the shops: John Stephen, Lord John and Toppers – we looked very sharp and we were all in competition to get something cool – if you saw someone wearing something you already had, that was it.'

Keeping track of the look as it changed literally on a daily basis had Mods constantly preoccupied with refining and updating fine points of fashion if they were to keep ahead. For Mick Tanner, an 18-year-old tailor's cutter from Stepney, originality of dress was paramount to owning to an identity. 'Before, tailors used to invent the styles and everyone bought them. Now we invent them and the tailors are going out of their mind trying to keep up. I started wearing crepe, nylon cycling jumpers because they were cool for dancing. All the tickets wanted to know where I got them – but if I'd told them they would all have been down the shop tomorrow.' Before John Stephen, who made modernistic off-the-peg clothes affordable, and John Michael who made crafted into a luxury, the look had to be invented rather than purchased as an accessory to Mod identity. Mick Farren recalls of the times: 'When I was a youth there were two things going on: I was at St. Martin's, so you saw girls doing fashion and got them to make you shirts, based on things you'd seen; and then there was also the Mod thing, the second generation Mods shooting down the East End and getting some old tailor to knock you up a jacket exactly like this picture of Buddy Holly, please guv, with the short lapels and the three buttons.'

Others like the young, Bloomsbury-born, grape-bunched curly-haired singer Steven Demetre Georgious, a.k.a. Cat Stevens, became obsessed with John Stephen's clothes to the point of changing his name to Cat Stevens, on the way to aspiring to the pop stardom that came to him in his late teens, dressed as the perfect statement for John Stephen's dandified suits and foppish shirts in the mid-sixties.

The new masculine experience of recreational shopping, popularised by John Stephen, was as dependent as much on the heady optimistic economy of the times, and the fact that there was no unemployment, as it was on Stephen's radical re-make of the conventional presentation of masculinity. Intimidated by John Stephen's accelerated hold on the look, the retrograde nucleus of sober tailoring, Austin Reed, around the corner in prestigious Regent Street, opportunistically employed the services of the pop artist Robyn Denny to create an imposing red, blue and white mural which read 'Great big biggest wide London,' epitomising the confidence of the capital at the dawn of the 1960s, as a means of attempting to update their downgraded image. Denny's bouncy, vitaminised collage composition set a youthfully chauvinistic tone for Britain at the time, while artistically suggesting explicit debts to Stuart Davis' American proto-pop murals, and Ellsworth Kelly's immense painting New York No 1, exhibited at the United States Information Service's Grosvenor House Gallery in November 1958. But no loud consumer statement from a reactionary menswear outlet, reduced to pop bannering to substitute for lack of original invention, could compensate for Michael McGrath's ingenuity in releasing to the press black and white photographs of Mick Jagger and Keith Richards, sharing the contemplation of a newly purchased item secured inside a familiar white John Stephen carrier with its black typographical JS logo. The instantly recognisable John Stephen look had by the early 1960s permeated men's fashion in an unprecedented, outrageously maverick way, rocking its securely conventional pivot, and opening a gateway into the times and into the collective needs of a youth set on differentiation through adopting the affordable Carnaby Street look. Stephen's small, lividly-coloured shops had by now written their trademark signatures into the precinct's architecture, so much so that the name John Stephen was now inseparable from the place he had singularly transformed from its run-down origins into the epicentre of youth culture. John Stephen had, on his part, succeeded in laying claim to a complex so edgy and hyperactive in its pilled-up purchase on the look, that it was for the next decade to redeem dead-end south-east Soho from a no-go impoverished workroom and red light district into the most energised fashion-conscious precinct on the global map.

4

SCOOTER ATTACK

As a sign of personal success, on account of the fashion supernova Carnaby Street had become, John Stephen and Bill Franks upgraded their home address from Sussex Gardens, initially to an apartment in the World's End sector of Chelsea's newly fashionable King's Road, before moving into a spacious five-room apartment at 59–60 Jermyn Street, behind Fortnum & Mason in St James' Piccadilly. The mansion block in a high-end residential street was also home to prestigious shirtmakers like Turnbull & Asser, where the artist Francis Bacon had shirts custom made, and T.M. Lewin whose speciality shirts were an inimitable deep-sky Gaulois blue. The third occupant of the spacious St James' flat, was John Stephen's other, newer boyfriend, Frank Merkell, who had met John in 1962, and graduated into working for him by managing the John Stephen His Clothes in Queensway. The apartment, given unconditionally extravagant interior design by Myles Antony, with its white pergola, dark blue carpeting throughout, oak panelling and a glass table in the living-room, also contained a grandiose Edwardian four-poster bed, and was decorated with John Stephen's eclectic taste in antiques: figurines, objets d'art, vases, figurative paintings, Greek statuettes, and a prominent bronze greyhound on a smoky onyx plinth, much of it picked up on impulsive shopping forays at Portobello Road and Camden Passage, Islington, as well as at Christie's auction rooms, where Stephen was a regular bidder. The flat, one of a luxurious Mayfair block entered through heavy mahogany front doors in a building cushioned into unrelieved interior silence by sumptuous Bordeaux red carpets, was considered sufficiently ostentatious a novelty to merit a feature in *Woman's Own*, in the series 'Meet Top People at Home'. As the lead-in to situating John Stephen within the flexible frontiers of a home that also acted as an informal workspace, Edith Blair compacted some of the designer's most notable characteristics into a compressed resume. 'He intently works out with his cutter the exact line of a coat lapel or a shoulder seam,' she wrote, 'sells in his shops shirts of every colour down to deep purple, exotic white corduroy jackets – yet himself wears only dark tailored suits, white shirts. Never tires of shop talk; even his girl friends are rag trade experts.' And in the tradition of his innovative shop design for His Clothes, three white walls and one slab of depth-resounding purple, Myles Antony gave the St James' living room, three white walls and one wall decorated with the Byzantine-patterned fabric that also covered the two imposing 8ft long settees. With his intense dislike of formal business meetings in clinically designed spaces, John Stephen's need for a demonstratively spacious living-room was in part prompted by his equally modernistic approach to his group, which was to conduct impromptu directors' meetings at home, with much of his recreational time given over to the late-night discussion of configurative ideas affecting fashion. Dressed cutely for the interview with Edith Blair in a scarlet wool cardigan, white shirt, black knitted tie and black mohair slacks, Stephen, personifying his own edgily debonair line, spoke precisely of his sociable needs at home for space. 'Often a dozen or more people come back here for coffee or a drink after an evening out. The two big settees facing each other take several of them, and give a good conversation group.' The living room also featured tall white louvred shutters, while the dining-room table, as an ostentatious Myles Antony splash, stood surrealistically inside a sculpted wrought-iron pergola purchased from a junkyard. Stephen's bedroom was done in brown and red, the walls painted a soft tan; the sumptuous duvet a golden brown linen union scored with red, and having tailored pillow covers, a small round bedside table covered in red felt, and the lampshades likewise a matching red. Two built-in pine wardrobes with slatted sliding doors held Stephen's functional rotation of 40–50 customised suits in predominantly dark colours. Something of Stephen's obsessive nature, bordering at times on acute microphobia, and brought out in his insistence on the regular dusting even of concealed spaces in all his shops, was manifested through his interview comment on the vigilant maintenance of his clothes. 'Remember to line slatted doors inside with hardwood,' he advised. 'I didn't to begin with, and found dust got on to all my clothes.' There was additionally a second bedroom done airily in white and yellow, again incorporating white shutters that screened out the diagrammatic mapping of pipework facing the back wall of another building. An additional room, with soft tan walls, served as a study, the sofa converting into a bed, the colour statement employing shocking pink and red checks in the fabric for the curtains, lamp base and settee cover. Rows of military and theatrical prints, purchased by Stephen on his compulsive antiques shopping binges, filled the settee wall of this room, while the other wall was shelved with Stephen's collection of crime thriller paperbacks as a panacea for periods of chronic insomnia. Home catering was kept to the minimal, on account of his unremittingly exhaustive work pressures, with Stephen professing that he usually phoned a restaurant, 'probably Chinese – and they send round dishes of hot food, and a waiter to serve.' The flat was home too, to John Stephen's inseparable companion, a white German Shepherd dog called Prince, who was also to feature prominently in photo shoots as part of the personal iconography associated with Stephen's Carnaby Street emporium. The immaculately groomed Prince, fed on tinned lobster from Fortnum & Mason's, would accompany John Stephen to work, and be taken sometimes as his singular guest to the Private Room at the Ivy, London's chic celebrity restaurant at 1 West Street, Covent Garden, or to Le Caprice in the heart of St James', or on special occasions to the Rivoli Bar at the Ritz. John Stephen and Bill Franks had also acquired a weekend house at Marine Drive, Brighton, having opened a shop there at No 7 East Street, which was dependent for success largely on summer trade. Brighton, as a town, had an interesting precedent in gay-oriented clothes with a boutique called Filk'n Casuals that dated back to the late fifties, and sold styles of clothing similar to Bill Green's Vince and John Stephen's, including red socks, purple ties, casual shirts, jackets, trousers and bikini briefs for men. Stephen and Franks also established a retail precedent by becoming the first London shop to open on Saturday afternoons, at a time when stores uniformly closed their doors for the weekend at 1.00pm, the spectacular increase in fanatical weekend shopping in the street meaning that visits to Brighton proved to be a recreational luxury rather than an established custom. And as part of his escalating investments, John Stephen briefly took a stake in a Health Food Interest in 1963, something precipitated by Cranks initiating the first vegetarian restaurant in London, round the corner from Carnaby Street in the newly-fashionable Newburgh Street in 1963. Another splinter-interest at the time was Stephen's setting up a car-hire firm, with a core fleet of Jaguar Mark 10s as its ostentatious incentive to clients, called Status Car Hire. He also sub-let a blank-walled property in Ganton Street, one of the alleys running across Carnaby Street, that had at one time been used for the refrigerated

John Stephen, the creator of pop flamboyance, dressed quietly in suits, pastel shirts and ties worn with impeccable taste.

storage of fur coats, and which he now let out as a tobacco kiosk to Frank Welby, of Inderwick's, gay partner, and as a complex of tiny local workrooms.

A near neighbour to John Stephen at 8 Duke Street, St James', throughout the late sixties, and an inveterate Savile Row man, who favoured custom-made suits, was the infamous writer and junkie, William Burroughs, who in an arrangement not unlike John Stephen's ménage à trois, also lived with two men, his then partner Ian Sommerville, and his new boyfriend Alan Watson. When the two moved out due to volatile emotional hostilities, Burroughs took up with a young Irishman called John Brady, a Piccadilly rent boy and compulsive shop thief who Burroughs had met on the site of the notorious Piccadilly meat rack. Brady had little or no interest in writing, and was like so many of the Dilly boys essentially heterosexual and working as rent on the black banana-curved railings simply for money. Burroughs' intense dislike of what he considered to be Britain's parochialism was also accelerated by the same repressive sexual climate to gays that Stephen and Franks also experienced as an adverse symptom of the times.

Worried by his irredeemable cigarette habit (the permanently-wired designer was smoking on average 50 Dunhill or Benson & Hedges Gold a day), John Stephen switched to smoking premium *Romeo y Julieta* cigars, a steady supply of the aluminium-tubed cigars arriving in their wooden boxes of ten from an account Stephen had established with the tobacconist Franco & Hunter. But no matter his newly acquired celebrity, John Stephen retained simple tastes at home, starting the day with salted porridge, as a continuity of his Glaswegian upbringing, used basic Wright's Coal Tar soap, his one grooming luxury being a dab of Chanel cologne purchased at Liberty, and no matter how hard he drank at night, began his working day at 7.30, his public image always one of inscrutable perfection. Lunch for both John Stephen and Bill Franks was usually a local affair, with no time taken out from their working day, and most often comprised a chunky home-made sandwich from Mrs Miller's Snacks in Foubert's Place, or a John Stephen favourite, the salt beef sandwich with its generously proportioned spill of red fins purchased from Blooms in the same old Soho alley. Myles Antony remembers, as typical of John Stephen's unaffected lifestyle, being telephoned by him one Sunday morning and asked to go over to Jermyn Street for lunch, and finding John Stephen sitting on the couch in a T-shirt and his suit trousers, peeling potatoes in a bucket, and asking Myles for assistance with the sprouts. But underneath the polished façade of independently-realised success on a scale unparalleled in contemporary design and its attendant hype, John Stephen was inwardly finding it hard to manage the obsessive anxiety disorders, including severe hyperactivity, that were to result in the manic highs he experienced as the pressures of escalating success ripped into his constantly overexposed and fine-tuned sensitivity. On a constant prescription regime of the benzodiazepines Valium and Librium as tranquillisers, and using the hypnotics Phenobarbital and Limbertol for disrupted sleep patterns, Stephen's hyperactivity was for much of the sixties precariously managed by pharmaceuticals. There was the additional strain too, of keeping his homosexuality concealed from the media, a necessary precaution in the viciously homophobic climate of the early sixties, and to counteract potential press innuendo, John Stephen, listed as one of Britain's most eligible and elusive bachelors, was strategically photographed with glamorous pretend girlfriends in teen magazines, as a way of keeping his public image straight.

With two shops newly opened in the fashionably bohemian King's Road, at 97 and 201, and one in South Kensington, and with his purchase on Carnaby Street extended to six shops, including the newly opened Mod Male, managed by Kenny Slater, John Stephen was in 1963–4 to experience the beginnings of the scooter invasion of a still un-pedestrianised Carnaby Street, as Mods transformed the street into the epicentre of their omnivorous fashionista mania.

Mod Male, as the shop patronised by the scooter boys, and situated at 47a Carnaby Street, was a tiny cutting-edge boutique, its orange interior pulsating for a season with the sound of the Rolling Stones' *The Last Time*, the riffy power chords and contagious pop hook as immediate and modern as the sunlight arriving that moment in the street outside. Mod Male, true to the ethic established by John Stephen and Bill Franks, was run by two teenage Mods, Ken Slater from Stamford Bridge, and Keith Lewis from Harringay, who when visited by a journalist were dressed at the time respectively in gingham button-down collar shirts and orange and lavender denim hipsters. Denim shirts in a variety of colours including cerulean and shocking pink were the fashion in early 1964, together with denim slacks in off-beat but attention-seeking colours like tan, dusty blue, silver-grey, burnt-orange and lavender, all shades new to heterosexual menswear, and making their hypnotic debut in John Stephen's arrestingly innovative windows. Writing for *Top Boys* magazine, one of the innumerable fashion-conscious monthlies to which he contributed freelance journalism, Michael McGrath commented with all the heady serotonin-boosting uplift of encountering a John Stephen design, totally new in its originality, and quite literally a first for men's shirts, 'I was knocked out by the shirts combining navy blue with Black Watch tartan … You can either have the body in blue with the Black Watch at the collar,

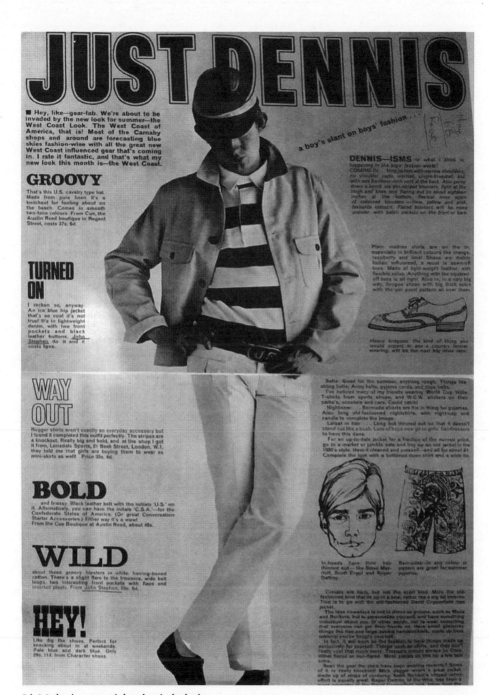

JUST DENNIS

a boy's slant on boys' fashion...

■ Hey, like—gear-fab. We're about to be invaded by the new look for summer—the West Coast Look. The West Coast of America, that is! Most of the Carnaby shops and around are forecasting blue skies fashion-wise with all the great new West Coast influenced gear that's coming in. I rate it fantastic, and that's what my new look this month is—the West Coast.

GROOVY

That's this U.S. cavalry type hat. Made from pure linen it's a knockout for fooling about on the beach. Comes in smooth two-tone colours. From Cue, the Austin Reed boutique in Regent Street, costs 37s. 6d.

TURNED ON

I reckon so, anyway. An ice blue hip jacket that's so cool it's not true! It's in lightweight denim, with two front pockets and black leather buttons. John Stephen, do it and it costs 6gns.

WAY OUT

Rugger shirts aren't exactly an everyday accessory but I found it completed this outfit perfectly. The stripes are a knockout. Really big and bold, and at the shop I got it from, Lonsdale Sports, 21 Beak Street, London, W.1, they told me that girls are buying them to wear as mini-skirts as well! Price 33s. 6d.

BOLD

and brassy. Black leather belt with the initials 'U.S.' on it. Alternatively, you can have the initials 'C.S.A.'—for the Confederate States of America. (Or great Conversation Starter Accessories.) Either way it's a wow! From the Cue Boutique at Austin Reed, about 48s.

WILD

about these groovy hipsters in white herring-boned cotton. There's a slight flare to the trousers, wide belt loops, two interesting front pockets with flaps and inverted pleats. From John Stephen, 59s. 6d.

HEY!

Like dig the shoes. Perfect for knocking about in at weekends. Pale blue and dark blue. Only 29s. 11d. from Character shoes.

DENNIS—ISMS is what I think is happening in the boys' fashion world

COMING IN The jacket with narrow shoulders, no shoulder pads, slanted, single-breasted, and with no fastened-down vent at the back. Also going down a bomb are thin-striped trousers, tight at the thigh and knee and flaring out to round eighteen inches at the bottom. Flared once again in coloured trousers—lime, yellow and pink favourite colours. Flared trousers will be more popular with button pockets on the front or back.

Plain madras shirts are on the in, especially in brilliant colours like orange, raspberry and lime! Shoes are made in Italian influenced, a mood is sawn-off from. Made of light-weight leather with flexible soles. Anything with the squared-off toes is all right. Also in, in a very big way, brogue shoes with big thick soles with the pin point pattern all over them.

Heavy brogues, the kind of thing you would expect to see a country farmer wearing, will be the next big shoe rave.

Belts: Good for the summer, anything rough. Things the sling belts, Army belts, pyjama cords, and rope belts.

I've noticed many of my friends wearing World Cup Willie T-shirts from sports shops, and W.C.W. stickers on their parka's scooters and cars. Could catch!

Nightwear Bermuda shorts are the in thing for pyjamas. Also long old-fashioned nightshirts, with night-cap and candle to complete the image.

Latest in hair Long but thinned out so that it doesn't stand out like a bush. Lots of boys now go to girls' hairdressers to have this done.

For an up-to-date jacket for a fraction of the normal price, go to a market or jumble sale and buy up an old jacket in the 1930's style. Have it cleaned and pressed—and all for about £1. Complete the look with a buttoned down shirt and a wide tie.

In heads Tops their hair thinned out—the Steve Marriott, Scott Engel and Roger Daltrey.

Bermudas—in any colour or pattern are great for summer pyjamas.

Cravats are back, but not the scarf kind. More the old-fashioned kind that tie up in a bow, rather like a big fat bow-tie. This is to go with the old-fashioned David Copperfield type jacket.

The idea nowadays is not to dress as poncy, such as Mods and Rockers, but to personalise yourself and have something individual about you. In other words, not to wear something that everyone can get their hands on. Have something personalise things like that and I have noticed something, make-up from material you've bought yourself.

In fact, it will soon be the fashion to build things made up exclusively for yourself. Things such as shirts, sort that don't really cost that much more. Trousers should always be tailored flared or non-flared. Most people go out for a few bob extra.

Next the gear the class have been wearing recently? Some of it is really knocked out Mini Cooper—such a great jacket made up of strips of corduroy. Now that's what I mean.

It's Mod, it's camp, it's butch, it's the look.

running down the front and at the cuff, or have the Black Watch body with the blue trimming, or the same shirt is available made completely of tartan at the same price.' In various other fashion columns like *Flamingo Magazine*, McGrath eulogised on the diversity of John Stephen's designs for 1964, pointing up the mix of tropical and temperate colours, utilised by Stephen as part of his ingenious, upbeat palette for a decade already accelerating away from conventional moral and fashion protocol like a Lamborghini. McGrath drew attention to Stephen's ubiquitously popular gingham button down collar shirts with a V design over the pocket, that came in variant shades of blue and white, pink and white, grey and white, red and white, black and white, offset with coloured mother-of-pearl buttons as a detail adding flair to a fabric already given a whole new remake by its inclusion in Stephen's repertoire of generously pronounced collars, with a 3in height, and a 4in roll collar terminating in the button-down point. Stephen had originally made his first high-collar shirts after watching his customers attempt to pull their collars up high above the lapels of a jacket for emphasis, and carried this detail over with endemic success as individual to his exhaustive range of shirts. Much of John Stephen's early facility as a stylist depended on design accidents, his intuitive perception working with an observation made in a customer's needs, or by overhearing a comment as to how a style could be improved, or made additionally attractive, by someone trying on an existing garment in the shop. By working the floor Stephen adeptly acquired insider knowledge as to his young customers' preferences, and was through this method able to anticipate their incessantly resourceful needs.

The columnist also noted Stephen's ubiquitously popular black and white block-striped matelot shirts, his Acrilan sweaters in red, beige, brown or charcoal grey, his leather and French elephant cord waistcoats that came in vermilion, dark blue and black, Madras jackets in a variety of broad-striped pastel shades, collarless leather jackets – sleek skins that came in thundery colours of navy blue and black and purple and cotton striped polo neck sweaters that were available in either blue, brown or red combined with black stripes. Black and white dog's-tooth hipsters, twill trousers and petrol-blue denim shirts with tab and button-down collars were amongst the other eminently noticeable attractions on offer at Mod Male for John Stephen's voraciously competitive Mod clientele, all of them lending a new definition to the concept of cool, and saturating it with defiant colour and celebratory attitude.

By 1963–64, when the look was no longer exclusive to a cult, but had been shaped into a public image for Mods, rents had escalated in Carnaby Street from £10 a week to £70 or £100; and Stephen who employed no designers, and for lack of a formal office conducted his business transactions opportunistically on the pavement, was the street's principal occupant, with six shops in his name, the lead one, The Man's Shop at 49–51, being managed by the stunningly attractive Anglo-Indian Pat Simms, who went on to become a croupier, and whose sister Lorna and brother John were both to find employment in John Stephen outlets. Stephen's other shops, nominally His Clothes, Mod Male, Male West One, Adam and Domino Male, were all small, stunningly designed, and regularly stripped of stock at the weekends by the scooter attack of Mod enthusiasts. John Stephen's early menswear rivals in the street, Nathan Spiegal's Paul's Male Boutique at 39 Carnaby Street, that always according to Bill Franks, smelled of Aqua Da Silva, and the street's originator in terms of men's boutiques, Donis, at 23–24 Carnaby Street, run by Andrew Spyropoulos, a shirt manufacturer with a factory in the street, who had opened Donis in 1957 as the first of the small boutiques to open on Carnaby Street, offered little opposition to Stephen's ruthless dynamic in linking his designs to the spectacular coefficient of pop. At first considered transient by traditional tailors and conservative retailers, Stephen was by now the intransigent rogue gene in menswear, whose flash-forward ideas they were forced to follow or risk slow extinction. Stephen's impetuous dynamic was a quality that had him sign, seal and deliver for a property in five minutes, only later informing his partner Bill Franks of the temerity of his impromptu decision. Department stores such as Peter Jones, Bourne and Hollingsworth, Harrods, and even Liberty opened 'boutiques' within their stores, and even traditional concerns like Austin Reed and Simpsons were forced to follow in Stephen's indomitable wake or go under. Stephen too, had survived the incineration of his premises, The Man's Shop, at 49–51 Carnaby Street, a fire gutting the shop one Saturday night in September 1963, when he and Bill Franks were watching a screening of *Saturday Night and Sunday Morning* at the Warner Cinema in nearby Leicester Square. Undeterred by the extensive fire-damage, Stephen had retrieved saleable stock, sold it off at a reduced price, and with characteristic alacrity refitted the shop within a week of the catastrophe. And despite attempts on the part of the trade to undermine John Stephen's clothes as lacking in durability and fine tailoring, and placing ephemeral fashion appeal before qualitative design, *Queen* magazine nonetheless rated him sufficiently proper to list in Society: The Index, in their superior Tailors category, together with Vincent, Henry Poole, In Hong Kong, Hayward, Denman and Goddard, John Michael, Blades, Hawes and Curtis and lastly John Stephen Custom built.

Amongst the stylistically cool tailors listed, John Michael, who had started as a women's fashion designer in his mother's business before opening the first man's boutique called Sportique on the King's Road, at No 170, in 1957, was also the owner of the proto-gay outlet Sportique in Soho's old Compton Street, and was, like John Stephen who followed him into the King's Road, one of the earliest proponents of the male boutique. The old Etonian John Michael, a.k.a. Ingram, whose clothes were high-end modern but reticent by Carnaby Street standards, altogether lacked John Stephen's pioneering drive towards the democratisation of clothes, and sold expensive but distinctly individual lines to young Chelsea aristos who went for his skin-fit hipsters in blue and silver tonics. John Michael's specialities included French-style tweed jackets, cut very straight with three high-fastening buttons and a single vent, fly-fronted shirts made out of Swiss voile with penny-round collars and detailed stitching, Gucci shoes and sumptuous Louis Vuitton luggage. He stocked rails of sensuously rippling pure silk Jacques Fath ties, Levi's in various shades of indigo, blue and stone-grey, and soft-skinned MacDouglas leather jackets. Richard Young, a friend of Mark Feld's at the time, was so attracted to the shop that he managed to secure a job there, drawn to the Sportique ethos by the art-house feel of the place, and by its themed window displays dressed by Charles Schuller. Young remembers, 'It was where I first came across gays, art, cinema, theatre and a much heavier feel of rock'n'roll. We had Bob Dylan and the Band coming in, Mick Jagger, Keith Richards, John Lennon – who I sold a black roll neck jumper to – and David Bailey. His models would come in to buy Levi's jeans after a shoot. Dylan came in 1965 and bought tons of stuff when he transformed his image. I had to deliver it to the Westbury Hotel. On the cover of Highway 61 Revisited, there's a picture of a guy next to Dylan wearing a striped T-shirt. I sold him that shirt.' John Michael's inimitably suave look catered for emergent Mods influenced by styles they'd seen worn in French or Italian films or on jazz album sleeves, and included sharp suits, narrow ties and spear-pointed collars on pastel shirts. Andrew Loog Oldham, an early customer at Stephen's His Clothes, as well as regularly eye-jabbing the John Michael windows as a compulsive browser doing virtual shopping, remembers with tonic enthusiasm that 'Sportique's fey clothes were ludicrous unless you were swarthy, wealthy and gay. John Michael, on the other hand with its formal grey flannel suits, and striped or gingham round-collared, fly-fronted, well tailored shirts, was another fashion plate we could ill afford, but we badly wanted. So I did starve a little for a superlative skinny wool-knit tie and gingham tab-collared shirt.'

Scoring by the quickness of his invention, and with an imagination that outstripped his contemporaries for trailblazing ideas, Stephen's example of the independent boutique run on the principles of quirky individual autonomy in defiance of regulated haute couture inspired a new proliferation of London boutiques opened to meet the Big Bang explosion of demand for individually-styled clothes by a fashion-obsessed youth. Sniffing the Chelsea potential that Quant had instigated for young women through the opening of Bazaar, John Stephen, preceded only by John Michael, had opened men's shops there at 97 King's Road, and His Clothes at 201 King's Road, establishing another lead in mapping out the topography of the city's principal fashion shopping-zones. Stephen, who had singularly created Carnaby Street as the gravitational field for the Mod milieu and was equally responsible for the extravagant hoopla associated with the place, was also the first to take innovative menswear to the King's Road at a time when it had become the locus for bright young things and dissenting arts college bohemians. Chelsea's King's Road had largely through the Quant flagship become the edgily antagonistic counterpart to Stephen's Carnaby Street, scoring in indigenous wealth, but unable to compete in clothes originality with John Stephen's democratisation of fashion for the young office workers and shop assistants who comprised the Mod hardcore who spent regularly on a weekly basis. London SW3 was given an additional heady endorphin boost by the publication in 1963 from Secker & Warburg of Virginia Ironside's topical novel *Chelsea Bird*, in which the heroine for lack of money sews her own home-made imitations of Mary Quant's flagrantly controversial clothes, wishing instead she could buy the originals at Bazaar, and goes compulsive window-shopping late at night with her friend, deciding in the process that Kiki Byrne was livelier than Bazaar. With her promotional photos, like those of the early Rolling Stones, taken down on the Embankment by a bibulously entrepreneurial Jeffrey Bernard, Virginia was photographed 'in almost every glossy magazine and every paper – in my miniskirt, on top of ladders, walking down the King's Road in high boots, in black fishnet stockings, cross-legged in studios.' Chelsea had the edge on bobbed micro-skirted girls in thigh boots, but judiciously and devotionally, Stephen went in there for men, establishing much the same precedent as he had done at Carnaby Street, by observing no formulaic protocol, and by targeting his clothes at the opportunistic spending power of enthusiasts prepared to change their image on a weekly basis to keep up with whatever was urgently new in his displays. The tone of Stephen's two King's Road outlets was necessarily modified for the Chelsea set, and concentrated more on suits, slick watches and cuff-links as accessories, with the Myles Antony interiors featuring coach lamps, brass, purple drapes and quality. Stephen's

Carnaby Kinks

Debbie Delacey and Mick Avory (the Kink's Drummer)
wearing new John Stephen gear

Clothes details — page 22

uniformly excruciatingly low-rise trousers for men, were a feature in both his Soho and King's Road locations, and were cut to sit on the hips and crotch like a tonic or mohair grape skin, and were the first of their kind, as well as being scandalously provocative in manifesting sex appeal for men. According to Stephen's friend, Mary Quant, as the progenitor of leggy appeal for girls, 'there was no one day when the mini first happened. I made the skirts shorter and shorter all the time and Chelsea girls loved to wear them because all the best legs come to London. The King's Road became a catwalk for the mini. Many people disapproved of the miniskirt but after Courréges also designed a miniskirt collection it became perfectly proper except in Italy where there was uproar about the mini and a riot in Rome on our visit to collect the Piavolo D'Oro fashion award in 1966.' John Stephen's hipster trousers for men excited corresponding attention on account of their erogenous attraction and were as equally provocative a fashion statement for men as Quant's crotch-teasing fluttery micro-skirts were for girls on a breezy King's Road Saturday afternoon. Encouraged by Stephen's unstoppable momentum as trend-setter, other boutique owners started out on similar lines, working independently and relying on brightly painted shop-fronts and bizarre window displays to draw attention to increasingly responsive foot traffic. Lee Bender opened Bus Stop in a former Cullen's grocery store on Kensington Church Street, and painted the front scarlet and gold, as the first of twelve shops, Jeff Banks opened Clobber in Hampstead, and James Wedge provided the highly influential, tiny shops, Top Gear and Countdown, at 135a–137 King's Road, opening a gateway for Ossie Clark's superior Quorum, named after an underground gay magazine at the time, that like *Jeremy* with its offices in Carnaby Street, was in circulation only to the cognoscenti. Barbara Hulanicki's success with Biba evolved along lines similar to John Stephen in that she had her teenage assistants wear the same sort of clothes as the customers who shopped there, the whole democratic impromptu atmosphere of life on the street being recreated in the shop. Hulanicki was also the first to introduce a communal changing room into her shop, as a means of accelerating the number of in-store purchases by having up to ten girls at a time trying on clothes, rather than the traditionally segregated two or three fitting rooms that slowed down any notion of rapid-fire sales.

But in 1963–64 Carnaby Street smelled of money, hair lacquer, the crisp notes of shirt cotton, the more complex musty tones of suede and velvet, and the sharp nostril-splitting tang of sleek leather skins. Entrepreneurs from wholesalers, sketchbooks in hand, sat on camp stools outside Stephen's newly dressed windows, busy lifting his conceptions for dispersal into mainstream

The Kinks raided John Stephen's boutiques for clothes. Their 'Dedicated Follower of Fashion' became the mid-sixties soundtrack to the street.

fashion. The popping exhaust smoke of scooters chugging into parking spaces vacated by other often recognisable faces in the Mod coterie, segueing off into the gridlocked West End traffic, their white, pink or dark blue John Stephen carriers, individually designed by Myles Antony, stashed into rear baskets, was the most recognisable sound on the air-waves rising above the sustained ambient roar of the Regent Street/Oxford Street intersection. Mods got high on the recreational élan of shopping for clothes, but Carnaby Street was by this time becoming a mini war-zone with violent run-ins between Mods and antagonistic Rockers disrupting trade in the busy constricted shops. On occasions staff were threatened with knives and even axes, as insurgent gangs of up to thirty leather-jacketed greasers ripped into a single boutique, gutting clothes racks and wrecking fixtures on the trail of their Mod antagonists. Ugly street fights erupted outside shops, intimidating pedestrians, tills were raided by the marauding leather vandals, and John Stephen was forced to write to the Police Commissioner asking for the street to be regularly policed as a precautionary measure to constrain violence. The police responded by placing plainclothes detectives in the crowd as a means of being on the spot if violence exploded, a method that worked short-term, without being in any way a final solution to settle animosities. Gang warfare continued to rage in the street on Saturday afternoons between the steaming homophobic biker-boys, and the no less fisty Mods, despised by the contingent of leather boys for their effeminate style of dress and their purist intellectual ideals. The situation however, was hardest on the John Stephen managers who found themselves the polarised targets of Rocker threat and lacerating verbal and physical abuse. John Stephen was obliged too, in view of apprehending 20–30 shop-lifters a day, to employ security for his shops in the form of two guards who maintained a vigilant scrutiny of his network of saturated stores projecting his name as a signature written into the architecture of the street.

In the early 1960s British fabrics were at their best, with T1 quality corduroy selling for as little as one shilling (ten pence) per metre, high grade velvet for a pound a metre, and the unlimited range of colours allowing for creative experimentation in all fabrics, most of which were purchased locally in Soho. For the new generation of designers like John Stephen it was the optimal moment in which to launch attention-seeking colours for a young generation sold on the compulsive pleasure-purchase of shopping for clothes that were shockingly state-of-the-art new.

An integral part of the John Stephen success was the visual dynamic injected into his displays by Myles Anthony as art director and display manager, and it was Myles together with his team of six young assistants who was responsible for dressing all John Stephen's London shops on a rotating monthly basis, with the discarded Carnaby Street props then used as display in the provincial shops. Antony would on occasions socialise with John Stephen by visiting the Two Decks in Soho's Rupert Court, where after a dinner of steak and chips, the two would go upstairs to watch a drag act provided by Alan Haynes and Tony Osbourne called Campelot. Stephen, who never took off his jacket or loosened his tie, remained inscrutable to Myles, who commented on his perfectly maintained façade, 'because he never spoke about his problems, you thought he didn't have any.' Carnaby Street in the early 1960s was the safe precinct for Mod-adopted androgyny, and the street itself provoked a partial gay response in straights, as well as being a renowned cruising area, with gays and straights meeting along a seamless line of fashion. Some pop stars like Billy Fury, Cliff Richard, Dave Clark, Mick Jagger and Brian Jones wore makeup openly, as something complementary to their status as celebrities, and Myles remembers how even straight managers and models used for his photo-shoots were curious to experiment sexually and try gay sex as indicative of aspects of the reinvented masculinity they were experiencing.

Interviewed by *Style Weekly* in June 1964, Myles Anthony remained unapologetic about the overt homoerotic theme that continued to pervade John Stephen's windows, much to the consternation of the local police. 'Women's dress manufacturers realised a long time ago,' Anthony explained, 'that pictures of beautiful girls wearing clothes can sell them faster than any other method. I simply use the same technique with boys. But having too sexy a display has brought our windows under fire from numerous display teams.' And with reference to the blow-ups of attractive male models that were a regular selling-point in John Stephen's windows, Myles Anthony went on to explain his working method. 'In order to get the best out of photographic display I dress in the suspended Swiss style in groups, balancing merchandise, photos and space. This can take an enormous amount of work when one is organizing dozens of windows at a time, but the result is worth it.' Anthony's window displays featuring semi-nude boys in micro-briefs were the subject of regular controversy, and after receiving an admonitory call from the police telling him that his display of teenage blow-ups in the window of the John Stephen shop in Old Compton Street was offensive to the public, he countered the allegation by informing the police that what he found 'personally objectionable was all the big tits on show as part of the Soho sex-trade.' For Myles Anthony, John Stephen also symbolised the prankster – the man who would do silly things like run into the shop, grab something like a shop-lifter and run out into the street to catch the managers out as failing to be vigilant.

By 1964 the popularity of John Stephen's clothes was generating as much as £4,500 to £5,000 per week, per shop, as opposed to the £100 a week he had generated on first opening in dead-end insignificant Carnaby Street. John Stephen's own manic sensibility appeared to have infected an entire youth culture with the fanatical impulsive momentum to strip the racks for weekly purchases with a compulsion that interfaced their creator's g-force velocity of invention. If Stephen appeared to risk burn-out by overtaking himself too soon, then he constantly proved his critics wrong by the apparently untiring resourcefulness of his creativity, and by keeping Mods coming back day after day to search their colourful reflections for self-appraisal in his shop windows. The self-regarding Mod teen meeting his own identically dressed image in the display of His Clothes or The Man's Shop, as confirmation of the look, was of course central to John Stephen's marketing strategy and a system fully endorsed by Myles Anthony's feedback as window dresser. 'At other times we've found that displaying pictures of unknown models in their teens can prove as popular as stars. But it is essential that the boys used are similar to our average customer and not too sophisticated in appearance', Myles Anthony told *Style Weekly*, with the authority of well-tested experience. The boys employed as models for fashion shoots rarely came from agencies, but were often junior members of staff, photogenic customers, friends of Mike McGrath's or rent from nearby Piccadilly Circus, all of who possessed a similar street credibility to John Stephen's teenage clientele.

John Stephen's undisputed purchase on the look, together with the sheer volume of his creative output, understandably shocked his menswear contemporaries into a state of panicked abeyance, requiring a desperate collective re-think on their part as to how to compete with his charismatic popularity and retail monopoly on the younger market. Bill Franks insists that commercial gain was never their prior incentive, and that success happened independent of systems and without the application of any studied business acumen, as an unstoppable phenomenon of the times that pushed them forward impulsively on overdrive and overreach to meet the demands of a generation sold on the idea of competing for the look. And John Stephen, according to Myles Anthony, was incredulous about his iconic status in the fashion world, constantly surprised that he could do it, and invariably in doubt as to the merit and continuity of his achievement. Stephen's inseparable identification with a street he had transformed into the epitome of cool, combined with his debonair pop star looks, daily and opportunistically

John Stephen and admiring P.A, look at a model of the John Stephen Store that housed his offices in Carnaby Street.

exploited by the image-addicted paparazzi, invariably invited detractors and pejorative criticism of the quality of his clothes, and the unfounded accusation that his shirts and trousers fell apart after a first wearing due to inferior workmanship, began to circulate as bad press amongst the trade. According to the novelist and fashion critic Nik Cohn, who was also a regular customer, John Stephen, 'in the effort never to lose speed or excitement, got stuck in the visual equivalent of triple forte. All subtleties were forgotten, any possible pleasure of texture or line. Instead, there was automatic frenzy. Each new style was made wilder, more gimmicky than the one before; each window screamed louder than its neighbour. In no time, a limit had been reached and, from then on, the effect was like a jammed car-horn, blaring so ceaselessly and mindlessly that one doesn't even hear it.'

While the need for a constantly sustained thermal of excitement fuelled the undertow of Stephen's chain-smoking, street-fuelled creative stimulus, fine tailoring and personally-selected high-quality fabrics were, despite opinions to the contrary, a distinct part of his trademark. The Carnaby Street name came to be downgraded in terms of remiss tailoring by the arrival of later, purely commercial speculators, like the market trader Warren Gold who set up the lucrative Lord John, Irvine Sellars with his Courtauld-backed Mates brand and Sidney Brent of Take Six, all of who were in part responsible for an amalgam of propagated myth, and in some instances fact, that Carnaby Street placed showmanship before durable quality. A similar charge was levelled at the maverick King's Road entrepreneurs, with John Pearse who formed part of the Granny Takes A Trip syndicate, conceding to the charges of certain fabrics splitting because of their fragility. 'Well,' Pearse acknowledged, 'actually, certain trousers that we made did fall to bits as well, very quickly, but nobody ever complained about it, because that was part of the thing. It was velvet, and you'd become like some tattered troubadour the next day, you know. Some things did fall apart, and everything had to be so tight, that seams could burst, especially on velvet.'

As a physical location though, as well as a piece of archetypal Mod psychogeography, Carnaby Street in 1963–64 was still predominantly a Mod precinct, a barrio of rundown brick buildings, that had somehow made all the right connections at the exact moment of change to the way in which men presented a new expression of masculinity. Its culture was still traceable to its small, individualised, edgy origins, before its gradual evolution as the sixties progressed into a touristic colour-soaked extravaganza, overtaken by hippie preoccupations with an imaginary stoned East, owning to an idealistic culture filtered through the reading of Herman Hesse's ubiquitously popular novels like *Siddharta, Journey To The East* and *The Glass Bead Game*, in which the players all wore floral-patterned kaftans, and chased their dreams through contrails of acrid marijuana smoke.

In a *Weekend* article from 1964, John Stephen was noted as an exemplar of his own fashion by having in rotation in his personal wardrobe in Jermyn Street, 14 suits, 5 sports jackets, 4 casual jackets, 24 pairs of trousers, 48 shirts and 70 ties. That his renowned bachelor status was confirmed in the feature carried with it the implication that a man so singularly concerned with his appearance had to be gay. Stephen's brilliantly sustained and rehearsed interview persona – he always presented clothes and by extension Carnaby Street as his personality – and deflected all personal questions unless they related to work, remained an impenetrable façade throughout the exhaustive media circuit on which he found himself launched for the entire 1960s, with his equally hyped-up PR Mike McGrath, calling him at three and four in the morning to programme in interviews for the shattered insomniac to undertake the next day.

John Stephen was, to his advantage as premier Mod stylist, every bit as preoccupied by the look as the pop stars and their obsessive fans he dressed through his newly leased Carnaby Street shops like Male West One and the Drug Store, on the corner of Beak Street and Carnaby Street, fitted with an in-store café used for recreation by celebrities like Cliff Richard, Billy Fury, Sandie Shaw, Phil May of the Pretty Things, and Mick Jagger and Keith Richards. But in the context of his buried and highly secretive private life John Stephen increased his drinking proportionate to the quotient of his acclaimed celebrity. He was in addition intolerantly possessive, and despite winning Bill Franks' acquiescence into having Frank Merkell accepted into their partnership, he was demonstratively jealous if Franks showed any aberration from fidelity on his part, and on one occasion smashed up the Jermyn Street flat after Franks had confessed to going out to a Queensway club to look for a sexual partner. Myles Antony too, remembers an occasion at The Man's Shop in 1961, when after Franks had permitted a young man to try on shorts in the shop, Stephen after the customer had left exploded into a brief supernova of possessive rage. But to Rosalie Shann, writing for the *News of the World*, John Stephen remained the perfect enigma with his defensive fielding of personal questions, and his invasively projected charm. 'He looks like James Dean,' she enthused, 'with his brooding handsomeness. He is serious and nervous, chain smoking those small cigars you buy in a flat tin box. He dresses conservatively in a two-year-old light grey suit. And he talks almost apologetically in a soft voice which is still very attractive Scottish.' What

Shann understandably omitted to mention was that John Stephen rarely if ever spoke about himself, preferring always to keep to his profession, clothes, and to name-list the celebrities who visited his shops, a flamboyantly prestigious roster which by now included Shirley Bassey, Judy Garland and Marlene Dietrich, as three spectacular showbiz divas drawn out of sexual ambivalence to the androgynous nature of his clothes. Stephen claimed in interviews that he had no hobbies and that work was his relaxation, but he was an inveterately voracious reader of thrillers, speed-reading the likes of Ian Fleming, Graham Greene, Agatha Christie, and even cult literature like James Leo Herlihy's *Midnight Cowboy* and William Burroughs' *Naked Lunch* in bed, and found an outlet for his aesthetic preoccupations through the serendipitous collecting of antiques. Stephen regularly bought on impulse bronze Grecian and Egyptian heads, art-deco ornamentation, figurative paintings, decorative terracotta, and amassed a personal hoard of cuff-links, gold chains and diamond-chipped tie-pins from Regent Street and Bond Street jewellers. Stephen the aesthete wore hypnotically glowering blue diamonds on thin gold bands on each hand, as an indicator of his love of jewellery, and enjoyed dining at good restaurants like the Seven Stars in Coventry Street, Soho, Overtons restaurant in St James', Franks in his local Jermyn Street, and the Fisherman's Wharf at Chelsea Wharf. Stephen's gastronomical propensities were largely for shellfish, his preference being for mussels, and if they were not on the menu, then for lobster or crab. In 1964, the John Stephen board of directors, photographed drinking Moet & Chandon champagne at a board meeting in Stephen's Jermyn Street apartment, comprised Dean Rogers, Myles Anthony, Angelo Uragallo, Frank Merkell, Keith Dodge, Bill Franks and John Stephen, nearly all of who were in their twenties, and were formally dressed for the camera in dark suits, white shirts and dark silk or knitted ties. The all-male youthful conclave, with Stephen and Franks the only shareholders, drawn together at a particular moment in time that represented the optimum pitch of the first-wave Carnaby Street inspired look, symbolised a radical turning-point in British fashion in that for the first time youth was being dressed by youth as the expression of a new aggressively ageist cutting-edge generation. John Stephen had almost without precedent succeeded in sexualizing clothes for men, and suddenly it was the over-30s who found themselves excluded, and actually discriminated against, rather than arbitrating over lines of traditionally conservative menswear. John Stephen's clothes were uninhibitedly sexy, drawing from Andrew Loog Oldham, the perfect snake-hipped customer, the recollection that Stephen 'racked up huge sales by retailing clothes so body-conscious and sexy that it was less of a problem to afford them than to fit into them.' Oldham and his blocked, periodically psychotic business associate Peter Meaden, who shared an office space at 44/46 Maddox Street, had applied unsuccessfully to do independent PR work for John Stephen, who he found manically speeded-up to the point of adrenalin meltdown at a brief meeting at the Seven Stars in Coventry Street, a wired state that Oldham who also suffered from bipolar disorder recognised as an aberrant, if obligatory component in the chemical soup of all aspiring tycoons. And it was here of course, that the altogether better earthed and stabilising qualities of Stephen's partner, Bill Franks, came into such beneficial play by grounding Stephen when his overreach grew too obviously delusional, and his system-smashing ambitions threatened to override the business, that for all its outwardly showy, exhilarating success, was heavily in debt to wholesalers and its financial investors, and had resisted an offer by Whiteley's to buy them out in 1964.

The opening of the John Stephen Custom Made shop in 1964, at 47 Carnaby Street, was another fashion first for John Stephen, in that it provided a service in which the customer brought in drawings, cut-outs from magazines, or simply the idea of a garment to be reconfigured by Malcolm Bohla in the basement workroom at His Clothes, or put out to one of the innumerable tailors in the precinct, with a three-piece suit sometimes being made by three separate concerns. The duration for realising customised orders was in most instances, two days for a shirt, three hours for a pair of trousers, and a week that included three fittings, for the completion of a suit. Like all John Stephen shops, Custom Made was aesthetically pleasing, exhibited rolls of fabric and a number of display mannequins dressed by Myles Antony, one of them in Lord Nelson's beige waistcoat, that Stephen privately owned, and had a blue and white interior with the changing rooms and fixtures put up as was the custom by Bill Franks' brother, Brian, who was by trade a carpenter and joiner. After selecting a fabric and undergoing three fittings, the suit, given the availability of cloth, would be ready to collect in ten days. What it meant was that Mods who had conceived of a design to outstrip other Faces could have their individual pattern realised almost immediately, and for pop stars concerned with always dominating the look, the shop provided them with kick-start facilities as to how best to appeal to their fans as ace fashion icons.

John Stephen's one serious rival in custom-made shirt making at the time, was the renowned Philip Stevens, who operated from small premises in Soho's Broadwick Street, along similar lines to John Stephen's facility in encouraging customers to configure their own signature styles. In 1964, *The Mod*

magazine assiduously reported, 'still on shirts I've discovered where Mick Jagger, the Beatles, Dave Berry, PJ Proby, The Animals etc have their shirts made. It's a little workshop right in the centre of London's Soho, where Philip Stevens, his wife and assistant turn out the most fantastic out-of-this-world shirts. They make them up from odd scraps of designs cut from magazines and sketches the boys have designed themselves.'

The less fortunate amongst aspiring pop stars literally raided the Carnaby Street dustbins after dark for rejects by way of assembling a stage wardrobe. According to David Bowie, who was still the underachieving David Jones, he first met Marc Bolan in the early 1960s, and was introduced by him to dustbin shopping. 'At that time,' Bowie recalled, 'Carnaby Street was going through a period of incredible wealth. Rather than replace buttons on their shirts or zippers on their trousers, at the end of the day, they'd throw them away. So we used to go through the Carnaby Street dustbins around 9.00 or 10.00 at night, and get our wardrobes together.'

Largely due to John Stephen's brokering purist ethic as Mod proponent, as the decade evolved clothes continued to dissolve class distinctions, with youth creating its own subversive autocracy through its particular dress code. Writing of the Beatles and their attachment to a dandified image as seminal to their accelerated success as a band, Renee Fox in the *New York Times* commented, 'Their long fancy Edwardian clothes suggests a sort of sophistication that contrasts further with their homespun style of performance. Much has been made of their poor, lower-class backgrounds in Northern England, yet they are accepted by the upper-crust, having attracted the auspicious attention of the Queen mother, Princess Margaret, Mrs Nelson Rockfeller, and President Johnson.'

But a generic resistance on the part of the older generation to the Mod look remained endemic, and the preconception that Mods, no matter how sophisticated their look and intellectual leanings, were uniformly cultureless, persisted through the early 1960s, with the suavely chauvinistic, rat-pack aficionado Dean Martin, using the Rolling Stones booked on his televised *The Dean Martin Hollywood Palace Show* in 1964, as the butt-end of deprecatingly sarcastic jokes aimed at ridiculing their long-haired girlie appearance. Martin's innuendos, implying that the Stones were indubitably gay, a deliberate subversion of the look on the part of the climacteric host, had Keith Richards describe his arrogantly offending host as a 'right fucking offer.' Youthful defiance amped-up by the intransigent visual image provided by the Rolling Stones as the epitome of its punky, amoral, bad-boy attitude, had now gained in ascendancy, and with John Stephen as its shape-shifting

John loved cuffs and cufflinks, both prominent here as he dresses a mannequin.

designer, youth culture was now a magnified entity fully exploited by the media as an unsettling but lucrative novelty phenomenon. And for John Stephen in 1964, it was business as usual. *The Observer* ran a photo-feature on John Stephen, drawing attention to his putting Mods in the taboo colours, for men, of pink and lavender, and in providing more subdued daytime shirts in greys and blues with deeper-coloured collars and cuffs. Stephen spoke of the marine-themed collection he had put together for the winter as a way of introducing Mods to the sailor look, previously only associated with camp. 'Jackets,' Stephen assured, 'will be navy blue, double-breasted, with big vents, or in tough-looking corduroy with epaulettes. Sweaters will have a deep V. Trousers will be 16 inches wide from the thigh down; shirts will have long-pointed button-down collars.'

By now John Stephen had his own factory in Kilburn, where he supervised the cutting of trousers and jackets, his maverick status allowing him still to make up limited editions of as few as six or twelve of a garment. Shirts were manufactured for him by the Irish concern Omar Shirt & Collar Company, who also produced quality shirts for Stephens Brothers, the fabric and pattern being delivered to the manufacturer for completion.

If Carnaby Street was still local in 1964, then it was starting also to attract celebrity-spotters looking out for the likes of Mick Jagger, Phil May of the Pretty Things, Sandie Shaw, Dave Clark, Ray and Dave Davies of the Kinks, all busy shopping for pink and ice-blue ruffled shirts, red leather waistcoats and blazing red tartan hipsters worn with wide leather belts. Stephen had also designed candy-striped watch straps as an accessory to striped blazers that came in an inexhaustible combination of delectable confectionary colours, and could be worn to complement block-striped sailor vests and Madras cotton blazers. Each of Stephen's shops had its own characteristic flavour, usually dictated by managerial preferences, and Peggy Lee was the noted voice issuing from Bill Franks' favourite His Clothes, when an *Observer* journalist reported on the street's daily hyperactivity of dedicated customers and attendant film-crews. The same reporter noted that Male West One was selling 'snappy sports shirts and slacks,' from a décor of orange felt hangings, and that sounds in this boutique were supplied by an abundant stream of Beatles' records. At John Stephen's Man's Shop, art nouveau prints and Nat King Cole set the style, and slacks in black and white glint tweed worn with pink long pointed collar shirts were best sellers. In the newly created Mod Male, the journalist observed of the shop's ambience that 'tiny blue-beat pork-pie hats with miniature brims lie in a corner, fast going out, while scarlet polo-necked sweaters and gold shirts hang on rails on their way in.'

STOP PRESS FORECAST
From John Stephen, head
of the John Stephen
Organisation:
"Flowered ties are finished
and op-art will predominate,
with flaring ends,
odd cut-outs, etc. Jackets
will get more and more
nipped-in . . . . shirts
stay patterned, but what
sort of pattern is still
top secret . . . as for
trousers, bell-bottoms
are dead, it's hipsters all
the way, straight and
simple."

◄ Jimmy Tarbuck, the cheeky Liverpudlian tipped to be one of the
biggest show-biz successes of all time, is all togged up
in the latest male mod gear. "All together, it's a bit much,"
says Jim, "but any one item could sharpen up a more trad
outfit." Surprise tactics are the mod's trademark—like the
combination of non-matching patterned shirt, tie and belt,
or one unexpected item like op-art cuff-links or those
sensational fly buttons.
Carnaby Street experts form two schools of thought about
male plumage—some say floral shirts, jazzy socks and
pastel-shade underwear are the fore-runners of even more
colourful and (dare we say it?) effeminate trappings; others
claim that quiet fabrics in an extravagant, Regency-type cut are
on the way in. So the Beau Brummel in fine worsted checks
may be the next lad to grace the fashion scene.
Jim's gear, from the feet up: square-toed shoes by Mr. Merrywell,
59/11; button-thro' fly-fastening trousers, Cecil Gee,
99/6 ("I'll be raped in these," he cried); leather waistcoat
from John Stephen Store, Carnaby Street, W.1, 7 gns.;
flowered fun-shirt from a selection at Woollands, 89/6;
fur fabric double-breasted mini-coat designed by Hardy Amies
for Hepworths, £18/5/-; and corduroy cap, John Adam Boutique,
Civil Service Stores, Strand. W.C.1, 2 gns.

Out-and-out mod—or casual trad-man? Whatever your personal style,
these two likely lads should give you something to think about (and
your nearest and dearest a few snappy gift ideas at the same time)

COUPLE OF SWELLS

Caps and floral shirts – John Stephen's idea of feminised masculinity was the look, and found an
unlikely model in the youthful Jimmy Tarbuck.

The reporter noted that as for interior design 'the walls are pasted with pop stars, and the music comes from the Rolling Stones.' And with an insider's knowledge to the fact that 'all the trousers from the Stephen factory come without a bottom hem and hang on shop racks in this unfinished state until someone buys them,' the acknowledgement was that after being sold, 'they are carefully measured to the customer's length and the workroom in the basement of His Clothes turns them up in a matter of ten minutes.'

Carnaby Street and Mods as a collective were given an additional publicity incentive when on 9 August 1963, ITV debuted *Ready Steady Go!* as London's premiere Mod music show, a Friday night routine of informal party-going and scene-making in which the top bands were given the enthusiastic endorsement of the 19-year-old ex-secretary presenter Cathy McGowan, whose eye-level black fringe, panda eyes, untameable vivacity and miniskirted pins were matched by a personality that brimmed with the euphoric liberation of sunshiny sixties teen spirit. McGowan who regularly featured on the cover of every teen magazine such as *Rave, Jackie, Fabulous, The Mod* and *Melody Maker*, became as much a glamour icon of her times as models like Jean Shrimpton, Chrissie Shrimpton and Twiggy, only she appeared more personably accessible, more a direct, unpretentious Carnaby Street product, electrified by the excitement of the moment, and spontaneously prolific in the use of enthusiastic adjectives like 'cool,' 'fab,' and 'smashing.' With the weekly show engineered by Vicki Wickham and Michael Lindsay-Hogg, who as directors were responsible for booking the artists, as well as selecting and showcasing the sharpest-dressed Mod dancers secured from scouting clubs like the Scene and the Flamingo, *Ready Steady Go!*, with its youth sensibility specifically targeted a pop enamoured audience. With pop art sets designed by Nicholas Ferguson, and the theme tune changing on rotation from Manfred Mann's anthemic '*5–4–3–2–1*,' to The Who's *Anyway, Anywhere, Anyhow*, to *Three Hundred and Sixty-Five Rolling Stones*, an instrumental by the Andrew Loog Oldham Orchestra, the show was indirectly a John Stephen fashion shoot, in that both the performing bands and the dancers were dressed predominantly in his clothes, or if purchased elsewhere, in derivations of his style. The thermal of hysterical excitement generated by performing artists of the likes of the Rolling Stones, The Who, the Kinks, the Small Faces, the Animals, Jimi Hendrix, Ike and Tina Turner, Otis Redding, John Lee Hooker and all of Motown, caught unrepeatably performing in Studio 9, at Television House in Kingsway, London, became the central focus of the week for upwards of three million viewers. And as cool arbiters of tomorrow's taste the floor was presided over by Mods wearing John Stephen gingham shirts, in a variety of colours, from blue to pink, to red to green, vented Italian jackets, crew-necked sweaters in pastel shades, white leather shoes bought at Ravel, all dancing their characteristic the block, a complex dance in which the person rose on the left heel and right toe, twisting the feet and coming forward with the whole body. The movement graduated to rising on the right heel and left toe and twisting both feet again, arms raised to shoulder level, left palm turned in, right turned out. The body was then bent forward, right foot placed behind left, spiralling back at the same time, and completed by placing the left foot in front of the right, relaxing the knees and swinging the right arm across the body.

Cathy McGowan, the show's pin-up presenter, at 5ft 4in inches, patron of John Stephen shops, Foale & Tuffin and Biba, and due to her looks and her cutting edge fashion sense, black Mary Quant kohl and eyeliner, black polo-necks, dyed black jeans, and mini-skirts worn eight inches above the knee, soon acquired the eponym 'Queen of the Mods,' and was a crucial style catalyst in bringing Mod fashions, and particularly John Stephen's clothes for men, to a nationwide audience. McGowan, who had evolved from the fashion department of *Woman's Own* magazine, had unanimously secured the role of TV presenter by answering 'fashion', without hesitation, to a question from Elkan Allan, RSG's executive producer and Head of Enter-tainment at Rediffusion, as to whether sex, music or fashion were more important to teenagers. McGowan's affable on-screen personality, neither patronising nor ingratiating to the stars she interviewed, her image appearing inseparable from theirs, quickly won her iconic status, to the degree that she had her own fashion range at British Home Stores, as well as nominally endorsing a portable makeup set known as Cathy's Survival Kit, a blue and orange case designed to slip into a handbag, and containing lipstick, mascara, eyeliner, eye-shadow and a pencil. Like John Stephen, with who she was strategically photographed in Carnaby Street, as the Mod emporium, McGowan's celebrity relied in part on a cultivated air of mystique, with both celebrities at pains to prevent any media access to their private lives. McGowan, who received over 600 fan letters a week, remained, like John Stephen apparently unaffected by success, preferring to continue living at home with her parents in Streatham, South London, and despite giving her name to a line of Cathy McGowan shirts, jeans, tights and even a celebrity look-alike doll, remained, like John Stephen, remarkably resistant to her endemic popularity. And in the same way as John Stephen had succeeded up to a point in democratising clothes, so McGowan democratised pop, her ordinary, chatty sensibility possessing the facility to normalise pop

stars and strip them of their inherently megalomaniacal tendencies. Like Stephen, McGowan, who married secretly in 1967, was from an uneducated background, and Elkan Allan, executive producer of the show, remembered not without with reservations that, 'she was awfully gauche and raw and desperately nervous, but she was worth taking on because she was obviously switched on in a teenage way.'

With its full-on slogan, 'The Weekend Starts Here,' *Ready Steady Go!* was viewed weekly on Friday evenings from 6–7pm, as a live showcase for the hottest emergent bands, and helped establish the concept of the weekend as a recreational zone for Mods given over to shopping and clubbing, which for most of them meant a wired-up Saturday afternoon visit to Carnaby Street, to strip the racks of whatever was new and visually appealing, before presenting their new clothes' assemblage in one of the cluster of preferred Soho clubs. *Ready Steady Go!*, as a televised fashion shoot, was in some ways the stylistic gateway to John Stephen's exuberant fashion empire, a subliminal message that if you were a Mod, then the majority of clothes worn by the audience and bands on stage were purchasable from Stephen's escalating chain of Carnaby Street shops. In an odd, tangential way, McGowan's look complemented John Stephen's, in that both were essentially shy, obsessively nervous individuals, who as introverts found themselves idolised by an extrovert generation of outgoing teenagers. In reality, neither Stephen nor McGowan were clubbers, Stephen's private life as a gay man being conducted underground at Piccadilly, while the naturalistic McGowan found stability in a monogamous relationship with the actor Hywel Bennett, who appeared in sixties films like *The Family Way* (1966), and *The Virgin Soldiers* (1969). Like John Stephen with his perennial bachelor status, McGowan's apparent availability was part of her selling-point as a leggy teenage icon, habitually employing her hand like a windscreen wiper to flick the cliffhanging black fringe from her kohl-saucered eyes, as she introduced hot London favourites like the Rolling Stones, the Pretty Things and The Who. Barbara Hulanicki, whose Biba store opened in September 1964 was a McGowan must, recalls that 'the girls aped Cathy's long hair and eye-covering fringe and soon their teenage faces were growing heavy with stage make-up,' as they crowded into hip London venues like The Scotch of Saint James, Tiddlydolls, The Chalet Suisse and Tiles on Oxford Street.

In 1964, it was the Kenny Slater-managed Mod Male which pulled in significant revenue for the expansive John Stephen empire, the shop finding dedicated celebrity patronage from members of the Pretty Things, the Davies brothers from the Kinks, Mick Jagger and Dave Clark of the

John Stephen opened Tre Camp in 1965 as an outlet for his ambidextrous women's designs.

Dave Clark Five, one of the most successful of the 1960s British Invasion bands and the vanguard of the 'Tottenham sound,' whose Mod haircuts and constantly mutating John Stephen clothes, including white cotton polo-neck shirts that buttoned up high on the side with a four-button fastening, gave them prominent live and television appeal. The sartorially observant Dave Clark, who was self-regarding to the point of having had a face-lift at 24, was a devoted John Stephen customer, who bought formidable quantities of knitwear, shirts and trousers from Mod Male and His Clothes, and had a particular propensity for suede-fronted jumpers in every available shade. On one occasion he purchased fifty before an American tour, manifesting an obsession the equal of Stephen's in creating a single item of knitwear in such abundant contrasting colours.

As a stagy ostentatious addition to his trademark silver Rolls Royce, regularly parked outside His Clothes in the way that Elvis Presley had a lipstick-pink finned limo stationed in the drive of his baronial Graceland, John Stephen in 1964 purchased a purple and gold chrome Cadillac, with the customised registration plate, KGC 5D, the KGC standing for the sobriquet, King of Carnaby Street, as the first American import of its kind. A typically impulsive Stephen's purchase, procured through Leck's as the agents for £8,000, the glitzy, almost extraterrestrial big American car, with customised ergonomics, was delivered directly to the door of His Clothes in Carnaby Street, as the first Cadillac to be awkwardly introduced into the London streets, and without immediate payment to cover the costs, the car was deposited awaiting a cheque. Interestingly, John's enduring friend and initial patron Ada Harris also favoured American-styled cars, and drove a roomy pink Vauxhall, as the British equivalent of Americana, its chrome fixtures and proportions considerably diminished by Stephen's audacious plum Cadillac with its Hollywood film-star connotations. Its impracticality apart, in the narrow complex of Soho streets, the car proved to be valuable eye-candy to the showbiz props incorporated into John Stephen photo shoots taken on site in Carnaby Street, with the car often parked outside the Roaring Twenties Club, situated in the basement of The Man's Shop, a West Indian club whose nocturnal clientele comprised black GIs and negro jazz players drawn to the Soho milieu for the music. A love of ostentatious cars featured strongly in the Stephen/Franks image-repertoire, with Bill Franks having purchased a James Bond-inspired silver Aston Martin DB5 for £6,500 in 1963, gunning its constrained potential across town, before a boyfriend turned the car over at Hyde Park Corner. Franks replaced the nuked Aston Martin that he had purchased from David Brown at Piccadilly with a white Alfa Romeo sports

A lucky customer gets personal attention from the dark-suited ultimate Mod hero.

car that proved equally hostile to restraint, oiled up in town, and was finally traded in for a classic silver grey Bentley.

1964 found John Stephen at his creative apogee, his transgressive designs for young Mods going even further towards dissolving the boundaries of gender. By the late summer of 1964, his shops were brimming with candy pink and ice blue shirts with 3in deep collars and fly-fronts, the barrel-cuffs secured with block-shaped jewelled cuff links, leather waistcoats made in twenty-four colours, including salmon pink and Louis XIV red, paisley or navy blue and white polka dot shirts, sleek leather trilbies, and distinctly butch Mersey jackets in elephant cord, sleeveless and collarless, with leather fastenings and giant brass buttons.

The polka-dot shirt, popularised by the likes of Bob Dylan and Brian Jones of the Rolling Stones, was a John Stephen original for men, and quickly taken up by the ambitiously entrepreneurial John Simons and his partner Jeff Kwinter at their reputable cult shop Clothesville, in Peace Street, just off Pettitcoat Lane in London's East End, situated in the basement of a garment manufacturer. Simons who would go on to open the eminently smart and upmarket The Ivy Shop in Richmond, sold amongst highly selective stock, polka-dot and paisley tab-collared shirts, reefer jackets, tight peacoats, and eye-catching knee-length Burberry corduroy raincoats in various colours tagged with customised proto-punk labels like 'Cary Grant Never Wore This Suit,' or 'Edward G Does Not Shop Here.' Simons got East End Mods into polka dots, while Stephen led from the West End. The polka-dot pattern had first become common on women's clothing in the late 19th century in Britain, when polka music was fashionable, giving rise to the name of the pattern, although there was no direct association between the two. Rarely associated with formal wear, John Stephen reversed the notion of polka dots as a largely playful fabric, and combined the shirts with velvet ties and dark blazers. Polka dots had been given a distinct 1960s boost by the Paul Vance and Lee Pockriss song, *Itsy Bitsy Teenie Weenie Yellow Polka Dot Bikini*, that Paul Hyland had taken to number one on the Billboard Hot 100 in 1960, the ludic bubblegum lyric telling the story of a shy woman posing in a minimal polka-dot bikini. True to his obsession with dictating variants of colour, Stephen designed his shirts in navy, black, scarlet, green, pink, purple, and orange with white polka dots, brown with orange polka dots – an immediate best seller, and innumerable permutations of coloured dots including scarlet and turquoise on a white background. And while the equally popular paisley pattern owed its origins to the Scottish weaving town of that name, the design dating back to the 16th century, its use in menswear had largely been confined to ties and scarves. John Stephen saw the potential to make the extravagantly whorled and swirly heart, teardrop and snowflake-shape pattern into a fabric for shirts that proved so popular that they became for a time almost a Mod identity. Nik Cohn was witness to the seamless update of fashion displayed in Stephen's windows, observing that, 'every time you past a John Stephen window there was something new and loud in it, aurally loud too. Inside his numerous Carnaby Street shops blared the shifting soundtrack of "Swinging London:" the Yardbirds, The Who, the Pretty Things, the Small Faces. Outside, he strategically placed racks of clothes as bait, and through his doors passed aristocrats, gangsters and pop stars, and among the latter the Beatles, the Rolling Stones, the Kinks and the Bee Gees.'

By 1964 Carnaby Street was on the periphery of going international, a phenomenon that when it occurred two years later, turned Mods against the street with an enduring antipathy to its growth-pattern of commercial incentive. While founder-members of the street like Bill Green, who had opened a second Vince boutique in nearby Foubert's Place, Nathan Spiegal with his 'Paul's Male Boutique,' and Andrew Spyropoulos with 'Donis,' remained as prototypes, together with John Stephen's Big Bang effect of continuous expansion, rivals were starting to appear in the form of Henry Moss and Harry Fox's 'Lady Jayne,' Irvine Sellars' 'Mates,' and Warren and David Gold, who much to John Stephen's consternation called their opportunistically-opened shop 'Lord John.' Warren Gold auspiciously commissioned the street artist and psychedelic mural painter David Vaughan, together with Douglas Binder and Dudley Edwards, (a.k.a. Binder, Edwards, Vaughan) to customise the façade of Lord John into a pop art mural. Vaughan, whose mural paintings regularly got him into trouble with the authorities and was arrested and charged twenty-two times for wilful damage in the course of the 1960s, exploded colour across the white front of Gold's Lord John boutique, his fluid line and boldness of tone working texture fluently into the flamboyant Carnaby Street ethos. Vaughan succeeded in creating what looked like a rainbowed Indian chieftan's headdress patterned with stars and meteoric gemstones splashed across two white facades, the mural continuing over the building's boarded-up windows on the top two floors. Despite John Stephen taking out a writ to prevent Warren Gold appropriating his name as a brand, Gold was permitted by law to trade under the deliberately plagiarised name of Lord John, claiming dubiously that his nickname at school had been John, and quickly succeeded in becoming a serious competitor for Mod attention, and by far the most commercially popular of the non-John Stephen enterprises resident in Carnaby Street. The 25-year-old controversial figure, Warren Gold, was an opportunist who had started in clothes with a stall in Petticoat Lane in the early sixties, and quickly earned East End Mod approval. By 1964 he had two shops in Carnaby Street, and three in Camden High Street, and although lacking John Stephen's manufacturing facilities, he designed in conjunction with manufacturers, his designs remaining exclusive to him for two or six months. Like John Stephen, who had a monthly fashion tips column in the *News of the World*, invariably ghosted by Michael McGrath, Gold had a similar monthly in the *Glasgow Daily Record*, and relied like John Stephen on editorial mention in the music and fashion press as a valuable means of generating publicity, his Carnaby Street shop finding the energetic patronage of the Small Faces, who as omnivorous teenage style icons filtered most of their immediate earnings into a constantly saturated account with Lord John. Warren Gold's stalker-like obsession to emulate John Stephen extended not only to using his name, but to wearing expensive jewellery and to owning a Rolls Royce, with the ostentatious showman in him taking to shining the car's headlights on his shop windows after dark. A rag-trade plagiarist whose ideas were largely cloned from Stephen's windows, Gold was sufficiently assertive a personality to win a dedicated pop clientele, with Micky Dolenz of the Monkees on one occasion forcing a passage through a crowded Carnaby Street to buy six suits impromptu from the shop.

Although the ebony chocolate sound of Motown was a cultural appropriation indigenous to Mod culture, and cooked in their collective genes on the dance floor, 1964 produced an affirmative London sound, a raw, energised R&B garage brew electrified with pop hooks, and often recorded locally in Denmark Street, characterised by the likes of the Rolling Stones, the Yardbirds, the Pretty Things and the Kinks, all of them committed exponents of the John Stephen look, raiding his boutiques for candy-coloured ruffled shirts and green, white and red houndstooth vented jackets. The Stones, who started the year with a top three hit, their demonstratively sexy version of Buddy Holly's *Not Fade Away*, coloured by wailing harmonica and brash maracas, predictably made it to the top spot, a chart apogee repeated in the same year, with two additional blues covers given pop makeovers, *It's All Over Now*, and *Little Red Rooster*. With their intransigent attitude and sexually ambiguous look fusing street credibility with spotty rent boy image, the Stones more than any other band were the prototypically skinny exemplars of John Stephen's untutored line. Jagger's outrageous nudist hipsters compacting a protruding crotch into low-rise, worn with skinny-rib crew-neck jumpers fully complemented Brian Jones' eye-level fringed blond bob and dandified shirts teamed with boldly striped John Stephen Madras jackets. The band's uncompromising sartorial melange, bringing Charlie Watts' sharply tailored Ivy League suits into contention with flagrantly sluttish flame-red leather waistcoats, pastel shirts with 6in pointed button-down collars, black and white check hipsters, fitted velvet jackets, invariably featured foppish accessories worn provocatively mean.

The Pretty Things, whose proto-punk garage blues rivalled the Stones for intense earthy grittiness, and who rode high on the charts with the muddy stop and start, lurchy R&B scorcher, *Don't Bring Me Down*, dressed almost uniformly in John Stephen's clothes, confessing in interviews that whatever money they earned was spent shopping in Carnaby Street. Contemporary photos of the band show them wearing blue, pink and burnt-orange, fly-fronted tab-collared denim shirts, with their recklessly alcoholic drummer, Viv Prince, often choosing scarlet shirts teamed with black knitted ties, leather waistcoats and the mini-brimmed trilbies that Stephen had made popular in black and dark blue felt. Living collectively in semi-squalor in a house at 13 Chester Street, in London's plutocratic Belgravia, the Pretty Things exemplified the Mod ethic of placing clothes as a singular priority on their list of necessities. In fact, Phil May, the band's controversially androgynous singer, was so preoccupied with John Stephen's fashions that he announced to readers in *Disc* that he too was thinking of going into design. 'Opening a shop is something we've been thinking about,' he announced, the interviewer remarking on the bright red and pink tie he was wearing with a dark shirt. 'I had a spate of doing some clothes for myself once, but it took so long, that when I wanted some new clothes I just rushed out and bought them ... Designing for girls will be especially interesting when we get around to it. I think girls should dress to suit their personality, not the terrible fad of following fashion. I would design with a particular girl in mind. I think you've got to. Actually the most marvellous thing I ever saw was Anita Ekberg wearing a red dress.'

Even first-wave Mod purists with their allegiance to imported soul and Motown were forced to take note of emergent London bands like the Action, led by Reggie King's deep-fried vocals, Chris Farlowe and the Thunderbirds, The Spencer Davis Group, and the artily experimental the Creation, all of who were filling London clubs like the Marquee with their own strains of blue-eyed soul that seemed very bit as deviantly hot as their black progenitors. In the same way as the look had mutated, so Mod music had also gone hybrid, its initial predilection for the black underclass as role-model heroes having been transposed in part into sympathies with an equally subversive white underground. Educated on the black sounds made popular by Guy

Stevens at the Scene, London's aspiring young musicians found that they too could undermine class by achieving their own blues-drenched pop as a way of working at eroding social repression. A whole teenage subculture buried by inveterate decades of suppression found in sixties fashion and music the tools with which to rebel against the existing *status quo*, becoming in the process ageist and defiantly antagonistic to conventional moral attitudes. Mods were fashion-conscious to the degree of judging a band as much on its appearance as on its music, and pop stars unable to compete with the look experienced an immediate decrease in popularity amongst the high-flying chart contenders.

In 1964, the conflicting gang violence that had raged on a small scale in Carnaby Street and in areas like Notting Hill, between Mods and Rockers, escalated into full-scale beach warfare in the much publicized 'Battle of Hastings', on August Bank holiday, when the sedate seaside town of Hastings was ripped up by the dual sonic attack of scooters and tanked-up motorbikes aimed towards the waterfront, where the grey English Channel uneventfully licked the compact pebbled shore. There had already been run-ins between Mods and Rockers, most notably at Clacton-on-Sea, Essex, on 27 March of the same year, when the pilled-up Mods by strength of numbers more or less wiped the promenade with their leather-jacketed, macho-posturing rivals. Mod/Rocker battles had become by now a feature of the press, and over the Whitsun weekend, 15–18 May, members of the two groups had fought hard and bloodily at the seaside resorts of Brighton, Margate, Southend, Bournemouth and Clacton, much of the action being shot by the principal Mod photographer Terence Spencer. For all their feminine concentration on style, it was invariably Mods who came off best, often chasing their greaser antagonists into a helter-skelter head-on flight into the sea. There were ninety-seven arrests at Clacton alone, and at the infamous Battle of Hastings, where riot police were flown in for support, nineteen youths who admitted to taking part in the riot were sent to detention centres, while another three were jailed for criminal offences. Mods as renowned style elitists, were also caught fucking in alleys in seaside towns, and developed a reputation for being aberrant sexual outlaws, a conception that was outwardly the antithesis of their image as purveyors of the inscrutable look and of ordered epicurean living. The infrastructural shift in the Mod ideological axis was remembered by the seminal Johnny Moke as a betrayal of rigidly maintained ideals. 'From then on, and I mean 1964/1965, it wasn't modernism anymore, it was something very different. Attitudes changed within and without the group, and it wasn't any longer about being identified as a Mod. It was more about being a member of a gang, and that was never our concern. We were into style, fashion and music, and the next thing is that the whole movement's focused on Clacton or Brighton beach ... Those people calling themselves Mods were just a tribe, they weren't concerned with setting themselves apart in the way that we were always on the move and one step ahead, and never part of a gang.'

One redoubtable Margate magistrate in sentencing Mod offenders, referred to them as 'long-haired, mentally unstable, petty little sawdust Caesars,' while sensational tabloid headlines like 'Day of Terror by Scooter Groups,' and 'Riot Police Fly to Seaside,' and '19 Delinquents Sent to Detention in Mod Town,' were deliberately sensationalised by the media to give Mods the unflattering image of rampaging vandals, teeny hoodlums who fucked in public, took drugs and were a generically dodgy tribal menace.

Faces were invariably loners, individuated by a disciplined application to modernistic ethic, and the formation of organised gangs went contrary to their largely non-political programme, as much as the collective invasion of Carnaby Street, where John Stephen continued to accelerate the populist update of the look. *Time* magazine in their 10 April 1964 issue, reported with topical enthusiasm, tempered by a necessary degree of reserve, that 'The fashion Mecca for Mods is Soho's Carnaby Street, where a string of shops offers pink denim shirts, crimson leather vests and blazing red tartan pants for ultra-slicks. Most of the shops are owned by a young entrepreneur named John Stephen, who has wholeheartedly embraced Detroit's idea of planned obsolescence. Pants are pegged one month, bell-bottomed the next. To the individual who keeps up, says one of Stephen's managers, "style can change every week. But some suits are in style for months."'

And for John Stephen, as a measure of independently-achieved incentive, business had reached an unprecedented commercial apogee in 1964. Stephen's unparalleled success as a maverick style-guru to pop fascinated the press, largely because in the subversive spirit of the times it dispensed with all retailing norms, including the refusal to accept cheques by way of payment. *The Investors' Chronicle* was as perturbed as it was intrigued by Stephen's celebrity, and remarked derogatively of Carnaby Street, that 'it's hard to find, you can't park, all the shops depend on the same market, compete directly, and there is no conventional advertising.' The reporter's surmise was that the constituents of success lay in part with Stephen's small, closely-controlled production lines, and that he made a 60 per cent mark-up, and took cash only as the method of payment. *The New Statesman*, while equivocating over Stephen's durability as a design-tycoon catering to pop, conceded that his popularity had succeeded in attracting to the area , 'ex-Savile Row men, who make suits for Polanski, Stamp, Curtis, Caine and other heroes of our time. If they don't make your suits man, you just don't rate.' The inference was that John Stephen represented pop kitsch, and that celebrities with a more discerning eye for quality still chose bespoke tailors who were Mayfair trained and had modernised sufficiently to cut cloth that was considered cool even by the sharpest new actors like Terence Stamp and Michael Caine. The general implication, maintained by the trade, was that John Stephen, as a retail opportunist, was too preoccupied with commercial change to be taken seriously, and treated clothes rather like pop singles, as transient hit-or-miss affairs, although his chart status remained impressively consistent. Stephen too, was regarded as suspect on account of his lack of recognised training as a designer, relying instead on his brilliantly intuitive apprehension of what was right for the times. In the mid-1950s when John Stephen and Bill Franks had opened shop unassumingly in Beak Street, Soho at the time was full of concealed gay bars in basements and attics, places like the Alibi, the Hunstman, Take 5, the Apple No 9, the Casino and the notorious Mambo in Greek Street, that had provided them with a consistently regular local clientele. Ironically, the publication of the Wolfenden Report in 1957, recommending to the government that 'homosexual behaviour between consenting adults in private places should no longer be a criminal offence,' worked initially against gay men by perversely encouraging the frequency of police raids on queer meeting places. Hunted and in fear of exposure from police threat, gay people went underground in cellars usually run by black people sympathetic to the gay cause, and for reasons of repression similarly disaffected with society. By the 1960s, John Stephen and his friends could on occasions find sanctuary at Le Duce in Soho's D'Arblay Street, a club run by Peter Burton, and a safe location for Mods, no matter their sexual preference, who could dance there all night on Saturdays. The basement room had a strict door policy and gay men and straight girls danced in unison, both blocked on amphetamine, until a dead-beat red sun rose over the extended quiet of Soho on an uneventful Sunday morning. The trademark club music at Le Duce, and synonymous with gays, was black, Jamaican blue beat and Tamla Motown, as best suited to dance. As Soho was carved up by East End and Maltese gangsters, so the scene moved west to the Gigolo in the King's Road, where a long cellar doubled as a prototypical back room; the first of its kind to be incorporated into a club. Gay Mods were, with the exception of a preference for lilac shirts, largely indistinguishable in dress from their straight counterparts, both choosing to wear clothes that were unapologetically feminine in their emphasis on the new.

John Stephen, in his characteristic Italian-style suits, was an occasional visitor to Le Duce, where the full-on soundtrack was Jamaican blue beat stars like Desmond Dekker and Prince Buster, as well as US soul groups like the Supremes, the Miracles, and Martha and the Vandellas, and where the only white music played was by the likes of the black-influenced torch diva Dusty Springfield. Peter Burton, who managed Le Duce remembers that the tropical fish in the wall aquarium kept dying because clubbers out of necessity threw their pills into the water whenever there was a police raid. Most of the drug dealers in Soho's D'Arblay Street were Mod girls, because of their facility to use their looks to coerce prescriptions out of doctors. John Stephen's recreational poison was whisky, often drunk with the incentive of dry ginger as a mixer, whereas serious Mod clubbers could buy over the counter at the all-night Boots at Piccadilly Circus, tubes of Preludin, a slimming drug with an amphetamine basis, or a tin of ten amyl nitrate capsules, intended to treat angina. But speed, given the street name purple hearts and black bombers, remained the *de rigueur* Mod drug, its accelerated effects on stimulating adrenalin counteracted by the use of barbiturates like Mandrax as downers. The most popular night anthem in John Stephen's fugitive night world, was the Jimmy Ruffin song, *What Becomes of the Broken Hearted*, a Motown number with a specifically gay theme, a hit soaked up by Mod dancers and brooders at Le Duce and the Scene, where clubbers wanting to maintain a chemically-induced high would actually remove the wadding from Benzedrine inhalers and dunk them in drinks. Although the concept of gay liberation appeared to parallel the notion of free love in the 1960s, gay people like John Stephen were of necessity forced to stay closeted, or risk the backlash of a vindictively discriminating public. The quirky idiosyncratic record producer, Joe Meek, who was a regular at John Stephen shops, and who like his fashion guru rarely deviated from the acceptable format of a tailored suit, white tab-collared shirt and dark knitted tie, also cruised Le Duce and the Apollo for the transient camaraderie and bitchy competitiveness such places offered. There, Mods danced not only to the block, but to variations like the fly, the mashed potato, the locomotion, the pop pie, the limbo, the hitch-hiker, the shake and the frug, which became the staple dance of the late sixties. Joe Meek, who first shot his landlady before turning the gun on himself, on 2 February 1967, and who was responsible for the homemade extraterrestrial sounds of innovative hits like *Telstar*, was also the subversive producer of *Do You Come Here Often?* as the B-side of the last Tornados single, *Is That A Ship I Hear?* An extraordinary slice of taped spoken-word camp initiated between two hissy queens bitching in the toilet at Le Duce, Meek's underground slap at Columbia records in giving voice to a still sexually outlawed community, also represented the shadow aspects of Dilly life that John Stephen was forced to accommodate in order to survive, no matter that he had grown professionally successful through his unremitting designs in outwardly dissolving the barriers between how young gay and straight people looked.

But by 1964, the sheer scale, impact and hustle of Carnaby Street as the jostling epicentre of Mod fashion had succeeded, no matter its detractors, in elevating an obscure Soho alley into the most exhilarating colourful and stimulating thoroughfare in London, and if the social elite still preferred to purchase bespoke tailoring at boutiques like John Michael's Sportique, or Blades in Mayfair, where suits cost upwards of £70, it was John Stephen who effortlessly continued to dictate the look. He had come a long way towards realising his ambition of designing for his generation, was able to buy umbrellas at Swaine Adeney Brigg, drink a Chateau de la Bizalierre 1955 or a Chateau Grillet 1959, be invited to Annabel's or the Athenaeum, dine at the Ivy, with Prince sedately curled up as a white storm of fur beneath his table, drop in to Cartier or Asprey for cuff-links, have his hair done at Robert James', but essentially remained unaffected, his simple upbringing and astute business acumen reminding him always that clothes should be affordable and directed at the young, as the style protagonists who wore his inventions. It was the working class contingents of Mods, whose scooter-attack ripped up the West End at weekends, their fanatical clothes incentive directed at Carnaby Street, and the barrio of little shops Stephen had built out of a single room on the second-floor at 19 Beak Street, who meant business, and who overtook his boutiques like addicts in search of the next hit – a jumper, a shirt, a pair of edgy hipsters, a stagily vented jacket to beat all others, and a look that would turn heads in every fashionable, colour-soaked London club or street.

5

SEE MY FRIEND

In a 1965 feature in *Disc Monthly*, John Stephen appeared photographed outside Mod Male in Carnaby Street, his left arm resting casually on the bonnet logo of his maroon-upholstered Rolls Royce Silver Cloud, the revered 'Spirit of Ecstasy' logo, in the form of a woman leaning forwards with her arms outstretched behind and above her, symbolising the precisional speed and luxury of a car that was still in the sixties the exclusive prerogative of the rich. His expression is one of momentary complacency, his innate shyness visible in the acute sensitivity of his features, but for the moment dissolved by the total absorption of consciousness in addressing the camera. There's a rare note of what appears like self-realisation in his eyes, as though it's suddenly occurred to him that he is the singular reason why the street never lets up in purchase-tempo, and that its muscle never relaxes even on Sundays, when window-shopping amongst Mods calculating their next week's purchases replaces spending power. In the second of preparing for the camera, distraction has caused him to go missing, momentarily, before reconnecting again with himself and his immediate surroundings, as though newly recreated in front of his eyes. His hair is fastidiously groomed, and blown back in a springy un-gelled quiff, a style lending attitude made popular by the likes of James Dean, Tony Curtis and Montgomery Clift. He is wearing an unbuttoned narrow-lapelled three-button suit with a dark overstripe, a slimline silk tie and a pastel shirt with round collars. The clothes are the conservative end of his line, worn with constrained but impeccable panache. He is for the moment the epitome of Mod cool, the self-made creator of the Carnaby

Street look, who owned eighteen shops, employed over 200 staff, had two factories, one in Kilburn and one in Glasgow, and was busy eating into the American market by opening John Stephen stores within stores, as retail outlets for his clothes. Stephen had also secured a highly lucrative licensing agreement with Rex Truform to manufacture his clothes under licence in South Africa, with Rhodesia being the only state excluded, on account of its sensitive political situation with Britain.

With eight shops in Carnaby Street in his name, as a rebuke to the quality tailoring of Savile Row, the place was starting to be called Stephen's Row, and its macaronic design legislator the eponymous King of Carnaby Street. The street was also becoming essentially pop, and on opening Male West One, in October 1965, the blues singer Georgie Fame acted as a 'model' for clothes chosen for him by Chrissie Shrimpton, sister of the runway model Jean. Amongst the glitterati who attended the reception were luminaries in the popocracy like Cathy McGowan, Chris White and Rod Argent of the Zombies, Rod Stewart, Spencer Davis and members of Unit 4+2. Georgie Fame was photographed wearing a white polo-neck jumper, a hip-length suede jacket with a button front and two patch pockets, tonics and voguish beige suede desert boots.

As an opportunist attempt to capitalise on the street's name in 1965, five 20-year-olds, John Cahillane, Steve Milners, Kip Smith, Andy Andrews and Ronnie Ross, all of who had worked in Carnaby Street outlets, either for John Stephen or Warren Gold – John Callihane, the vocalist, having been a window dresser for Stephen – formed an emergent pop band appropriately called The Carnabys, with John Stephen dressing the band in Op Art jackets and broad red and white striped shirts, that looked according to Cahillane like 'animated barber's poles.' The short-lived band who attempted to fuse the influences of The Who and the Kinks, cut one critically acclaimed single, *Jump and Dance*, before deliquescing in the general saturation of largely derivative mid-sixties pop bands who lacked individuality and cutting-edge durability.

One of the consistently sharpest dressers of the epoch, Andrew Loog Oldham, and also one of the few clothes detailists who has total recall of the period, then managing the Rolling Stones, recollects in his second volume of autobiography *2 Stoned* attending an entrepreneurial business meeting at the Ritz Hotel in London's Mayfair, and to the consternation of the manager, worried about the hotel's reputation, wearing the unlikely combination of Pierre Cardin boots with an energetically embossed John Stephen suit. 'I wore the choco brown Pierre Cardin butter leather boots and a rich brown and dull gold-striped double-breasted suit with inverted pleat, covered buttons, flared sleeve and trouser cuffs with slashed pockets on the trews and jacket,' Oldham recalls, reliving the thrill of having shocked the formal environment by his dress. But the look, and its attendant attitude, was still a minority expression, exclusive to the young, and generally disdained by an older generation, whose preconceived ideas of masculinity were at considerable variance to the spearheading effeminacy of the clothes adopted by the renegade bandits Oldham managed – the infamous and socially reprehensible Rolling Stones. Something of the alienation they had achieved by wearing shoulder-length hair and Stephen's skinny-fit Carnaby Street hipsters, ruffled shirts and waisted blazers was captured by Nik Cohn in his spontaneous account of seeing the Stones arrive for a concert in the drizzly docklands of Liverpool. 'They had their hair down past their shoulders and they wore clothes of every colour imaginable and they looked mean, they looked just impossibly evil. In this grey street they shone like sun gods. They didn't seem human, they were like creatures of another planet. Impossible to reach or understand but most exotic, most beautiful in their ugliness.'

Both Stephen and his optimally-trained managers had by now grown expert in anticipating the needs of their celebrity customers, who came to the street without minders, signed autographs if hustled, but generally dissolved into the Mod amalgam skinning the racks for what was instantaneously new. With accustomed authority Stephen spoke of some of the fashion requirements of his pop star clients to Disc. 'Cliff Richard, for example, was instrumental to bringing mohair jumpers into prominence in 1959. He bought them all from me and is still one of my best customers. He's quite easy to satisfy. He just comes in and, without an assistant, looks around the shop, picks out what he wants and goes.' Stephen then proceeded to itemise the needs of other prominent pop stars who in the course of patronising his shops had become personal friends, fluently at ease with himself and his managers, and totally absorbed in the excitement of Stephen's Row. Ray Davies of the Kinks, he acknowledged, 'usually picks the band's stage shirts. Dave Davies buys slacks. Dave is a very easy customer. He comes in, tries on a jacket and takes it. But his brother Ray is slightly slower choosing. He seems to give more thought to his purchases, and remain very deep.' And of the lividly eclectic fashion demands of The Who, looking always for clothes as pyrotechnical as their turbo-driven music, Stephen commented on their individually various looks. Roger Daltrey he considered to be the most sober in his tastes, although he was one of the first stars fronting a band to wear a striped linen

John Stephen had his own horse-drawn carriage to arrive in style, when he wasn't seated in his Rolls.

jacket. John Entwistle, the bassist, had, according to Stephen, a preference for coloured suede jackets, whereas lead guitarist Pete Townshend preferred casual sweaters and sharp trousers, while the drummer Keith Moon favoured T-shirts printed with targets and pop art slogans, their regularity as patrons drawing from Stephen the observation that, 'Every time they come in they go through the racks saying, "Got it! Got it!" Avidity, as a key factor in keeping up with the look, often on a daily basis, naturally extended to the Rolling Stones, but more particularly to Mick Jagger and Brian Jones as attention-seeking rivals in appearance. With his creative aesthetic also fine-tuned as a retailer to the necessity of profit, John Stephen raised natural suspicions over Jagger's habitual attempts to elude payment. 'Mick has to be taken on trust. He spends a lot of money with us, usually on the bigger things. Last week he was in for a suede shirt costing £19. He often goes out forgetting to pay and we have to remind him.' The band's pretty boy, Brian Jones, who more than any other rock star of the period personified androgyny in his presentation of masculinity, was altogether more discerning about specific clothes detail than Jagger, who increasingly became his style copyist, only with affected lippy attitude. 'Brian Jones,' Stephen added, 'is very fussy about what he buys and often has things altered to his design. We never produce for general sale any special designs which artists ask us to make. That wouldn't be right, as they want to be individual.' Stephen gave a 10 per cent discount to celebrities, and calculated that bands like The Who and the Kinks would on average spend £100 on each visit to his chain of Carnaby Street shops.

At the same time as his business up-scaled, so Stephen's alcoholism increased, as a signal response to pressure. Garrulous when drunk, but inveterately guarded about his personal life, Stephen at times would go missing on an alcoholic binge in the late afternoons, and have to be searched for in the Carnaby Street and Kingly Street pubs, like the Shakespeare's Head, The White Horse, The Marlborough Head and The Blue Posts on the corner of Ganton Street, by concerned friends and solicitous members of staff, with Bill Franks usually knowing instinctually which pub to target for the retrieval of his lapsed partner. Stephen, as a sixties progeny, largely drank spirits with mixers, Scotch and coke, Scotch and ginger ale, or for serious impact Bells or King George IV whisky with water and ice. The increasing demands made on his time by the media, the need to sustain a momentous full-on design programme if he was to continue to stay out front as proto-glam svengali to the popocracy, as well as coping with breakdowns and his concealed sexuality, were all pressures contributing to episodic cycles of burn-out in the iconic designer. Being gay in the sixties was like having to conceal valuable jewellery in a bank vault, as something that shouldn't come out. Although three of the foremost pop managers of the time, Brian Epstein of the Beatles, Kit Lambert of the Who, and Andrew Loog Oldham of the Rolling Stones, were either gay or bisexual, their places within the music industry helped cushion them from outright discrimination in the work place. Epstein used to dress up in drag at home and sing songs to Lionel Bart's piano accompaniment, and Lambert made kamikaze raids on the Piccadilly meat rack for obliging rough trade. These practices, like John Stephen's concealed gay life, were of necessity subcultural happenings, clandestine as the polari, or street slang, adopted by rent boys as a dialect with punters in the know, who would pay to take them into the nearby Regent Palace Hotel. The intimations of homosexuality in the Beatles' song *You've Got To Hide Your Love Away*, clearly aimed at Brian Epstein's criminalised world of cottaging, was a theme also addressed by arguably the first mainstream gay pop song, *See My Friend*, by the Kinks. A psychedelically inflected number incorporating Indian raga instrumentation, and a simple lyric set to a plangent refrain, the song expressed regret at the distance across the river separating two friends, 'friend' being the term in use for a same-sex male partner. Given that Dave Davies, the band's founder member, was openly bisexual, and his brother Ray pointedly camp on stage, the song that charted at No 10 in October 1965, registered the first real note of sexual ambiguity in 1960s pop. With their ruffled shirts, fitted velvet jackets, and in Dave Davies' case Anello and Davide customised thigh-high leather boots, the Kinks looked the part in describing longing for a friend, and not friends, as has erroneously crept into the title of reissues of the song on subsequent Kinks' releases. Largely dressed by John Stephen, the Kinks succeeded in dandifying the Mod look, adding long double-breasted, velvet collared Regency style jackets, satin, tulle and crepe shirts and a paintbox palette of splashy silk ties to their dressy permutations of the Mod repertoire. Nearly all the models used for John Stephen fashion shoots were photographed in his clothes by the versatile Stephen PR, Mike McGrath, often at his Wentworth Mansions apartment in Earls Court Square, or on-site in the Carnaby Street locale. McGrath's Earls Court flat was situated conveniently almost opposite the basement club Masquerade that combined a restaurant with a club, and attracted a gay and showbiz clientele, including John Stephen and the reclusive Brian Epstein. Stephen would, after a night at Masquerade, often visit McGrath socially for late night drinks, at his red and gold painted bohemianly raffish art-deco flat, as would the equally taciturn Brian Epstein, capable according to McGrath of saying nothing for up to two hours at a time, accompanied by his friend Chris Curtis. McGrath, as a child star turned

Pop trio, Brian Auger, Julie Driscoll and Long John Baldry wearing John Stephen's designs.

fashion journalist and photographer, had first interviewed John Stephen for the magazine *She*, and immediately established a sympathetic rapport with the painfully introspective Glaswegian. A naturally, histrionically camp extrovert, McGrath, who wrote for an inexhaustible roster of magazines, as diverse as *Woman's Own*, *Boyfriend*, *Man About Town*, *Fabulous* etc, was possessed of exactly the right sort of personably effervescent chutzpah and indomitable enthusiasm for clothes necessary to push the John Stephen organization forward, celebrities attached, into its continually sustained apogee of unrivalled 1960s invention. McGrath's detailed typed captioning on the rear of promotional black and white photographs sent to editors, proved an understated but highly influential way of promoting Stephen's clothes, in which the innuendo was implicitly gay, and the model's current pursuits, if he was pop, usually noted. McGrath, who readily filtered his adventurous fashion tips to his employer John Stephen, photographed and gave effusive hints on style to most incipient talent, including the young David Jones, a.k.a. Bowie, who, dressed in a formal suit and tie, was advised by McGrath to dramatically colour his stage act if he was to be noticed. Likewise, the upcoming Reg Dwight, as pianist for Long John Baldry, looked irremediably ordinary to McGrath at his Wentworth Mansions flat, wearing a lumpy blue duffel coat and blue jeans, before going on to find an acclaimed solo career as the ultra-flamboyantly-dressed pop star Elton John. The young Rod Stewart, likewise a charismatic member of Baldry's Steam Packet and a John Stephen clothes aficionado, was another late-night visitor to Wentworth Mansions, a Face who combined style with hard-drinking, unruly attitude. McGrath, in his capacity as John Stephen's PR, met them all, those on their way up and those on their way down the stairs, many of them like Heinz, Mark Wynter and Eden Kane, all indomitably looking the part in their John Stephen's clothes, but unable to sustain careers beyond a single ephemeral hit.

In 1965, as an addition to his expansionistic policy, John Stephen opened the spacious Teen Store at 52–55 Carnaby Street, with its notable chocolate and white interior designed by Myles Anthony, making prominent use of a gothic peacock motif lifted from Antony's enthusiasm for the newly rediscovered work of the decadent *fin de siècle* artist and friend of Oscar Wilde's Aubrey Beardsley. The shop with its medium price range also incorporated an innovative record bar on the ground floor and a leisure wear department for girls into its predominantly male-themed emphasis on the look. Stephen also chose to introduce a limited range of cosmetics for men into his accessories line, including a John Stephen cologne, pre-shave and after-shave lotions, and talcum powder. It was there in a shop brimming with racks of off-the-peg prime mohair, velvet, corduroy and linen suits, that the normally taciturn Saul Sofar, who had been taken on as a questionable, petite junior at the age of sixteen, and who out of perverse lack of self-esteem refused not only casual conversation but also the right to take holidays, proved to be a demonstratively competitive salesman, who could work the floor with unrivalled success. Sofar attributed his coercively persuasive facilities with customers, the opposite of his usually introspectively paranoid state, to the fact that he was alone there, in a one-to-one situation with the client, and in the act of selling without the chronic aspects of self-consciousness that limited him in any formal social context. Mike McGrath's personally typed invite to Phil May of the Pretty Things, to attend a party for the opening of the Teen Store, on Wednesday 6 January, between 6.30 and 9.30pm for a champagne launch was unapologetic in its use of gossipy unadulterated camp. 'Phil my boy, It's all happening on Wednesday evening this week at the John Stephen party in Carnaby Street to celebrate the opening of the Teen Store. Besides the fashion press, several thirsty writers from record papers are likely to be in attendance and a few of John's pop world customers. So we'll hope to see you white-jeaned and at your lovely best ready for the photographers who pounce on you. Have sent an invite to Brian. And Mr Baldry is likely to be in attendance to chat up the local talent.'

For Mods 1965 was the year in which the increasingly pyrotechnical and anarchic The Who released the anthemic Shel Tamy-produced single *My Generation*, with Roger Daltrey's speed-freak affected stutter and Pete Townshend's windmilling power-chords, turning the song into a two minutes compacted delirious expression of Mod philosophy. *My Generation*, with its aggressive charged-up incitement to live optimally within the unrepeatable moment spoke directly through its lyrics to the kids who John Stephen dressed. 'People try to put us d-down (talkin' 'bout my generation)/ Just because we get around (talkin' 'bout my generation)/Things they do look awful c-c-cold (talkin' 'bout my generation)/Hope I die before I get old (talkin' 'bout my generation). Touching on the raw vagal nerve of the generation divide, The Who's seething refutation of age, following on from their earlier amphetamine-dazed *I Can't Explain*, was the street ideology acclaimed by all self-attitudinising Faces as their kind of poetry. Making a statement that impacted like a sonic tsunami, Townshend's rejection of moral reactionaries to the look was etched with incisive clarity: 'Why don't you all f-fade away/And don't try to dig what we al s-s-say/I'm not trying to cause a big s-s-sensation? I'm just talkin' 'bout my generation.' Riding high on a shock wave to No 2 in the charts, the record's commercial spin-off for

John Stephen was immediate in terms of a generation starting to consolidate its own definition of itself, based in part on the clothes he had singularly created. With The Who appearing dressed on stage like a John Stephen fashion shoot, *My Generation* as a song encapsulated indirectly something of the accelerated speed not only of Stephen's designs, but the unstoppable momentum created by the look. The heady mix of Pete Townshend's subversive lyrics, combined with Roger Daltrey's rushed vocal attack, together with the percussive meltdown of Keith Moon's drumming, and John Entwistle's cavernously descending bass chords, had The Who appear through this song to power the whole scooter-led Carnaby Street ethos forward into the mid-sixties orange sunshine optimism of a generation flagrantly proud of its disaffection from the past. With a chorus affirming, 'This is my generation baby,' The Who through their Mod identification helped open a gateway for teenagers to express themselves through a culture based almost entirely on the declaratively new.

With the British beat invasion led predominantly by the Beatles and the Rolling Stones making significant incursions into the American charts, and bringing the entire John Stephen look to a fascinated and acquisitive American youth denied outlets for his must-have clothes, John Stephen made his American debut by opening his first boutique within an enormous department store called Dayton's in Minneapolis in August 1965. The way forward had been prepared through Colin Rock, the UK representative of American Merchandise Corporation, who in conjunction with a US visit by Bill Franks, had on the strength of samples, taken over £70,000-worth of orders for John Stephen clothes. Not that the issue was a simple one, and on account of differing trans-Atlantic physique, height and weight, new patterns had to be made for all garments issued for the American market, something that was time-consuming and led also to the inevitable copying of the samples by American retailers, who had them cheaply manufactured in the East, and in the process downgraded the quality and the Stephen signature. With franchises in seventeen American stores, Stephen launched his stagy celebrity debut in New York with a full-scale fashion show at Stern Brothers in Manhattan. In addition *Look Magazine* ran a four-page feature called 'The Minneapolis Mods,' on how John Stephen's smart but innovatively dandified clothes for men were about to dominate the American youth market. Stephen's growth status was given an unexpected and additional boost in the States by his debut felicitously coinciding with the furore created by the Rolling Stones' frenetically conquistidorial tour of America in 1965. With Mick Jagger and Brian Jones both wearing form-fitting checked hipsters, with plain jackets, or vice versa, chosen from the Stephen workrooms, practically the first question fired at them by an adulatory and incredulous media, was related to where they bought their clothes, to which the affirmative answer, was 'John Stephen of Carnaby Street.'

A pathologically nervous John Stephen, sedated by prescribed Valium and on a serious Cutty Sark whisky mission, was interviewed for over thirty minutes on the Johnny Carson show, watched by a rating of 40 million American viewers, talking about the look, and with ten of his outfits modelled on the show to exemplify the line of his radically remixed current designs. Stephen's appearance on the Johnny Carson show engendered such endemic interest in his clothes that the entire stock at Dayton's was liquidated in less than a week. In fact John Stephen's renowned celebrity was such that he cloned an American imitator called Harvey Block, who claimed aberrantly to be one of Carnaby Street's leading designers, despite his only link with John Stephen being that of a dangerously infatuated stalker, rather than a rival in competing with shape-shifting city-coloured Mod fashion. With typically cautionary modesty, John Stephen said of Block: 'I've never heard of him before, but there's quite a market for everybody, and as many Americans don't know the background or anything about Carnaby Street, there is always the chance someone will believe him.' At the same time, and more invasively, one of America's largest clothes retailers, McGregor Doniger, quickly responded to the John Stephen look by launching a line of clothes largely copied from Stephen's designs called Brolly Male. Their polka dot shirts at $5, London cue turtleneck sweaters at $13, checked wool hipsters at $18, and herringbone double-breasted jackets with epaulettes for $45, the styles offering no variation on the originals, were like most Stephen imitators, the rogue product of direct plagiarism.

Staying at the art deco landmark, the pre-eminent midtown Waldorf Astoria, when in New York, and in the absence of Bill Franks' psychological support, he having stayed behind to manage the London organisation, Stephen, strung out by insomnia and the innate social anxiety he experienced when meeting strangers, lived dangerously on the edge of precipitant breakdown for the duration of a tour that lasted for six chronically pressurised weeks of ruthless overexposure to the media. In America, Stephen, accompanied on part of the tour by his PR Mike McGrath, was jittery, shaky, hyperactive and glamorously limo-chauffered by the idolising media network to stores, radio stations and television studios on a racy, impacted publicity jag. Adding to Stephen's acute social anxieties was the hard economic fact that no matter how successful Carnaby Street appeared to the

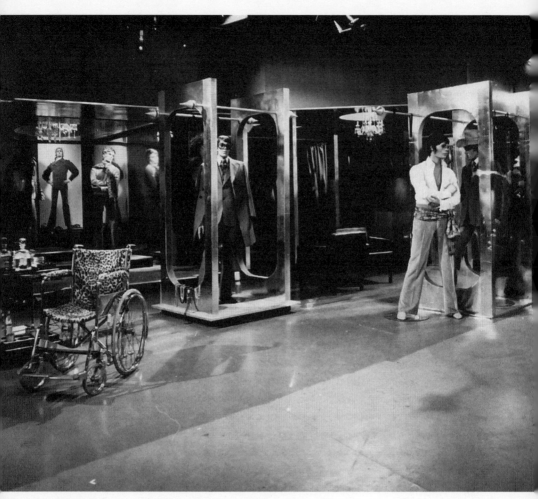

John Stephen's shops created alternative realities for his customers, decorative, modern and works of art in themselves.

public in commercial terms, mismanagement and a tendency on Stephen's part to over-expand without collateral had placed the entire John Stephen Organisation in severe financial jeopardy. At a time when John Stephen was being captioned 'The Millionaire Mod' in the States, Bill Franks in London was receiving as many as eighty threatening letters a day from creditors including writs due to substantial debts, many of them to suppliers. The John Stephen group owed £30,000 alone to Fermus, the Italian knitwear supplier, who generously agreed on Stephen's return to accept outstanding payment by monthly instalments, while continuing to supply stock. Faced with a potentially liquidating emergency, Franks had the good sense to call in Thornton Baker accountants as business consultants, whose initial survey drawn up by Tony Carratu and Grant Thornton, as partners, confirmed that the John Stephen organisation was a potentially good business, erroneously managed, overstretched and in chronic need of applied systems. Bill Franks remembers his beleaguered partner's frantic calls from his New York Waldorf suite in the early hours of the morning, desperate to know if they had sufficient credit to prevent going under, while at the same time continuing his promotional tour of the States as an undisputed success in marketing the John Stephen product.

It was inevitable given his innate vulnerability that Stephen should crack under consistent pressure in the States. Disorientated, displaced and unhappily celebrified, Stephen partially lost his always precarious hold on reality while there, and was most of the time drunk on his exhaustive, but highly lucrative media circuit. The only truly significant memory of the tour he retained, was that of a four-year-old boy at Carson's store in Chicago, presenting him as a memento with a miniature silver penknife with the logo Chicago Illinois attached, a gesture he interpreted as a redeeming token of humanity amongst the superficial high-flyers and vacuous glitterati with which he found himself constantly surrounded. Shattered by the experience, threatened by closure in London, and with his nerves shot through, Stephen had a severe nervous breakdown soon after returning to London. Of necessity he went into the Harley Street Clinic to recuperate for a number of weeks, where he was too delusional at first to even recognise his partner Bill Franks; the symptoms pointing to his first prolonged episode of mania, and initiating the recurrent cycle of manic depression from which he was to be medicated with lithium for the rest of his life. His employees were informed by Franks that Stephen was away on extended business, as a means of protecting a sensitive issue at a time when mental illness, like homosexuality, was treated as a virulent social taboo.

Although the look was exclusively a male fashion prerogative, with girls choosing to purchase John Stephen's ubiquitous unisex lines for lack of an alternative, Stephen by popular demand decided in 1965 to open a shop specifically for girls, on his Carnaby Street patch, called Tre Camp. The shop name, with its gay inflexion, nominally suggested fashions that were either travesty or clothes designed for girls who were eminently gay-friendly. With the shop exterior comprising a black and white plastic blow-up of an etching by Myles Antony suggesting the façade of a Jacobean palace, photographed, enlarged and then processed in Formica by the De La Rue Co, and with crenellated harlequin diamonds and whorled op-art circles adding to the decoration, the boutique with its plaster dummies wearing purple felt wigs was quickly highlighted as the street's optimal focal viewpoint. The interior of the tiny vaulted shop, no bigger than 13 feet deep, and 12 feet across, with a curved false ceiling, supported by pillars, with purple, white and pink helmets suspended from the ceiling, caused a press sensation, due to the incorporation of Antony's blowups of blond, butch, blue-eyed young muscle men dressed in white bikini briefs, lining the walls of the girls' fitting rooms. With suitable camp, Myles Antony explained: 'When girls pull that fitting room curtain we don't want them to feel neglected.' The shop's exaggerated camp fixtures, including a Pigalle-style nightclub board splashed with sexy star-sprayed pictures of boys, and a glitter sign reading 'Boys Boys Boys,' also featured a tiny pink stairway suitably leading nowhere, and an exclusive purple Tre Camp carrier boldly lettered with a white sans serif font. It was however Myles Antony's controversial body-beautiful blowups celebrating male physique, as a consolidation of the continued sexual ambiguity surrounding the John Stephen ethos, that unconditionally initiated a major press controversy. The shop was opened by the barefoot micro-skirted pop singer, from Dagenham, Essex, Sandie Shaw, renowned for her flatteringly long nyloned pins, and the fashionable curtain fringe partially obscuring her eyes, as part of an instinctual defence mechanism shielding her natural shyness. Dressed in confectionery millinery and a crochet mini-dress, and characteristically adopting her bare-foot gloss-polished toenails pose for the cameras, Shaw opened Tre Camp with all the girlie panache expected of pop, as a strawberry topping to a cake on a summer's day.

It was delegated to Stephen's other partner Frank Merkell to manage the women's line of John Stephen creations, and although Stephen set to work with his usual inventive flair, he was through his natural sympathies better suited to pushing innovative men's fashion to the cutting edge, rather than run against fierce existing competition in his girls' line. Mary Quant had already achieved the prototypical look for girls that Stephen had created for men, and the newly-opened Foale and Tuffin, at 1 Marlborough Court off Carnaby Street, with a shop-front lit by red, white and blue light bulbs, were running close to Quant as competitive stylists whose trousers suits proved hot property worn by celebrities including Susannah York, Cathy McGowan and Francoise Hardy. After being temporarily eclipsed by the unprecedented attention devoted to the fashionable male look, women's fashion was beginning to stage a comeback, and to consolidate its revival *Queen* in their autumn 1965 issue, glamourised extravagant femininity by featuring a blonde Parisian model wearing knee-length fitch and jaguar coats from the London furrier Maxwell Croft. The fitch skins worked horizontally, with roll collar and slim sleeves, in the new longer length for coats, while the spectacular jaguar coat had tailored reveres, slit pockets, long sleeves, and a narrow black kid belt that tied in a front bow, both exotic feline-skinned splashes being coupled with knee-high flat-heeled black suede boots from Anello & Davide, John Stephen's chosen Charing Cross Road shoeist.

By 1965, the John Stephen consolidation had led to the opening of outlets all over America, as well as in Rome and Oslo, and the Italian island of Ischia, where the street on which the John Stephen shop stood was renamed Carnaby Street, to honour Stephen's colourful liberating men's designs. Stephen, as the incurably reluctant jet-hopping pop-king of fashion, undertook nerve-zapping promotional tours of Norway, Sweden, Germany, France and Switzerland, as the look went international, with sensitively achieved modifications of style to suit the given market. Once again the deleterious effects of touring shredded Stephen's finely-tuned nerves, the shattering consequence of media exposure leading to the need for extensive periods of rehabilitation at the Priory, and a private nursing home off the King's Road. Stephen was during this period of acute stress assigned a private psychiatrist, Dr Dally, resident at the Middlesex Hospital, and who, rare for a psychiatrist, undertook home visits, as well as being available for telephone consultation if immediate support was needed. And as an encouraging sign of the radical dissolution of class distinctions, a Mike McGrath publicity photo disseminated to the press showed a modernised Lord Snowdon, in the company of Princess Margaret, wearing a John Stephen light blue linen jacket, with a high collar, four-buttoned front, two back vents and button pockets with inverted pleats, chosen for a trip to Sardinia; a jacket style that Stephen ran in heavier wool materials for winter wear in 1965. Snowdon's adoption of a Mod jacket was confirmation that the social revolution had advanced to the degree that the look had infiltrated the social hierarchy with the excitement of doing a new recreational drug. As distinctions of social background began temporarily to disappear, so aristocrats, pop stars, designers, dealers, clubbers and artists amalgamated into the hedonistic phenomenon of bright young things joined by the apparently common aims of liberating themselves from moral constraint. The apparent removal of obstructive class barriers meant in the words of the swank East End movie star Terence Stamp, that 'some yobbo like me could get into the Saddle Room and dance with the Duchess of Bedford's daughter, and get hold of her, and get taken down to Woburn Abbey to hang out for a long weekend and have dinner under the Canalettos with the Duke's sons.' Stamp, whose early career ran parallel with Michael Caine's, the two friends at one time sharing a King's Road apartment, had about him something of the defiant punk as well as Mod. Stamp spoke for the rebellious kids on the rise who John Stephen was dressing when he said: 'People like me, we're the moderns. We wear elastic-sided boots and we smoke Gauloises, we work hard and we play hard. We have no class and no prejudice. We're the new swinging Englishmen. And it's people like me who are spreading the word.' And as an additional endorsement of the new class acceptance, the William Hickey celebrity update column in the *Daily Express* announced, 'There's no harm these days in knowing a Rolling Stone ... some of their best friends, in fact, are fledglings from the upper classes.' The flagrant upending of social status at the time, creating an osmotic exchange between the previously segregated classes, had Marianne Faithfull remark of the chameleonic socialite Mick Jagger that he would indiscriminately accept invitations to 'dinners given by any silly thing with a title and a castle. He was as smitten as any American millionaire in the movies.'

What John Stephen had succeeded unconsciously in doing, in part through the creation of Carnaby Street and his seminal influence on making the King's Road into an energised, sexy locus for men's fashion, was to provide alternative centres of gravity to the conventionally respected markers of political and social power in Westminster and Belgravia. Stephen contributed through his extravagantly-colourful outlets in investing two unfashionable London thoroughfares with a look that was so contagiously powerful it succeeded in diminishing the social importance of traditional authority. Mods ruled by virtue of attitude and attitude meant clothes. As Mary Quant suggested, 'it was Mods who gave the dress trade the impetus to break through the fast-moving, breathtaking, uprooting revolution in which we have played a part.'

In 1965, dedicated Mods who got off on the fashionista scene still started the weekend trafficking for the cameras on *Ready Steady Go!* before moving

The white suit like you've never seen it before, four buttons, high-fastening and buttoned patch pockets.

The perfect interchange of knitwear for men and women. One of John Stephen's shops was called His and Hers.

on to the Scene Club in Ham's Yard until midnight, then switching to the Allnighter in Wardour Street to catch indigenous London R&B acts like the redoubtably gifted Georgie Fame and the Blue Flames, until the club closed at a blurry Soho 4am. Mod men still danced together, or alone, as a denial of conventional male/female partners on the dance floor, their partly transgressive act defying a law that three years earlier in 1962 had David Browne, manager of the Kandy Lounge in Soho's Gerrard Street, prosecuted in court because the club had been raided by plainclothes policemen who observed men dancing the twist together. And in 1962, despite Browne's counsel maintaining that the men concerned were dancing the madison, in which people of the same sex formed a line, Browne was found guilty and the Kandy Lounge closed. Mods, though, were reinforced by numbers, pills, cool and a saturated wall of sound that fortified them in their self-referential clubby ecosphere. Musically, 1965 surfed on the sonic wave of the Rolling Stones' sexual anthem *I Can't Get No Satisfaction*, and their equally addictive self-penned *The Last Time*, the consummate Motown danceiness of the Supremes' *Stop! In The Name Of Love*, the Beatles' *Help*, the Californian surf sound of the Beach Boys' *Help Me, Rhonda*, the plaintive dejection of the Kinks' *Tired Of Waiting*, the Yardbirds' Shel Tamy weirdo *For Your Love*, that kicked R&B into studio freakery, and for diehard Mods *Nowhere To Run* by Martha and the Vandellas. Mods, in their preference for Soul, Tamla and the beat merchants, largely resisted the invasive genre of American folk-rock, via Bob Dylan and his Mod-dressed interpreters The Byrds, who picked up their clothes in Carnaby Street, and stayed locked into the mahogany Motown dance grooves, and the British purveyors of R&B – the beat merchants who transformed a blues template into urgent melodic pop.

John Stephen's things of the moment for early 1965 were Victorian-style jackets with high collars and four-button fastenings and button-down pockets with inverted pleats, narrow trousers in white, lilac and pale blue, denim caps in colours like brick red, beige and navy blue, trimmed with braid in contrasting colours, roll-collar shirts in shades ranging from ice-blue to wine, hacking jackets in tweedy checks, candy-stripe casual jackets in cotton or seersucker, very fitted mohair suits, and waisted herringbone jackets in navy blue and autumn browns. To window-chasers with alert fashion radar, out were the previous year's styles, long pointed button-down collars, matelot vests, cavalry twill trousers, knitted silk ties, chunky Pringle sweaters, slightly flared trousers, pork pie hats, of the kind worn by Viv Prince of the Pretty Things, grey denim shirts and hectically coloured braces. Mods had assured weekly incomes, in that there were more jobs than people in Britain's new consumer society, in which shopping amongst the young was endemic, and Carnaby Street as the almost sci-fi shopping barrio, relocated from the future in the present, the only place for Mods to be seen. With the street no longer the closely-guarded milieu of kids from London's Stamford Hill and Shepherd's Bush, Mods from all over the country were starting to make Saturday pilgrimages to John Stephen's territorially congested alley, to discover first hand that the legend preceding the place was sustained by its reality. They could too, if they were observant, or happened to intersect with a felicitous moment, discover the street's progenitor, John Stephen, detached, critical, quizzing his customers' reactions to the racks, learning always from their instructive comments about his designs, and the modifications necessary on his part to successfully anticipate their next week's demands. For instance, when Stephen overheard one Mod remarking that his white hipster jeans would look sharper with one contrasting black leg, he had a short-lived rack of two-tone black and white jeans on sale in Mod Male the following week, in a limited edition of twenty, the small-scale immediacy of the enterprise made possible by the tailoring facility resident in the basement of His Clothes. It was precisely the unrepeatable nature of John Stephen's runs, transient, experimental one-offs, the product of a blinding inspirational moment, that had pop stars and Faces compelled by their search for the ultimate one-upmanship to obsessively scrutinise his shops, in the search for a single shirt or jumper, to place them for a day or at most a week, one jump ahead of the look. The vigilant eye of *Style Weekly* too, noted that in decorating His Clothes in September 1965, Myles Antony had artfully used swathes of a brown-red floral fabric, utilising it to effect on background screens, on dummies' heads and for large flower-shaped motifs positioned in the middle of the window, as typical of his display.

Meanwhile the acquisitive speed dealers had moved in on Soho, in a radius extending from Wardour Street to Cambridge Circus, many of them girls, who targeted Mod users as young as thirteen, dancing full-on at the Marquee on Saturday nights, before moving into the clubs around Greek Street, then on to a stand outside Tiffany's at 1pm. They also worked the circuit of Lyons' cafes around Piccadilly Circus, Leicester Square and Trafalgar Square, before moving south-west to sell their remaining pills to tired mini-skirted debs shunted out of high-end King's Road clubs in the early hours of Sunday morning. Some of the more expertly proficient dealers sold between 3,000 to 6,000 pills each weekend, stashing their earnings in the process into conveniently roomy pockets provided by parkas and crombies, or in the case of girl dealers, chunky Mary Quant handbags. Hard drugs like heroin were beginning to enter the London Mod recreational scene, and Bill Franks recalls that in the interests of keeping the business drug-free, John Stephen closed down the toilet facilities at their Drug Store shop after discarded syringes were found littering the in-store toilets.

As the pilled-up Mods continued to crowd into Carnaby Street, many of them making regular weekly visits to their chosen shop, so John Stephen's Kilburn factory that made up 90 per cent of his stock, ensuring its absolute exclusivity, worked on overreach to match the increasing demand for his clothes. With the Stephen properties now managed by Meadow, Schama & Co, the average shop site had escalated to rents of £100 a week, with fierce competition for space amongst competitors supplied by large manufacturers, who attempted to undercut Stephen's prices, while plagiaristically copying his line and selling their clothes nationwide. As a means of attempting to reinforce his independent logo, and as a partial vindication of his inimitable trademark signature on the street, the words John Stephen appeared on the windows of all his shops in Carnaby Street at this time, irrespective of their individual names. It wasn't only Mods who crowded into the street, but also celebrities like the blonde leopard-eyed gamine Brigitte Bardot, who filmed her Christmas spectacular TV show in the street, Garbo, Marlene Dietrich who chose candy pink slacks, Judy Garland who went for a dramatically angled leopard-print hat, as well as the legendary jazz singer Lena Horne, who bought a red collarless shirt from Michael Quinn, the manager who usually liaised with stars and helped advise on purchases. 'The whole hit parade appear to be his regular customers,' *The Glasgow Herald* reported of Stephen, on 14 July 1965, while the interviewer for *Women's Mirror* was in the same month taken to lunch by John Stephen at his favourite China Garden restaurant in Soho, where the blacked-out downstairs room was black in its entirety, including the walls, ceiling and floor, a uniformly decadent note carried over to the inclusion of a black tablecloth arranged on a black table. John Stephen's days were so crowded now, with only the briefest of holidays in Cannes, so manic with juiced-up impulse to stay at the top, that he accelerated through g-forces of adrenalised stimulus on a daily basis, his continuously boyish looks at thirty unmarked by the ravages of heavy drinking and a lifestyle that allowed for almost no form of relaxation. Apparently resistant to hangovers and the residual shattering that comes of drinking whisky to excess, Stephen, according to Bill Franks, had a system that quickly metabolised alcohol, leaving him alert in the morning and ready at 7.00 to rip into his working day. Carnaby Street had become by now as speed-crazed as the drug that fuelled the spearhead of the Mod contingent. Writing for *The*

Evening News and Star in June 1965, Ann Beveridge attempted to convey something of the milieu's vertiginous rush and frothy excitement, as well as its inscrutable cool in a paragraph aimed at capturing aspects of its unremitting full-on dynamic. 'Two long-haired Mods just beat me to the counter. Fixing me with a stare from their joint battery of black lenses, they swayed to pop blaring from a corner record bar and then sprawled on the floor to buy skin-tight white jeans. Crazy? Just Carnaby Street.' Beveridge's location was John Stephen's newly opened Teen Store, and clearly fascinated by the removal of gender distinctions that permeated the street's fashion, she added: 'Behind me an office girl, hotfoot from the city, emerged from a cubicle with her own choice in men's pants.'

By 1965, John Stephen had secured an undisputed and inexorable territorial hold on Carnaby Street, his fashion suzerainity extending to leaseholds on the Teen Store at 52–55 Carnaby Street, that sold male and female teenage clothes, the Village Store at 5, 6 and 7 Carnaby Street that sold ladies' wear, John Stephen Custom Built Clothes For Men at 9 Carnaby Street, John Stephen The Man's Shop at 49–51 Carnaby Street, His Clothes at 41 Carnaby Street, Adam West One at 47a, Domino Male at 46a Carnaby Street, and Tre Camp at 46 Carnaby Street, and the Drug Store on the corner of Beak and Carnaby Street that included a cafe and record bar. Continually opening in opposition to himself to up the ante of trade, the John Stephen topology of Carnaby Street in the crucial mid-sixties – he had also made significant property investments in the Earl's Court area – admitted competition from the likes of Lord John, but ruled by virtue of design initiative and staggering agglomeration of numbers. The street was John Stephen's, together with his city link Amore Marden, who took a stake of about £200,000 in 1965, with Stephen operating at optimal force, despite the fact that many of his small shops had been living with six months rebuilding orders for years. The sheer risk and impulsive temerity needed to configure the imposing building blocks of the John Stephen Organisation could only have been created by an individual who recklessly matched his creative chutzpah with the wired stimulus in business of a kamikaze. Stephen's suit could literally have been finned with flames, as he hurried in a volatile rush from one site to another on his turbulent patch, advising, noting, selling, designing, costing, and assuring that he turned round at least a third of his stock each week, with regular customers sometimes spending as much as £50 a week on clothes, while the average teen liquidated £10–£15 a week on the look, the equivalent of two thirds of their Friday night, cash-paid salary. John Stephen's life, inwardly rich and outwardly glamorous, remained singularly and unremittingly work-driven, and impenetrably enigmatic, his private life, as much as he cared to filter, largely confided to Franks, Merkell, and his intuitively sympathetic younger sister Rae. And while Bill Franks is adamant in insisting that both his and John Stephen's family were happy to allow for their relationship, and generally supportive of it, it was still a fact that had to be concealed like contraband from a society rigidly dominated by prejudice and an inherited moral aversion to gay couples. Stephen's milieu inhabited a necessarily paranoid world in which gay men adopted polari, or palare, as a private slang language, and one which featured strongly in the 'Julian and Sandy' sketches on the BBC radio programme *Round the Horne* in the late sixties. While a few words like 'bona' can still be seen in gay publications, as a throwback to the times, the constantly changing underground dialect interestingly differed in the West End from a posher theatre-speak, to the East End equivalent based on canal/boat speak. Outside of the concept of familial acceptance and the gay network that invariably prevailed over men's fashion, the likes of John Stephen and Bill Franks, as domestic partners, were considered to be an anomaly in an enduring and crushing sexual dystopia. Myles Antony remembers the prohibitive subterranean ethos of the times, and the lack of any acceptable gay milieu, even in a capital undergoing a radical overhaul of received notions of presentations of gender. 'The gay clubs of the sixties were awful and mostly closed at 11pm. If you didn't "click" by then, it was a trawl of the cottages or crowded tube trains, but it would never be a problem if you were even vaguely attractive. One of the more exotic clubs was the Two Decks. John Stephen and I went there a lot. It was really a supper club with a nightly drag floor show. It was owned by Allan Haines and was great fun. Gay coffee bars were few, I can only recall the Mousehole (very cruisy), and the Rouge et Noire in Foubert's Place. Once the big discos opened at the end of the sixties, all those boring small clubs closed.'

Estimating that as many as 5,000 customers might pass through a single shop in a week, Stephen worked on a system of high mark-ups, these, according to Victoria Brittain writing for the *Investors' Chronicle*, varying from 20–100 per cent depending on the item, with the norm being 60 per cent 'actual,' and working out at nearer 40 per cent after writing off failure. Brittain was sceptical of John Stephen or Warren Gold's long-term survival, or of the future of any of the vibrant, tiny, aquarium-coloured boutiques in Carnaby Street, burning like miniature Las Vegas excerpts under the uniformly lowering grey Soho skies. 'For the moment their future is uncertain,' Brittain wrote. 'They cannot stand still. To expand they must either go really big with branches in every little provincial town and export divisions as well (John Stephen's probable pattern); or like the efficient Mr Ingram or John Michael, they must trade up into an exclusive market.'

The largely disparaging summary, while praising John Stephen's US expansionist policy, with outlets like Daytons of Minneapolis, and Carsons of Chicago, nevertheless singled out Nathan Spiegel's Paul's of Carnaby Street, as the most efficiently managed of the street's boutiques, and the most likely to prove resilient to change, despite its clothes being derivative of Stephen's, only more conservative, with stock comprising perennially popular casual wear like jeans, needle-cord hipsters and Italian-styled V-neck and crew-neck knitwear. And as a deliberate put-down of the assumed inferior quality of Carnaby Street tailoring, Brittain suggested that upmarket purveyors of the look had their bespoke niches at the likes of Rupert Lycett-Green's Blades, who catered for rich bohemian Mayfair aristos, or the Fulham partners Dimitri Major and Douglas Hayward, who sold to the likes of dudes like Terence Stamp and Michael Caine, as cool proponents of the rich chalk-stripe suited gangster look, that relied on suits with strong attitude. Caine, whle adopting black horn-rimmed glasses, and dark suits, slim ties and white button-down collar shirts, combining killer tailored threads with a deadpan cockney delivery, was a Mod icon but not a Carnaby Street aficionado. The tendency to perceive John Stephen as little more than a meteoric ideas man, and ultimately as ephemeral as many of the pop acts he dressed, was an accusation uniformly levelled at him by critics suspicious of his controversially pioneering success as an untutored designer, who had broken totally with all received notions of men's retailing. It's usually an unenviable lot to attempt to subvert the *status quo* in any of the arts, and while Stephen may have attracted the entire sixties pop generation to his street, his virtuoso talents also received a contemptuous dismissal by a trade who considered him little more than an opportune punk making piratical raids on their traditionally established terrain.

One maverick visitor to the John Stephen Carnaby Street offices at the time was Karen Moller, who had taken to designing screen-printed semi-transparent paper dresses in zigzag and op art patterns, along with a commercial line of oily black PVC raincoats. In her self-published memoir of the period, *Technicolor Dreaming the 1960s Rainbow and Beyond*, Moller tells of her visit to an explosive Carnaby Street, dangerous to the system at the time as an overactive thyroid gland. 'Not knowing what to expect from that mythical Glaswegian Mod,' Moller tells us, 'I gathered together my commercial PVC raincoats, along with my most outrageous garments, and headed for his office. John Stephen, a small, gentle and unimposing man, sat at his desk that day, among a stack of drawings and papers. After a brief greeting, he nodded to me to get on with the show. Even though he was gay, the lack of a changing room was disconcerting. One after another, I modelled the garments, while he sat at his desk taking notes.' To help the young, impecunious designer, John Stephen, with characteristic generosity on discovering original talent, gave Moller a contract to supply a limited number of her disposable avant-garde creations to the American side of his chain of stores within stores.

In 1965, it was John Bates with his own label Jean Varon, who won the Dress of the Year award for a bikini dress with a revealing net panel, a creation modelled by Jean Shrimpton in *Vogue*, January 1965, the skimpy dress having a bikini top and short skirt knitted together in navy, the pattern being terra-cotta and orange on navy cotton. John Bates, unlike John Stephen, had been couture trained at Gerard Pipard, and quickly won recognition amongst populist Mods for his costume designs and jumpsuits worn by Diana Rigg for the TV series *The Avengers*. According to *Get Dressed, A Useful Guide to London's Boutiques*, there were eighty such shops in central London alone, in 1965, with perhaps 2,000 in Greater London, as a whole, as the indicator of an accelerated uptempo clothes pandemic that owed its origins in large to John Stephen for sexualizing colourful men's retail, and to Mary Quant for liberating women's clothes on much the same erogenous principles, and with an equally flagrant disrespect for couture. Both had begun and continued with the same subversive conviction that legislation by the big houses had to go, and that as part of democratizing fashion and updating it to suit the needs of the immediate moment, it was essential to go straight to the customer to determine their needs. But for Faces, John Stephen's decision to design for women through opening Trecamp, and the Teen Store in 1965 severely disrupted the gendering of the street, where men were the key patrons of innovative retailing done by the John Stephen Organisation. In a subtle way the decision was interpreted by Mods as a betrayal of their male domination of the street, and viewed as a concession to consumerism, no matter that Stephen's overtly homoerotic photographs of musclemen in the changing rooms of Tre Camp still further promoted the ideal of a subtextual gay ethos to which Mods with their intimate male friendships readily subscribed. Anticipating Malcolm McLaren and Vivienne Westwood's prototypical punk hoopla at The Sex Shop, 430 King's Road, by a decade, Stephen's highly controversial fitting rooms at Tre Camp were a reminder that he had lost none of the cutting edge, disruptive street credibility that had originally attracted Mods to his back-alley shops in a surprise bonded fraternity in the early sixties.

London finally exploded into pop culture in 1965, and John Stephen's name and designs were inseparable from the impacted self-confidence youth felt in separating itself from the residual post-war austerity into which the older generation remained partially locked. Nigel Waymouth's Granny Takes A Trip opened in November 1965, at 488 King's Road, World's End, Chelsea, the shop's druggy art nouveau ethos quickly filtering off the social cachet of Chelsea's hip young elite, who, distinct from Stephen's Soho Mods, expressed reservations about Carnaby Street's undeniably sleazy glamour, publicity overkill, suspect tailoring and red light district origins. Waymouth, and his arty counterculture partners, John Pearse and Sheila Cohen, dealt largely in vintage clothes and stunning remakes of period revival, with the emphasis being on faux romantic aspects of Victoriana. The conflict between urgent pop art and retro nostalgia that themed the shop's dynamic was nowhere more evident than in the fundamental contradiction between its psych-edelically painted exterior, and its eccentric interior décor that included purple walls, a green tasselled light shade, a phonograph, a Victorian looking glass and a Victorian sun shade. Meanwhile, to consolidate the Chelsea backlash, James Wedge and Pat Booth opened two highly innovative shops, Countdown at 137, and Top Gear at 135a King's Road, a tiny shop near Café Picasso that had a black interior painted by Albert Finney and his friends, a concept that may have triggered the inspiration for the Rolling Stones' sitar-driven hit single *Paint It Black*. Pat Booth remembers the fascination that Top Gear engendered amongst the popocracy as a meeting place, rather in the manner of John Stephen's pioneering café-fitted Drug Store and Teen Store. Behind the high-flying Stephen in initiating this particular social facility, Booth recalls, 'the shop was a meeting place every single Saturday. For the first time shopping became a social event. John Lennon used to sit on the window-sill and put 78s on the old record player, and Mick Jagger had an account with us for all his girlfriends.' In contrast to Top Gear's funereal

*Granny Takes
A Trip – the
inventive home
of psychedelic
period revival
clothes. The
painted façade
of the shop
was frequently
redesigned.*

black interior, Wedge and Booth did Countdown out in polished silver metal, the space-age inflexions provided by the fixtures appearing intensely post-modern within the shop's compacted space. And even though clothes were seminal to the radical declassification of class taking place, Soho led by John Stephen still outran the pack for ideas, and was *de facto* Mod territory, as opposed to the wealthier King's Road, where period revival was the prevalent influence on Nigel Waymouth, as well as Ossie Clark's Quorum at 52 Radnor Walk, both of who provided styles filtered and re-modified for trust-funded dandies, with John Stephen viewed as their irremediably déclassé progenitor. Reluctantly, but inevitably, the mainstream fashion outlets were forced out

of financial necessity to rejuvenate their image by retailing modernistic lines, as with Austin Reed's Cue, managed by Colin Woodhead, Gordon Deighton's Trend at Simpsons, and Way In at Harrods. The Way In investment at Harrods featured an internal Quink-blue street of boutiques, covering 20,000 square feet of fashionable hard sell, all aimed at an affluent market, and promoting upmarket designs styled elegantly with Italian chic to target the more discerning and decidedly modern punter. John Stephen, with his untutored background as a designer and pop accessories, continued to be assessed ambivalently by his contemporaries, and viewed by some more as a maverick opportunist than an enduring style innovator. Writing for the influential *Design* magazine, Kate and Ken Baynes, with some degree of caution, recognised Stephen's Carnaby Street as the 'birth, however illegitimate, of a really thoroughgoing design movement,' the word illegitimate appearing to target the fact that Stephen was an untrained designer, while acknowledging that his legacy through Carnaby Street could rank with Bauhaus in terms of importance as a design legend.

The iconoclastic formula started by John Stephen, almost without any stock, of cutting out the buyer and going directly to the customer as the means of discerning popular taste, rather than anticipating their reaction to an arbitrarily imposed seasonal look, had by the mid-sixties been adopted by enterprising individuals all over London, as the temperature of clothes consumption amongst the young spiked up to hothouse equatorial. Nigel Waymouth, of Granny Takes A Trip, remembers that the endemic message of the times, was look at me, by which he meant, look at my clothes. 'We didn't realise it then,' Waymouth reflected, 'but the John Stephen revolution was a very gay thing. Youth wanted this way of dressing for themselves because it was a way of rebelling. It was the antithesis of Burton's: fast-moving, fashionable, very voguish and affordable. It was self-consciously trendy and camp in the same sense of the word. The clothes had their retro aspects, but basically they were new. If you want to point your finger at a common denominator in all the clothes, it was that they were pretty narcissistic, whether you were a Mod or whatever. The message was, "Look at me!"'

Nigel Waymouth, like Bill Franks, also defends the generic quality of Carnaby Street clothes, on the strength that the fabrics used were still manufactured in Britain, much of the flannel for John Stephen clothes coming from Dickens & Jones in Regent Street, which had a wholesale department on the top floor. At the time John Stephen refuted negative qualitative charges, 'as just a lot of crap, to be honest. As a matter of fact it sometimes worries me that our clothes do last for such a long time.' Nigel Waymouth

Cathy McGowan in a mini skirt of her own design worn several inches above the knee. The butch caps were copied from John Stephen.

recalls affirmatively that, 'although people thought of the clothes then as being roughly made, compared to now they were Savile Row standard. The quality of clothes is horrible now by comparison. Things were still made in England then, not Taiwan, with cheap threads and poor cutting.'

Carnaby Street was now in sheer volume of daily foot traffic the busiest street in London, with Mods and Stephen shop assistants literally running from shop to shop with trousers over their arms, film-crews shooting footage of visiting celebrities, Japanese reps assiduously photographing the windows for ideas to take home and copy, and a frothy plethora of international tourists drawn to the unremitting attraction of its gravitational field. Youth were swallowed into the alley's pull like matter sucked into a black hole, their fascination acute, their need to be seen and noticed imperative. As Beryl Hartland, writing for the *Daily Telegraph* on 28 May 1965, commented on the street's celebrity value, 'you can bump into Mick Jagger buying a sports jacket and Gerald McCann, the dress designer, carrying away a 1930s-style suit, Jo Grimond, Cathy McGowan and Sean Connery are all regulars,' and this was just her experience of a single afternoon's visit to report on the street's optimal, early summer fizz amongst hedonistic fashionistas, and more seriously clothes-committed Mods sighting each niche of the window displays, and hurriedly moving from shop to shop in search of the immediately new. Mods still lived fast and metabolised speed with the same accelerative rip as they injected fuel into their scooters, for a declarative, buzzy Soho getaway, their attitude given rev by their extravagantly sculpted gizmo-stacked Vespas and Lambrettas, invariably acquired on hire purchase from the likes of stockists like Jo Grimstead. Many of them continued to wear clothing so finely tailored that its subtle detail was altogether lost on outsiders, a winningly subversive prerogative that added to their mystique as a cult. The Faces remained the redoubtably diffident originators of style, distinguished by their attitude from the tickets, which as a collective, tended to wear conventional Mod uniform: Parka coats, Fred Perry shirts, cherry red commando boots and blue beat Mod hats. And to Faces and tickets on the Soho club scene, The Who with their Tuesday night residency at the Marquee, the Rolling Stones, the Yardbirds, the Small Faces and the Action, were the only white bands who qualified for Mod acceptance, largely on account of their ability to integrate the look into scorching R&B pop, often fired-up by chronic amphetamine abuse. 1965 was musically the year of Dobie Gray's infectious hit single, *The 'In' Crowd*, a Billy Page song, extolling the cool sassiness of being 'in' in the mid-sixties, and a number immediately adopted by Mods at The Scene and The Flamingo as a self-referential anthem. It was also the year when

Cathy McGowan's Mod-infused showcase *Ready Steady Go!* switched from mimed to all-live performances, adding not only credibility to the music, but incentive to weekly clothes spotters to search out compelling individual designs worn on the show the next day in John Stephen's daily stripped-apart and ingeniously-updated racks.

Speed was still the essential to Stephen's success, and the rapidity of his creative output remained unrivalled amongst his designer contemporaries for sheer colour-saturated invention. Interviewed at the time, John Stephen's refreshingly pragmatic approach to highly customised retailing was stripped down, intensely focused, and concentrated totally on the individual's needs. 'If a customer buys an article from one of my West End boutiques,' he affirmed, 'and it requires altering or the trousers need attention, the detail is done immediately in our workrooms at no extra cost. And if someone wants a garment they can't find in the shops anywhere, instead of them ordering it through a large manufacturer and waiting months, I can put it through my workrooms in a fortnight.' And speed, dictated by his chemistry, was the essence. A pair of hipsters could be made up by the flame-haired, 5ft 10in, mercurial Ivy Dean in three hours, whereas a shirt might be two days in the perfect structuring, and a suit two weeks.

In 1965, the offshore pirate Radio Caroline was illegally broadcasting pop to 7 million of the nation's youth, with some of the DJs encouragingly endorsing John Stephen's clothes in sound-bites, between airing the latest experimental singles, also being played contemporaneously at maximum volume in John Stephen's shops. The more pop and rock music gained a significant hold on the capital, the greater the spin-off for John Stephen's clothes, as the two energies fused in a mutually interfacing aesthetic. John Stephen could now afford holidays, on the rare occasions he permitted himself breaks, in Nice, Cannes and Marbella, was habitually seen dining at the upmarket Ivy and the Mirabelle in Curzon Street, Mayfair, and was a regular at the legendary drag artist Danny La Rue's celebrated Danny's Club in Hanover Square. The venue, which attracted celebrity names like Judy Garland, Shirley Bassey, Noel Coward and Elizabeth Taylor to its histrionically camp interior, where La Rue as part of his drag stage act performed travesty impersonations of the likes of Garland, Dusty Springfield and Barbara Streisland, only with an even greater capacity for optimal camp histrionics. John Stephen was now the most celebrated of the Mod designers, and Carnaby Street so inextricably linked to his name that the association was compounded into his identity. John Stephen was Carnaby Street, a thoroughfare lettered with his name and variant Bahaus-styled shop logos, on both sides of the street, and congested

to saturation point with a generation obsessed with the cool edge of his vitally modernistic clothes. And for Barry Fantoni in his guide to Swinging London, Carnaby Street was 'the storm centre of the excitement that has the whole world wondering about what has happened to the British, and the reserve they've always expressed ... In Carnaby Street the revolution is right here; in the bright sunlight of a smoky London day the main body of the revolution pass and re-pass, codifying the visual legislation of their declaration of intent today.' And by way of inventive John Stephen Christmas displays for 1965, *Style Weekly* noted that in the Teen Store, Myles Antony had used huge white candles against a background of gold outline Gothic windows, while at the Man's Shop he had employed dominant pink candles and white twigs to notable camp effect. Domino Male, as a bijou shop competitor, was unusually provided with a performing seal and ostentatious rotating glass ball as a hypnotic attraction. John Stephen and Bill Franks had arrived at this stupendous apogee in sixties fashion without ever having intended to do so, and by additionally staying small and independent, marginally deficient in business acumen, but singularly individual and unrivalled in their capacity to create designs that intimidated tradition, but thrilled their own generation into living so absorbed by the present, that they dressed to colour the moment with alacritous style and sartorial euphoria.

Contemporaneous with Stephen's persistently itchy need to expand, both in Carnaby Street and in the King's Road, as a means of consolidating his independent achievements, another opportunistically serious but acutely stylish men's boutique, Peter Golding's Just Men, opened in opposition to John Stephen's and John Michael's King's Road suzerainty at 9 Tryon Street in late November 1965. The ground floor of the Just Men shop was engagingly decorated in oak, beige leather, green baize and brass, with the upstairs saturated in Russian red baize, black corduroy and more glowering brass. Golding took Stephen's seminal lead in making the shop into an interactive fusion between customers and staff, as well as facilitating in-store stereo, with the music played encompassing everything from the Beatles to Bach. Designed with a considerably more resourceful budget than Stephen's brilliantly improvised stage-set Carnaby Street boutiques, Just Men was aimed to target the high end Chelsea market, its floors stocked with flared trousers, Peter Golding-designed tapered shirts, skinny Shetland sweaters in sea and sky colours, suede and leather suits, wide satin kipper ties, shoes and accessories, with all designs made exclusively for Just Men. Adding little to Stephen's repertoire, but making considerable purchase on his ideas, Just Men also featured a busy custom tailoring department with John Dacie and

Patti Boyd's leggy extravagance, showing off a dress designed by Ossie Clark for the Quorum Autumn Collection of 1966.

Charles Schuller creating lively trousers at £8 and individually customised suits from £30.

Opening contemporaneously with Just Men, Andrew Moussolo and Gerald McCann's The Gloryhole Boutique at 342a King's Road was another slice of exaggerated Chelsea aggrandisement aimed at capitalising on the fashion supernova that had overtaken sixties London. The puce-coloured interior decorated from the outside by a galaxy of twinkling multi-coloured light bulbs provided an almost extraterrestrial attraction to the steamy King's Road foot traffic, acquisitively and fetishistically window-shopping for the next hit purchase. Dusty Springfield, Patti Boyd and Rita Tushingham were amongst the celebrities who succeeded in turning over the spectacular Gerald McCann-designed dresses and coats, with the shop in keeping with 1960s unisex, quickly following with a colourful men's clothes section.

Pauline Fordham's new wave glitzy Palisades, at 26 Ganton Street, an alley off Carnaby Street, as still another offshoot of Stephen's localised dynamic, pulsated with a chrome-lashed, coloured lights flashing Zodiac jukebox, as a centrepiece attraction to the shop, as 1965 accelerated Carnaby Street as a location, into an unprecedented global centre for youthful fashion. Whether it was the nearby Foale & Tuffin at 1 Marlborough Court, Robert Krausz's Barok on the Earl's Court Road, or Biba with its stagy Victorian dressing tables and revamped furniture heaped with feathered boas, bags, accessories and lingerie, John Stephen's template of playing loud pop music in shops, and dissolving customer relations into a mutually recreational experience, had been copied all over London as the *de rigueur* prescription for fizzy retail attraction and escalating commercial profit.

6

DEDICATED FOLLOWER OF FASHION

In an issue of *Mod Britain '66*, Bob Farmer reported on the unprecedented vivacity of 'Swinging London,' as the tonic capital for clothes and drugs, quoting Warren Gold of Lord John, as saying, 'You can liken Carnaby Street to the Beatles. Everybody imitates us, but we're the originals.' In the same issue, Keith Moon of The Who, an insatiable Carnaby Street aficionado volunteered, 'We see Mods with eyes as big as saucers. You see drugs passed in any loo in any London club. I'm sorry I mentioned that, loos will be banned now.'

Whatever the preferred chemical, drugs as a must-have recreational stimulus directly influenced fashion, and the sharp, streamlined look favoured by Mods found its pharmaceutical interface in speed, as a clean drug documenting increased energy and euphoric states. Amphetamine also caused decreased appetite as a side-effect, and was medically prescribed as a slimming pill, as well as an anti-depressant, an additional gain as the Mod aesthetic statistically favoured size 14in shirt collar, 36in chest for jackets and 26–28in waist for trousers. In 1966, speed or purple hearts was still the staple Mod drug, although LSD had gained a limited recreational currency among British rock bands into its hallucinated cloud ceiling in the mid-sixties. The Rolling Stones had first hinted at the emergent infiltration of acid, as a hallucinatory drug, by recording the seminal *Something Happened To Me Yesterday*, and the Beatles too, in their initial acid-tinged number, *She Said She Said*, responded to the initiative, with a song reputed to have been inspired by a conversation with Peter Fonda during John Lennon's second LSD trip. The song appeared

Note the trailing window boxes, the superb Myles Antony displays and the John Stephen fusion of gender.

on the Beatles' cutting-edge *Revolver* album (1966), as a pointer to the acid-immersed psychic landscapes that would dominate their 1967 psychedelic classic, *Sgt. Pepper's Lonely Hearts Club Band*, as an album recorded over an epic 129-day period begun on 6 December 1966. The introduction of psycho-tropic drugs into street and club culture, including hallucinogenic substances like the shape-shifting LSD, would come to have a profound influence on the mimetic properties of colour and pattern not only in Carnaby Street designs, but in general fashion. London in 1966 was still, however, an amphetamine-based Mod ethos, with The Who subversively firing up racist tension, often induced by speed, amongst Mods with the line, 'I look all white but my Dad was black,' on the chart-impacting single *Substitute*, with Pete Townshend's windmilling riff ripping off Keith Richards' declarative guitar figure from the Stones' *19th Nervous Breakdown*.

The extent of John Stephen's domination of the men's London fashion scene in the mid-sixties is apparent from the listings given on the back of a receipt for a purchase made in His Clothes, in Carnaby Street, June '66, which as a piece of historic Carnaby Street memorabilia, is worth quoting in full. The receipt incompletely lists the John Stephen Store, 52/55 Carnaby Street, John Stephen Man's Shop 49/51 Carnaby Street, Adam W1 47a Carnaby Street, Domino Male 46a Carnaby Street, His Clothes 41 Carnaby Street, Male W.1. 38a Carnaby Street, His Clothes 189 Regent Street, His clothes 40 Old Compton Street, John Stephen Tailoring 9 Carnaby Street, John Stephen 33 Old Bailey Street EC4, His Clothes 63 Queensway W2, His Clothes 171 Earls Court Road SW3, John Stephen 97 King's Road, SW3, His Clothes 201 King's Road SW3, John Stephen 272 High Road Loughton, His Clothes 7 East St Brighton, and Tre Camp 46 Carnaby Street. Contemporary photog-raphy of Mods by Terry Spencer, who worked as a features photographer for *Life Magazine*, shot in Stephen's outré His Clothes, reveals the characteristic facial angularity of typical Mod features, with their habitual use of speed pinching all definition to the bone. Their eyes are blacked out by dark glasses creating a wraparound, post-human extraterrestrial look, as a number of ace faces concentrate their attention on a saturated trouser rack. Their crew-neck pastel jumpers are worn with feminine attention to style, and their attitude is cultish, alien, almost inaccessibly remote, their short haircut precisely geometric, and kept in place either by lacquer or by the use of sugar water, a trick of shaping the hair after washing it with a solution of sugar dissolved in water. These were the forward-looking proponents of Mod ethics, with fastidious Faces insisting on using a sheet of brown paper when sitting down on public transport to protect their trousers from spoiling, and particularly

in the case of the ubiquitously popular white jeans. Mods into the look experimented with wearing subtle makeup, as part of the gender subversion of the
times, not only in the Carnaby Street precinct, but also in the Soho clubs,
with the use of eyeliner and eye-shadow pointing a direct challenge to their
female counterparts. Mod girls tended to wear grey or brown eye-shadow,
to complement provocatively mascara-lashed false eyelashes, and were adept
at near enough copying their partner's choice of clothes and colours in the
fusion of unisex. Masculine androgyny as the spearhead of the constantly
updated look was still the line successfully developed by John Stephen,
both in his ingenious application of detail, and in his choice of fabrics for
men, with black leather underwear proving consistently popular; and as
the aesthetic that instantly differentiated his clothes from the chain-store
copyists. Leather jackets too, in black, red, navy blue and beige as the basic
colours, were made up for Stephen in a tannery on the corner of Foubert's
Place and Carnaby Street, the black leather jackets lined with poppy-red
satin, with five skins required for a jacket, and the cuttings used to make up
leather ties and underwear for Stephen's exclusive range of shops.

Constantly on the edge of burn-out, caused in part by the strain of
maintaining his public image at the expense of chronic social anxiety, John
Stephen continued successfully to live a double life, his undisputed reputation as the progenitor of the sixties look leaving the media predictably
curious about his private life, conducted with Franks and Merkell, and the
usual anthology of occasional boyfriends and pick-ups from the subterranean gay scene. Stephen though was severely internally scarred by the residue
of his first major breakdown, and subject to periods of acute paranoia as a
residual recurrent symptom. Myles Antony recalls these unnerving pockets
of mania in his sympathetic employer as characterised by an obsession
that people were cheating him, even down to his staff, who he suspected
of stealing and attempting to undermine his authority. Stephen's violent
mood swings were also characterised by a loss of all interest in food, and for
someone who at best only picked at the contents of his plate, the refusal to
eat only accelerated the negative aspects of heavy drinking. By way of some
relaxation from the perennial hype of business, Stephen and Franks were
regular visitors to the cabaret restaurant Talk of the Town, on the corner
of Charing Cross Road and Leicester Square, which featured many of the
popular artistes of the time performing solo, including appearances by Judy
Garland, Shirley Bassey, Pearl Bailey, Cliff Richard and Johnny Ray. Stephen
and Franks were in the audience to catch Garland's cabaret debut there, in
which the histrionic Garland, as a cryopreserved youthful 46, gave a raw

John Stephen was bipolar. His overstrained sensitivity looks on red alert here.

emotion-packed powerhouse performance to a sold-out venue, dressed in a bronze Beau Brummell trouser suit alive with sequins and gold beads. Garland as indomitable diva with the likes of Zsa Zsa Gabor, Johnny Ray and Danny La Rue in the audience, scorched her way through agonized torch songs like *Just in Time*, *The Trolley Song*, and *You Made Me Love You*, before sitting vulnerably cross-legged on the stage in black satin spike-heeled shoes to sing her trademark epic *Over the Rainbow*. The two also caught virtuoso nights there by the ad-libbing controversial black singer Pearl Bailey, who starred as matchmaker Dolly Gallagher in the all-black Broadway revival of *Hello Dolly!* before returning to the intimacy of cabaret, charming British audiences, including Stephen and Franks, with her flagrantly risqué, off-handed, impertinent style, laced with accentuated double entendres, during an extended cabaret run, complete with costume changes and a rainbow of feathered boas, at London's Talk of the Town.

Taking unconscionable refuge in the comfort-zone provided by personal wealth, Stephen, with the capriciousness of a pop star, refused to travel anywhere without the fortress protection of his Rolls, even taking it abroad for Swank American and Scandinavian promotional tours, and to South Africa where a highly lucrative licensing agreement had been secured with Swank. But no matter his plutocratic standing amongst a Mod clientele who were generally working class apprentices, shop hands and office boys in the workplace, whose weekend liberation into wearing detail-acute clothes for the hedonistic pursuit of clubbing, comprised individual revolution, Stephen's approach to retail remained pragmatically democratic. 'Where else can you go on a Saturday and get a pair of trousers that fit you?' Stephen emphasised, as a point of honour, in an *Observer* interview. 'They all come pouring off the M1 and get to Carnaby Street about midday. They want their clothes before they go off to Brighton.' Regular customers were individually known to staff, and their preferences massaged on a personal level, the prevailing air one of intimacy and friendship, as well as a mutually shared enthusiasm for whatever was new on the racks, which in 1966 included wide, dramatically coloured op-art ties, turtle-neck sweaters, flowered shirts and tight checked trousers.

1966 saw another first for John Stephen, in his creation of floral shirts and ties for men, in patterns not so different from the ones traditionally used by Liberty for women. The inspired use of floral prints for shirts, evolved from Stephen's usual method of purchasing a remnant from a local fabric shop, and having samples made up in the workroom, and assessing if the idea had staying power by placing the items in his windows. Stephen rightly predicted that Mod androgyny had advanced sufficiently to put men in flowers, a pattern almost exclusively associated with women. A compelling Mike McGrath publicity photo used Jeff Beck of the Yardbirds as the model for a high collared floral shirt with button-down collars, the typed caption on the back of the photo stating that the Yardbirds would be wearing John Stephen flowered shirts on their upcoming American tour, as an endorsement of cool. A variety of floral prints were used, varying from diminutive pink roses on a dark blue or black background, to a larger flower motif imposed on pastels, with matching and alternating ties made up in multiple variants. The unthinkable expression of putting men in flowers, and with such finely detailed qualitative taste, could only have originated from John Stephen, and was also a marker of the radically changing times. A shirt that even five years earlier would have invited homophobic abuse of the wearer, was now injected into the contagion of heady, shape-shifting Carnaby Street fashion, and quickly taken up by Mods in search of prettifying the look. Rarely credited by other designers for his extraordinary originality, John Stephen was by the mid-sixties the undisputed, constantly risk-taking dictator of what was new, in the way London dressed in the heady era that defined its fashion apogee.

Amongst John Stephen designs for 1966, emphasised by cute models on black and white promotional photos, were alpaca cardigans worn by the young singer Bobby Shafto, as well as mohair polo necks worn with waist-coats from the same fibre, loud op art ties in navy blue and red, and striped belts that came in a variety of candy-coloured combinations, and which were worn with check hipster slacks incorporating wool-reverse pleats on the front patch pockets, and a slightly flared vented ankle. As a complementary photo to Bobby Shafto's pose, the vivacious girl singer, Billie Davis, who had scored a Top Ten hit with *Tell Him*, was shot wearing a white Dralon sweater with crocheted sleeves, and blue tweed slacks, both available from Tre Camp boutique. Other Stephen notables for the climb-out velocity of menswear sales in 1966 included white suits, the hardest of all fabrics to maintain in any way pristine. In the apprehension of the fact, Stephen had white suits made up in a Terylene and worsted gabardine combination to be worn with polka-dot and floral shirts. 'Our sales have proved that, despite the cleaning bills, most guys are happy to have a white suit in their wardrobe,' Stephen commented on his anomalous choice of colour. 'The decision to be made is whether to buy one cheaply made of fabrics that look effective in a shop window, but prove exhausted after a few cleanings, or to choose a fabric that is more crease resistant and has the kind of body that isn't adversely affected by dry cleaning. As stunning as white suits can look, the cheaper kind can show creases very quickly. I've seen the results of someone wearing one of the

Nothing but a star: John Stephen was the look before he created it.

inferior versions at a party in a warm room, and who has sat down in it for a couple of hours. When he stood up there so many creases in the trousers and jacket it looked as if he had slept in the suit.' Eloquent at the time in contributing to the captions accompanying publicity shots of his new lines, Stephen promoted the idea of matching slipovers and cardigans contesting the sports jacket as a legitimate advance in innovative menswear. The sets came in black and white, or beige and brown, while for girls Stephen designed a square-necked jumper in botany wool with an exclusive Stephen zigzag motif dominated by four different colour blends, beige, chocolate, bottle green or navy blue. 'Right now guys are realising how comfortable matching knitwear can be,' Stephen speculated, 'and so much smarter than all those millions of jean jackets that have become a uniform. Anyone who wants to be more exclusive about their matching knitwear can simply make sure they bypass the chain stores and choose patterns they like best from some of the smaller groups of shops. Unlike roll collared shirts and neck scarves for men, it's a fashion that can't be a bad investment as slipovers and cardigans can be worn together, separately or for years.'

Despite the inordinate success of the John Stephen Organisation, publicity continued to be low-key and subterranean, and to exist largely through captioned photos released to the press, almost as a throwback to the era of Vince and John Stephen's first Beak Street catalogues, when advertising was of necessity clandestine and its dissemination sensitively targeted. It could be argued that the street's unstoppable popularity dispensed with the need for energetic publicity, a phenomenon that continued to unnerve the trade on account of its spectacular unorthodoxy. Stephen's topographically personalised alley also owed a large part of its success to the continuously subversive displays pioneered by Myles Antony, who, interviewed by The Outfitter for their 12 February 1966 issue, spoke precisely of his defiance of convention. 'I think one of the main reasons for the success I've found in display and shop design is that whether intended or not, I have defied convention. I have hung trouser dummies upside down, used pink as a background to men's clothes, used sexy photos, and painted dummies' faces purple, not to mention designing a shop that is a cross between a gothic cathedral and a cinema foyer.'

Interviewed by the fashion journalist Barry Fantoni, for the television series, A Whole Scene Going, on 26 January 1966, John Stephen was asked to describe the clothes he was wearing and to account for his choice. 'I'm wearing a roll collar shirt,' he replied, 'made of cotton, and a quilted tie, which isn't lined, on account of ties always getting crumpled at the cleaners. The jacket

I have on has a high button fastening, and the pockets are pouched pockets, because ordinary pockets literally bulge, if you're someone like me, who uses their pockets as a filing cabinet. I'm one of those people, who after a few drinks in a restaurant, become a restaurant kleptomaniac, and take everything including ashtrays and teaspoons. The trousers, like the jacket, are made in English check tweed, and the belt is a wide two-inch one.' All of the clothes were of course his designs, and the unexpected confessional admission of getting out of control after drinking, provided a rare insight into his scrupulously closed inner world, from which the media were uniformly excluded.

Carnaby Street had by now become the daily fashion equivalent of a live gig, and in 1966 the Small Faces actually set up equipment outside Lord John, plugged in, and delivered a short impromptu set, as part of the street's crazy, hyper, exuberantly state-of-the-art delivery. In the same year, Harry Fox's newly initiated Lady Jane boutique in Carnaby Street had live models changing and unchanging in the window of his shop as a lunch-hour attraction to the cynical, the girls in rotation peeling off to Mary Quant black see-through bras and panties. When the police pressed for a charge of indecency and obstruction, due to the amassed crowd formed outside the shop, the Marlborough Street Magistrate, Mr St John Harmsworth, acquitted Fox, by sympathetically affirming, 'You set up a good business promotion, but try to be less exuberant. In the circumstances, I cannot find it in my heart to fine you.'

Although John Stephen continued to dominate the precinct through his unfalteringly virtuoso designs, Carnaby Street was also taking colour from pioneering entrepreneurs increasingly attracted to the street's torrentially prospecting potential. The first wholly vegetarian enterprise, Cranks, opened a flagship restaurant called Salad Table at 22 Carnaby Street that year, as well as a second shop at 24, for the sale of vegetarian health foods, and additionally expanded round the corner into owning a self-service restaurant at 10 Ganton Street, as well as initiating an unprecedented wholemeal bakery and juicery at 17 Newburgh Street. Marion Foale and Sally Tuffin, two ex-Royal College of Arts fashion students, opened a small but devastatingly original outlet at 4 Ganton Street, with an all-white interior designed by Tony Laws, sliding mirrors from floor to ceiling, and with clothes hung on scaffolding construction, lit by 500 red, white and blue light bulbs. As one of the many rivals to Stephen's Tre Camp boutique, Foale and Tuffin were amongst the first to experiment with cutting trousers exclusively for women by reducing the number of pleats and darts so that they became closer-fitting, flattering sexy garments. The two also provided slim trouser suits worn with loose tunic tops in tough cowboy style corduroy and streamlined linen, sold to celebrities like Cathy McGowan, the model Patti Boyd, and Edina Ronay. As a note of their exclusivity at the time, Sally Tuffin commented on how, 'we were very careful with our sample fabrics. We kept the offcuts in bin bags. We were very aware that people shouldn't know what we were using.'

A contemporary mapping of John Stephen's monopoly on the Carnaby Street village, included highlights like George Malyard's theatrically camp Head Gear, Malyard having almost instantly made John Stephen's flowered shirts into a favourite, purchasing them on a daily basis in every available permutation of colour, with the same obsession that Brian Jones of the Rolling Stones manifested in the same period, by ordering dozens of floral shirt creations from Ossie Clark. Malyard designed chi-chi hats for girls and boys, and engineered a lucrative killing by acquiring a large consignment of French naval cadets' caps decorated with gold oak leaves that went into instant ballistic popularity, encouraging him to design similarly-styled caps in suede, leather, velvet, corduroy and denim. The opportunistic success provided by the seminal French naval caps was the equivalent to Malyard of John Stephen's felicitous acquisition of the thousands of un-saleable McCaul's polo shirts that had helped establish his little-known business in 1960.

At the time the windows of the Ravel boutique, owned by Raoul Chaussures of Oxford Street, like the other fashionable shoe specialist Monty Stewart's Toppers, were a multicoloured pedic architecture of block-heeled, round-toed shoes in purple suede, patent leather, two-tone, striped and quartered, as well as blatant design-candy like pop art plastic baseball boots in black and white with chisel toes, flat heels and long cross-over laces. With three Carnaby Street branches to their credit, the manager of Ravel, Leslie Wise commented on the street's spectacular attention-pulling magnitude, as a bonus on any of their other shops, and as producing 'twice as much business in half the time, while offering one quarter the comfort.' There was also Tom Salter's newly-opened Gear, a full-on hallucinated furniture and hardware shop, specialising in Art Nouveau, Tiffany lamps, chest-of-drawers and wardrobes painted in hectic primaries, huge gilt-foliated gas lamps, and oddities like coal scuttles in olive-green and glaring London Transport red. There was Rene, the florist, owned by Mrs Oscar Danin, Detroit Cleaners, Univeral Commissions, betting office, Como Snacks, coffee bar, the Bonbonaire restaurant, James Galt who sold toys, Lord John, Lady Jane, Irvine Sellars, Mates, and dominating it all, as a monolithic construct, the John Stephen Department Store, built to give space to the congested shopping crowds. Stephen had his offices located on the top floor, extending to a studio used by Myles Anthony and his team for constructing window displays, and incorporated a Kenco Coffee Bar into the first floor that sold men's clothing. As a way of endorsing his lucrative commercial expansion, at the expense of the tiny shops that had been his formative building blocks, Stephen argued for the necessity of space. 'We'd noticed that the still increasing volume of visitors was creating problems. Having six or eight people in one of my little shops gave them such a crowded look that potential customers had a habit of passing by. The department store provides plenty of room for browsing, and we've even had the space to put a café in the basement.'

Mods hadn't as yet dispensed with the John Stephen look, or Carnaby Street as their prime fashion locus and convening point on Saturdays, but the proliferation of imitators, combined with the street's dispersal into the beginnings of merchandizing – the John Stephen Department Store sold thousands of Carnaby Street imitation road signs to tourists – was beginning to chip at its cool ethic of gritty street cred legitimate to Mods. With the boyish looking, size-zero, Leslie Hornsby, a.k.a. Twiggy, dominating fashion photography with her androgynous, skinny, gamine features, the first hints of a possible Carnaby Street implosion were hinted at by some of John Stephen's most loyal customers, the Kinks, in their archly sardonic take on the street, the hit single, *Dedicated Follower Of Fashion*. As a lyricist, with an acute sense of how to dress sharply on and off stage, Ray Davies' perceptions of the optimally hip street to which he so regularly returned to invest in the look, were persuasively accurate. All of the narcissistic hedonism of the dandified Mod collective got translated into his overview of the Carnaby Street eruption into meltdown: 'They seek him here, they seek him there/In Regent Street and Leicester Square/Everywhere the carnabitian army marches on/ Each one a dedicated follower of fashion.' The distinctly bisexual intimations in the song of a man pulling 'his frilly nylon panties right up tight,' were also prescient of the mutation in men's fashion from highly self-conscious Mod to overstated dandy, that in time would, as the decade progressed, submerge the Carnaby look. Promoting the song live, Dave Davies of the Kinks wore thigh-length leather waders, with a shocking pink jacket, the sleekly gloved on boots being a copy of the style girls had elected to team with micro-minis, as an accented sexual turn-on. The song's flip-side, *I'm Not Like Everybody Else*, only further accentuated sexual ambiguity and outsider pride in its message, as Mod and gay fashions dissolved temporarily into a seamless unity

John Stephen's clothes, and their topological provenance, Carnaby Street, were at the centre of the salient thrust to reinvent masculinity, as the decade grew more assertively volatile in laying down its dual signature of clothes and

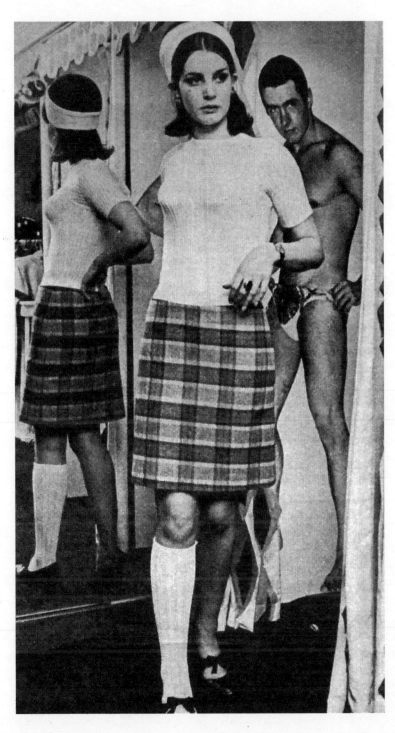

Myles Antony decorated the women's changing rooms with male blow-ups in skimpy briefs. You could fall in love while you changed.

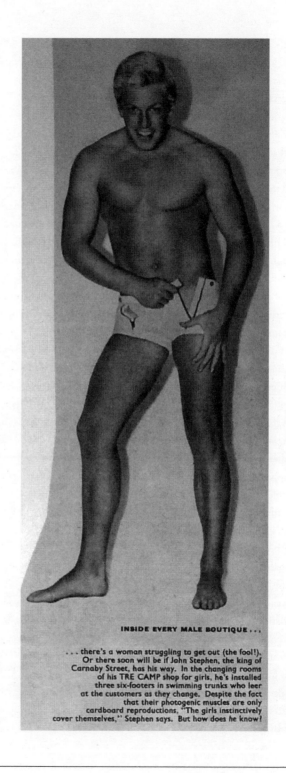

INSIDE EVERY MALE BOUTIQUE...

... there's a woman struggling to get out (the fool!).
Or there soon will be if John Stephen, the king of
Carnaby Street, has his way. In the changing rooms
of his TRE CAMP shop for girls, he's installed
three six-footers in swimming trunks who leer
at the customers as they change. Despite the fact
that their photogenic muscles are only
cardboard reproductions, "The girls instinctively
cover themselves," Stephen says. But how does he know!

One of the
notorious male
blow-ups in
Tre Camp, a
throwback to
beefcake.

music as the inseparable spearheads of its sexually questing advance. '1966 was a hot year,' Jon Savage writes of its confused gay and social milieu, and eclectic musical tastes, 'crowded with clamor and noise as seven-inch singles were cut to the limits of the then available technology. Hit 45's by the Yardbirds, the Rolling Stones, the Beatles, the Supremes, James Brown, the Byrds, The Who, Junior Walker, Wilson Pickett and Bob Dylan were smart and mediated, harsh and sophisticated, monomaniacally on the one or, raga-like right out of Western perception into the eternity of one chord. Everything was wound more and more uptight, as generational assertion reached a psychotic pitch.'

Meanwhile, John Stephen's original girls' boutique, Tre Camp, not only attracted a heavier influx of Mod girls to the street, but continued through the use of highly controversial homoerotic male blow-ups to perturb journalists through its deliberately bisexual disruption of gender. The interchangeable nature of Stephen's line between the sexes, together with the interior of a shop that parodied his rivals in the street catering for men, was a cause of real concern in an article in the *New York Tribune*, written by Hebe Dorsey in the attempt to undermine Stephen's deliberate contempt for convention in the shaping of unisex clothes. 'It's Tre Camp,' the journalist reported, 'even if the salesgirls don't know what that means. You can't blame them too much either, Tre Camp being a combination of tres (French for very) and camp (American for, well, camp) ... Inside the changing rooms are not the usual mirrors, but three blow-up, life-size pictures of boys. Handsome boys, who are what's more, in various states of undress. One, a blond Adonis type (and an art student in real life) is bare-chested and is sliding down his trunks zipper (which, however is placed sideways) while giving you a full, toothy smile. In the second fitting room, there is a slightly built and what the English call a sweet-looking boy, in trunks again, and taking off, – no, not his trunks – but his shirt, and looking at you in a sort of sad and deadpan way. The boy is the lead singer in a new beat group called The Carnaby.' The journalist was equally disturbed by Myles Antony professing that the genderless shop mannequins were 'bisexual. Their breasts and wigs come off – and we can use them in the boys' stores too.' It was inevitable too, that the characteristic detail Stephen applied to his men's creations became diffused into the complementary designs he created for women. A *Sunday Independent* feature for 17 April 1966, called 'The Quant Stephen Miracle', gave particular focus to the 27-year-old Myles Antony's controversially innovative window-dressing achievements for the John Stephen group. Described as wearing an expensively cut fawn double-breasted John Stephen jacket, Myles Antony informed Norman Barry that Stephen had 'achieved in seven years

what the Mayfair fashion people did in two hundred.' Justifiably unapologetic about his overtly homoerotic themed displays, Antony attributed his
flagrantly experimental risk-taking to the conditioning of the times. 'My
whole approach has been to bear in mind the age group and temperament
of our customers. I have tried to create windows to interest and amuse them,
bringing into the displays the uninhibited and exciting attitudes which make
young people tick.'

Of the moment, and no less attractive in their use of inventive colour
and dare than those of Quant or Foale and Tuffin, who were favourites of
Stephen's, Stephen's clothes for girls were nonetheless their equal in detail,
experimentally configured patterns, and often ahead of them in terms of
modernism, and the refusal to draw on period revival as the resources of
inspiration. For Tre Camp Stephen designed sharply-cut suits in two-tone
leathers and suedes, the beige suede offering a combination of purple, orange
or red at the collar, waistband, cuffs and hem. The leather suit, with both
suede and leather versions having two buttoned patch pockets on the yoke of
the jacket, came in navy or black, combined with white or lavender collars,
cuffs and waistband, and a pink, white or lavender skirt. The suede or leather
skirts were cut to an ultra-mini 14in length, as a defiantly sexual statement of
Stephen's forward-presenting modernism. Mod girls had by now adopted a
hairdo similar to their male counterparts, a backcombed, tiered effect, only
the style was shaped slightly longer at the sides and back, while leaving the
ears exposed, a cut taken to its androgynous extremes by Steve Marriott
and his band associates the Small Faces. Contemporary with the opening
of Tre Camp, the pop singer Julie Driscoll, the singer with Brian Auger
Trinity, who had gone Top Ten with a cover of the Bob Dylan song, *(This)
Wheel's On Fire*, was photographed with singers Long John Baldry and Alan
Walker, all wearing John Stephen clothes, in a club called Darling, the three
of them posed next to the scarlet Austin that housed the club's PA system.
Julie Driscoll was pictured wearing a purple crepe catsuit with orange bands,
the fly-fronted zip and trouser button designed to be interchangeable with
a man's trouser fastening. As a suitably camp flourish, Julie trailed a fringed
purple boa round her neck and shoulders, like a species of marine fauna.

Stephen's preoccupation with unisex also had him create personality-
shaping double-breasted needlecord trouser suits for girls, the high six-
button fastening and epaulettes on the shoulders, making them almost
indistinguishable from those he designed for men. In one photo shoot, Jackie
Blake, modelling the suit for John Stephen, lodges her chin on Eden Kane's
shoulder, drawing attention to his mauve and white striped fluffy collared

sweater, while he nonchalantly pretends to be engaged in reading Andrew Ewart's topical novel *The World's Wickedest Women*.

The singer Kiki Dee, who sang backup vocals for Dusty Springfield before going on to an acclaimed solo career, was another early photographic model for Stephen's alluring, limited edition lines for Tre Camp, and was photographed alongside Mick Avory, the fashionista drummer with the Kinks, wearing an antique leather culotte with a belted tunic top, to be worn with shirts or polo necked sweaters, and also in an antique leather trench-coat with epaulettes and an outstandingly extended back vent for signalling detail. As interestingly, Mick Avory was shot in a new Camelot-shouldered John Stephen suede jacket, his preference being stated for beige and green, while Stephen's appetent range of colours extended to turquoise, mid-blue, grey and brown, the fabrics in themselves creating a warm, mellow, in-store block of overwhelming colour. Not only was the cut of the jacket totally original, but Stephen again introduced a gender-free palette in suede never before associated with men, like green, turquoise, mid-blue, and grey.

Pushing his showbiz-like purple Cadillac, or gun-metal grey Rolls, into the West End from St James', John Stephen, the impeccably-dressed, formally suited Mod svengali, was riding on a high, the financial crisis of the previous year that had threatened the John Stephen Organisation with extinction, having been converted into profit by the systems implanted by Thornton Baker into an optimistic financial thermal that continued throughout 1966–67. Recessions throughout the 1960s occurred with air-pocketing regularity every two years, with concessions having to be made within the business to allow for any sustained lows, which in Stephen's case usually meant temporarily cutting back on publicity and suspending Mike McGrath's services for two or three months at a time as a compensatory measure. But 1966, like the Kinks' liltingly sardonic hit single, *Dedicated Follower Of Fashion*, was a high point for the John Stephen Organisation, with its look synchronistically dissolving into the style-hungry needs of the fashionista milieu, who were attracted on a daily basis to the street's gravitational pull. John Stephen was by this time a celebrity demanding constant media attention, and when in a moment of drunken recklessness, he uprooted a number of daffodils in his local Jermyn Street, the press blew the incident up into exaggerated proportions, with headlines reading, 'King of Carnaby Street in Jermyn Street Vandalism,' and 'John Stephen Drunk in St James.' And although Stephen endeavoured to maintain an anonymous public profile, stating memorably in an interview, 'please don't mention my name, mention my clients,' he had in fact become as popular as the bands he dressed, with such attention to style, his private life monitored by the invasive scrutiny of the media, and his photo appearing strategically with potential suitors, the girls supposedly on the edge of persuading Stephen to relinquish his status as one of the most eligibly handsome British bachelors amongst bright young things. Stephen though, more realistically, remained singularly obsessed by work, and the consolidation of his group, even to the point of turning up hours late for an interview won with relentless persistence on Mike McGrath's part with Godfrey Wynn, actor, journalist and presenter of *Housewives' Choice*, and one of the most influential journalists of the time, having been both a Downing Street and White House correspondent. The imperious and understandably indignant Wynn, who claimed that not even heads of state had kept him waiting, was left to sour, before Stephen showed, having given priority to attending his Brighton shop, where there had been an overnight break-in. That Stephen attached greater significance to a minor disruption of trade in his East Street Brighton premises, than the prestige that came with a favourable Wynn interview, indicates something of the extent to which he was unremittingly work-driven as the 1960s peaked in a furore of sensationally tonic colours bottled into his explosive Soho alley.

Triggered into action by Stephen's success in dominating the London look, Austin Reed, through the instigation of Barry Reed, somewhat cautiously opened the Cue shop, managed by Colin Woodhead, the name deriving from an advertising campaign involving the cartoon figure Cue, as the creation of Alan Aldridge, who was later to work in close association with the Beatles on *Yellow Submarine*. Imitating Stephen's integration of sounds into a shop interior, the Cue boutique was fitted with a Bang & Olufsen music centre that ripped out the latest in pop experimentation from the likes of the Stones, the Beatles, The Who, the Kinks and the Yardbirds. With a large goatskin rug as a centrepiece on the floor, modernistic chairs, cubist-style typography, and a flashing pinball machine in the corner, the severely-undermined traditionalists Austin Reed, alerted to John Stephen's innovative, upbeat retailing, hit in on the contemporary market with a range featuring looped alpaca cardigans, knitted shirts, white roll necks as an obligatory Mod constant, black and white vinyl peacoats, and a line of wickedly cut Italian-styled, two-piece suits. While lacking in Stephen's impulsive originality and street-edge, the upmarket Cue shop proved a commercial success, redeeming the otherwise obsolete Austin Reed traditionalist tailoring, by the patronage of the likes of Jeff Beck, and his bandmates, the Yardbirds, and by attracting the discriminating attention of a wealthier and slightly older market than Stephen's inveterate teen clientele. But if there was an enforced radical image makeover at Austin Reed, indicative of the times, then there was nonetheless strong resistance on the part of the directors to change. An internal note to shareholders from the company director, Barry Reed, expressed not only a semi-apologetic tone, but deep scepticism about the venture into modernism. 'I find it difficult to express this to you in detail,' Barry Reed wrote, his manner of reserve already a decade behind John Stephen's intransigent pioneering, 'but its purpose is to cater to young men who like to dress in more advanced styles than normal. To be frank, I have been quite surprised by the amount of business achieved in this small department. It means we have got coming into our Regent Street shop men who we never saw before.' Reed's attempt to coerce shareholders into the necessary acceptance of change was a fight maintained on every level of the enterprise, with Austin Reed's longstanding suppliers, Barran's of Leeds, initially refusing to execute Colin Woodhead's proposal to lower waistbands, sew on belt loops and taper trousers to the fashionable 14in width. Not that Cue found favour with all fashion critics, and Barry Fantoni conceived of it as a spurious pretender to originality and little more than a commercial adjunct to the scene, aimed cynically at rejuvenating a tired business. 'Some of the things are wild enough: white PVC macs and white Stetsons, which Woodhead himself prances about in. But many of them are loosefitting jet-age clothes that add fashion to function, garments as comfortable behind a wood-rim mini steering wheel as in a supersonic jet. Inevitably Woodhead's clothes look and feel best on his own kind of shape: skinny chest (38), sloping shoulders, narrow, flamenco dancer's hips. They are also aimed at his own age group, the post-teen, post-Carnaby age group that is carrying its demands for fashionable clothes forward into the seventies.'

Regent Street in the 1960s remained a shopping centre for the conservative elite, the Portland stone facades of its shops and department stores standing for quality in a fashionable precinct that prohibited change, revamped exteriors, or the least impropriety of window display. That an independent, like John Stephen, had a few blocks away in a no-go commercial area, succeeded in creating the look that Austin Reed was now forced to adopt, was something of an intractable conundrum to its shareholders and board of directors. The idea that a young Glaswegian, with only minimal training, had been instrumental in filtering London's entire style-hungry foot traffic into his downmarket corridor of shops, in a backwater only minutes away from the eminently Austin Reed Regent Street fascia, was in itself sufficient insult to their line, let alone having to make the concession to modify their styles, in an update attempting to compete with his market.

But the John Stephen look, no matter how it was approved by Mods, still met with resistance on the part of those hostile to change. Antipathy to any mode of dress seen as a desertion of masculinity, remained endemic. The interior designer, David Milnaric, recalls the social rejection he encountered at the time, for supporting the look. 'I remember going to Turnbull & Asser and having a bright pink shirt made, then being asked to leave the Cavalry Club for wearing it. This happened again in about 1966. I was wearing a white suit made by Blades, and was asked to leave Annabel's Nightclub for wearing a white suit.'

Liberty too, the imposing Regent Street fashion-house, with its Great Marlborough Street entrance backing on to the sustained segueing jostle of Stephen's Carnaby Street extravaganza, was forced to revitalise its traditional prints if they weren't to lose face to the prolific spending power of the new generation. To this effect they employed the services of Bernard Nevill, as consultant designer, to help rejuvenate their signature prints by injecting Islamic and Art Deco-inspired ranges of patterns into their generic patterns. Nevill's alluring combination of colour and fabric – he always worked backwards from the dress to the textile – succeeded, against the grain, in face-lifting Liberty into an artfully restrained but nonetheless commercial contender in the fashion race. Bernard Nevill, while rarely a Carnaby Street customer, was ultra-fastidious about his look and tended to use the high end designers to have his clothes made. 'I tried Blades, but the cut wasn't me,' he remembered. 'Michael Fish was very good for shirts, not so good for jackets. My tailors were Tommy Nutter (he was the most avant-garde): before that I had Welsh & Jeffries, just round the corner from Fortnum & Mason, Jarvis & Hamilton in Clifford Street, and Dege and Skinner of Savile Row ... I would spend hours or days going to Maxwell's my shoemaker and choosing the suede skins for my suede shoes. Going to Michael Fish and finding a piece of pale beige suede, I had a jacket made in it, and of course, and ties. The time involved was unbelievable. One suit made by Tommy Nutter, I slung a length of blue jeans cloth to him, and said make me a hand-stitched Savile Row suit in denim and he did, and following that one in panned velvet that I had especially woven from Liberty Prints, and dyed eau-de-nil, before having it made into a suit.'

The extent to which the 1960s fashion-conscious male would go to stand out in the crowd, was inexhaustible in its attention to finely-tuned detail. Hair too, was a significant gesture of cool, always cut short and impeccably groomed in John Stephen's case. Out of habit each Saturday afternoon, he and Frank Merkell would have their hair styled at Blow, in Henrietta Street, Stephen's hair, true to Mod ideals, being meticulously managed, sometimes

PERSONALITY

★ PAGE

Lord John, King of Carnaby Street, responsible for the gear that flows through the neon-lit mod paradise. But, surprisingly, he's not the extrovert that this kind of image suggests. Quiet and unassuming, he appears more of a courtier than a King. He's got a funny, spluttery laugh that's infectious, and bites his fingernails. His best feature are grey/blue eyes that are very direct. He doesn't talk all the time, but if he misses a point in the conversation, he likes to recap just to make sure. Born under Virgo, certain characteristics of his birth sign definitely apply in his case, like being an organiser and a shrewd businessman. John Stephen, tailor-made for success in a 1966 world, where you buy and live off the peg !

dry combed, but most often gelled into an unruffled fixture, as permanent as the hairdo presented by a James Dean or Elvis Presley. There is, phenomenally, no existing photo of John Stephen ever looking one fraction discomposed or out of style: the image sustained at the cost of time, and always modern, in the manner of those who set the times, rather than compete for the fashion lead. There is something permanent about John Stephen's image, in the way that certain faces not only define their epoch, but transcend it in the process of becoming a generation's iconic archetypes. Any photo of John Stephen taken in the period circa 1960–67 has, by sheer force of self-imposed, disciplined commitment to the look, to be a part of Mod iconography.

Meanwhile, Harrods, the departmental store for Coutts' account big spenders, sniffing the air of change that Stephen had courageously pioneered for a decade, as nothing less than the complete overhaul of masculinity, opened their Way-In shop in the store, as a necessary concession to the changing look, and, like Biba, green-lighted communal changing rooms as part of the liberating sexual currency of the times. Using John Stephen's shops as the basis for radically altered interior design in the mid-sixties, neighbouring boutiques in the Carnaby Street complex drew on progressively eclectic and outrageous sources to express the individual taste of the owner. The exterior of nearby Palisades in Ganton Street had a façade painted in fairground style by the artist Derek Boschier, while the interior screamed red, yellow, orange and purple, and counted amongst its fixtures, pinball tables, flashing lights and a working jukebox for vinyl 45s. On a more sophisticated level, John Michael called in Gerald McCann to design the interior of his 106 King's Road shop, with McCann inventively choosing Hessian walls, theatrical suede curtains, bronze fittings and aubergine paint for the walls. The boutique in the mid-sixties had become a design artefact, a zone for imaginative tourism, in which the consumer converted recreational shopping into an altered-state experience, with arresting colour combinations and sounds contributing to an ethos in which youth was the outright leader. Modern shopping for clothes, as a pleasurable rather than onerous experience, first introduced by Stephen's strategic approach of dissolving the barrier between assistant and customer, had by the mid-sixties become *de rigueur* as boutique ethic. It was John Stephen, who asked to describe the personable atmosphere created by his shops, synthesised their democratic qualities, by considering, 'nobody approaches the customer to ask them what they want. The assistants are all in casual clothes – in the case of the Mod Male in very Mod clothes. They just smoke and lean against the wall and put records on ... It's all very casual.' Stephen's initiating attitude to dissolving the intimidating presence that shop assistants often were, inhibiting the customer by their superior approach, was carried to laconic extremes in some of the unconventionally hip King's Roads boutiques, with *London Life* reporting, 'the success of boutiques depends on the originality of their stock and their relaxed atmosphere. Not only is there no hard sell, it is sometimes difficult to get any attention at all. The girls who work in them are invariably depressingly pretty, and manage to look always as if they are doing someone a favour by just holding the fort for an hour or two. They sit at the back somewhere reading magazines, entertaining their friends, or telephoning interminably about special orders of astrakhan mini-spats.'

1966 saw a former John Stephen employee, Michael Fish, who had worked for Stephen in the capacity of an assistant designer, open his 'Mr Fish' shop in Clifford Street, with the backing of Barry Sainsbury, his upmarket clothes carrying the trademark tag 'Peculiar to Mr Fish.' Fish, who was initially apprenticed to Jermyn Street shirt-makers, had started out making shirts often decorated with embroidery and ruffles for the celebrated Turnbull & Asser outlet, before graduating to the sensational hoopla surrounding Stephen's Carnaby Street, and dressing Terence Stamp in hectic Liberty prints for his role in the movie *Modesty Blaise*. Fish's expensive boutique, aimed prevalently at the moneyed Bond Street milieu, sold wide patterned kipper ties, decorative shirts, colourful suits in loud stripes and ethnic-inspired separates, and quickly became a renowned meeting place for the London boho glitterati. Pioneering the concept that dresses were equally suitable for men, and pushing hard on the notion, like John Stephen, of dissolving gender markers, Fish found an acquisitively supportive client in Mick Jagger, who was photographed on a Tangier visit in 1967, wearing a Mr Fish silk jacket with a hippy face painted on the back, and who was to wear one of the designer's chemises in white moiré over voile as a controversial fashion first for the Rolling Stones' unprecedented crowd-pulling concert in Hyde Park in 1969, as a memorial to their inspired musical founder Brian Jones. Fish too, scored a celebrity client in the ageless Noel Coward, for who he designed a customised single-breasted jacket with slightly curved lapels, made of bright purple hopsack weave (a Hessian-like effect) wool mix. The jacket was lined throughout with twill-weave silk printed in an all-over circle design in blues, greys and white, and fastened with two flat black buttons, with two smaller but similar style buttons at each cuff, and a deep flap covering the entrance to each of the two pockets, set at hip level.

The year was turning gold for John Stephen in Carnaby Street and on the King's Road; but the pressures over the controversial Myles Anthony windows remained. 'A newspaper phoned me the other day,' Stephen told

You meet strange people in Carnaby Street, but John Stephen seems undeterred.

Style Weekly, 'to find out if the police had asked me to remove young men modelling underwear from my windows. I told the reporter that our assistants were encouraged to wear clothes.' And as a sketchy portrait of John Stephen at the time, the Personality Page of *Boyfriend* highlighted his dominant characteristics as they appeared to the columnist. 'His best features are grey/blue eyes that are very direct. He doesn't talk all the time, but if he misses a point in the conversation, he likes to recap just to make sure. Born under Virgo, certain characteristics of his birth definitely apply in his case, like being an organiser and shrewd businessman.'

The same year, John Stephen added the Village Store to his agglomerate of Carnaby Street shops, situated opposite his Tre Camp shop, on two floors, selling girls' clothes and accessories made exclusively by John Stephen. With the original window display and pink and gold interior designed by Myles Anthony, Stephen again targeted the neglected component of society, Mod girls; the girlfriends of boys with an omnivorous, weekly-refuelled passion to renew the look. While outwardly expressing a preference of designing for men – and that year Stephen had conceived of marketing a range of transparent trousers for men, negating the idea on the grounds that it was 'too sexy' – he nonetheless designed with unstoppable enthusiasm for his girls' line, only on a smaller, compacted scale, and one that endorsed unisex as its dominant characteristic. Stephen's boys were girls, and his girls boys, in the designer's popular interchange of bisexually-orientated clothes. In Stephen's design repertoire the Mod male remained the peacock in his alley, and his girlfriend the inevitably lapsed and slightly disparaged fashion counterpart, who at best interfaced her boyfriend's superior notions of style. The same year, Stephen designed a scent exclusively for men; the cologne intended to be the first in a chain of toiletries for men, and coming packaged as a square chunky bottle in a white box lettered with the name John Stephen in black. The tangy, citrus-dominated scent, achieved a slow-burn popularity amongst John Stephen customers, but was discontinued after eighteen months on account of its being too far in advance of the times to create a sustained men's market.

That John Stephen was by 1966 beginning in essence to desert Mod culture could be argued by an advertisement posted in *Queen*, depicting a more soberly dressed city-look, inappropriately titled 'Portrait of a Hippy'. The young executive-type model, more King's Road than Carnaby Street, was shot wearing a white high-collared shirt, with a paisley patterned tie and matching handkerchief in the pocket of his high-buttoned, narrow-lapelled suit jacket, and with his short hair as the groomed paradigmatic antithesis to the hippy. The ad caption too, was a confused mix of contradictory values, as though Stephen had temporarily lost the plot. 'He's been seen in Carnaby Street. And worse. He actually buys clothes there. From John Stephen. Says not many people know about the more sober side. Keeps talking about jackets and suits, trousers, shirts and ties. Quality brand names and superior fabrics, wool and worsted, cashmere and mohair. Tailored discreetly and cut with flair to John Stephen's discerning designs. Says John Stephen suits him well. But he doesn't spread it around. Afraid his wife will find out that John Stephen can offer the same quality to women too.' The attempt to endorse the John Stephen custom-built line, as having quality equal to that of Gordon Deighton's designs for Trend at Simpsons, featured on an opposing page of the journal, reads in part like a self-negating concession to the idea that Stephen and Carnaby Street were the purveyors of inferior quality clothes, an idea first introduced into currency by opponents in the trade anxious to undermine Stephen for his endemic popularity.

The advertisement also played on the fundamental dichotomy of Stephen the man, who was both the creative advocate of uncompromising innovative Mod fashion, and also, as expressed through his own taste in clothes, a conservative favouring classic lines, and somebody whose personal dress sense invariably expressed the reticent aspects of modernism. One could argue that the separation of interests in Stephen – often a pronounced characteristic amongst style-chasers – Mary Quant, Calvin Klein and Yves St Laurent tended to dress down – was brought about by the imaginative aspect of the person projecting theatrically as the compensation for an otherwise repressed personality. According to Bill Franks, Stephen on holidays refused even to wear casual clothes for the beach, insisting on retaining his suited appearance, with his one concession to beach wear being the abandonment of his tie.

By 1966, the competition amongst London's trend-setting boutiques to access the lucrative fashion market for the clothes obsessed young had grown acute in terms of design rivalry. The increasingly outmoded tailors, Simpsons of Piccadilly, like Austin Reed, sensing their imminent demise if they failed to upgrade to modernism, brought in Gordon Deighton to introduce a new line for Trend that included twill double-breasted jackets, black slacks with a white boucle chalk stripe, lilac crepon and pyjama-striped shirts with separate white collar and cuffs, grey herring-bone suits with waist-high slanting vents, and silk ties in exotic flower prints. John Stephen, with his informal virtuoso approach to matching youth's needs with fine-tuned fashion radar and an entirely self-taught and maverick business acumen, had by virtue of his escalating success provoked the city's large-scale boardrooms into down-mooded, humiliated consternation. That Deighton's designs were almost a direct imitation of Stephen's mattered little in the need for the store to save face, and present a cool image to its younger clientele, who found Carnaby Street too pop for their look. The almost ubiquitous attempt on the part of copyists to homogenise Stephen, an accelerated process of outright saturated plagiarism was reported by the *Glasgow Herald*, lamenting that mass market capitalisation had killed off individual creativity in an exploitative nuke. 'The zest has gone from Carnaby Street, the loss of vision in the street means that male fashion is at the moment without a leader and become respectable. Big business, the establishment of the outfitting world, has moved in. Every store now has its male boutique offering second-rate reproductions of Carnaby Street styles without the novelty, the gaiety or the zaniness that typify the originals.'

In the effort to beat off the rogue traders who constantly trafficked ideas from his windows, Stephen continued to create one-offs and limited runs, often in small measures of fabric purchased from Ian Mankin on Commercial Road. Much of Stephen's pleasure as a designer came from the instinctual selection of remnants that contributed to the making of three shirts or a pair of slacks that proved unrepeatable, in that they would be gone from his windows within hours. Some of the unjustified neglect given Stephen by his fashion contemporaries doubtless originated from his insoluble link with the pop world, which at the time was viewed by the establishment as a transient phenomenon, and as an aberration of taste that would quickly lose significance. John Stephen, as the man who dressed rebel icons like the Rolling Stones, who were also considered amoral influences on youth by the media, was through his poppy designs relegated by consensus to an ephemeral fashion moment unworthy of gravity or critical respect. 1966 was the seminal altered-state year, in which John Lennon instigated public outrage by telling London's *Evening Standard* newspaper, that the Beatles were now more popular in celebrity status than Jesus Christ, a statement considered so flagrantly controversial that it subsequently triggered en masse burnings of Beatles' records in the Bible Belt of the Southern States. Issued with death threats by the Ku Klux Klan, the group's third American tour lived under a penumbra of violent protest, with John Lennon forced to undergo a public humiliation at the Chicago Press Conference on 11 August. John Stephen's inveterately symbiotic link with rock music led to his clothes being featured on a number of record sleeves that year, including the Rolling Stones' first self-written album, *Aftermath*, Cream's *Fresh Cream*, the Beatles' *Revolver*, the Kinks' *Face to Face*, the Small Faces' eponymous album, and *Animalism* by the Animals. Diffused across the photographic artwork for these sleeves were the floral, paisley and polka-dot shirts first made popular by Stephen, so too the wide belts and elephant cord hipsters, the leather flying jackets, the black knitted ties and polo neck knitwear that he had made popular in the permanent Italian summer feel of his London West End shops, tiny, alluring, and hypnotically beautiful as a tropical aquarium.

That rock music through its image and creative expression openly embraced recreational drug culture, be it speed, cocaine or heroin, helped feed reactionary opinion amongst the media that it was a genre corrupted by the excesses of hedonism the young were provoked into copying. That John Stephen was a leading proponent of the look adopted by rock and pop stars thought to have a deleterious influence on youth, tied him indirectly to the whole suspect sixties counterculture phenomenon. Too identified with the movement to ever be properly separated from it, John Stephen was submerged by his times; sucked so deep into their undertow, that he never properly resurfaced to receive the credit due for his exceptional originality in creating the look.

John Stephen, acutely sensitive of his brand reputation and exclusivity, took to the courts in 1966 seeking an injunction restraining Joseph Gold (Pall Mall Ltd) and Warren Allen Gold from trading under the name Lord John, but was unsuccessful in his objective to have the shop's name changed; and in the same month, Anthony Augustin O'Shea, a 20-year-old John Stephen shop manager, was fined £10 at Marylebone when he pleaded guilty to stealing £7 and a tie belonging to his employer. O'Shea at the time was earning £13 a week.

Meanwhile the energetic impact on sales created by pop stars wearing his clothes on stage continued to benefit Stephen with unnerving regularity. In his monthly *News of the World* column, ghosted by Mike McGrath, Stephen reported that after Long John Baldry had done a TV show in the North, wearing a grey suede lumber jacket with medallion buttons, twenty-eight girls took a Saturday coach trip to Carnaby Street with the incentive to purchase identical jackets. Another gossipy fashion moment comprised the fact that Mick Jagger had just recently bought a maroon and white check jacket, to be worn over plain maroon slacks from His Clothes; and that John Stephen's younger brother Alex was currently working in Mrs Ada Harris' menswear shop in Tooting, the same Ada Harris whose patronage had been paramount to John Stephen in his formative years in Beak Street, when her regular orders for his skinny-fit hipsters featuring horizontal pockets had sustained the business. In fact without the providential custom of Ada Harris

Kiki Dee, and Mick Avory of the Kinks, get into leather and suede. The skins were prepared in nearby Ganton Street.

as patron it's unlikely that John Stephen would have survived long enough to make the hesitant transition from relative Beak Street anonymity to the successful pitch of Carnaby Street.

The Outfitter also reported a film noir robbery and subsequent segueing car chase across St James' at 4am, one rain-drenched winter morning, following the theft of £600 worth of clothes from John Stephen's Domino Male shop. Two men driving a black Ford Anglia had abruptly pulled up at speed, shattered the window with a brick, filled the car with a confection of clothes grabbed from the display, and squealed off into the night pursued by police, before crashing the car in Arlington Street, and being detained. It's significant too, in terms of clothes appeal, that it was always Stephen's windows that were regularly broken, and never those of his rivals on the street. Called to the site to have his shop boarded, John Stephen with characteristic humour pinned his usual postscript to the boards: 'They couldn't wait for us to open.'

John Stephen predicted that shades of purple, mauve and lilac were the colours to best flatter men in 1966, and to this effect designed shirts, slacks, velvet jackets, ties, belts and sweaters in variant shades of mauve including dark purple and resonant violet. He was thirty years old, and unchangeably youthful, presided over Stephen House in Carnaby Street, but remained privately inscrutable, his sexuality necessarily closeted, and denying him any legitimate claim to making public the facts of a personal life invariably conscripted into a regime of relentlessly self-disciplined work. There was no way of getting at Stephen, no least give in his brilliant professionalism, and the hard facts of alcohol and periodic breakdowns, and a life spent with two devoted partners, were sensitive areas concealed from his public.

In fact, things had reached a crisis point in the triumvital Franks/Merkell/Stephen relationship, with Stephen and Merkell constantly having fierce altercations fired-up by their respective drink habits, and with Bill Franks finding himself taking on the role of intermediary in their incandescent drink and row wars. After a particularly vicious row that was the culmination of weeks of escalating liquor-fuelled run-ins, the distraught Stephen, after storming to his room and slamming the door shut resoundingly, took a massive overdose of Mogadon and Valium on top of the copious amounts of scotch he had drunk, and immediately lapsed into unconsciousness. Alerted instinctively to the fact that something was wrong, from the change of mood-temperature in the flat, Franks on going to Stephen's bedroom, discovered the empty bottles of tablets on which Stephen had overdosed, and frantically contacted emergency services. Rushed by an ambulance burning its siren in loud sonic alert, its blue emergency neon flashing in the London night, Stephen, who had stopped breathing on arrival at the hospital, was placed on a life-support machine, with Franks sitting up all night at the hospital. The prognosis was that Stephen was unlikely to survive, and that at some stage the machine would be switched off. With Bill Franks and Stephen's sister Rae maintaining a constant vigil, and desperate to facilitate some action that could be of use, Franks was advised to talk to Stephen in the hope that his friend would as a subliminal response somehow reconnect with consciousness. After what had been days of Stephen lying void in a coma, and having been told in preparation that the machine was to be unplugged, Franks after speaking to Stephen for a number of hours, noted a premonition of response, a flickery intimation that his coercive voice was getting through, like contact with deep space, and alerted a disbelieving nurse to the fact that Stephen was starting to come out of disconnect. Franks continued with his familiar reassuring voice to coax his partner through the re-entry to full consciousness, and achieved the result that medicine had discounted: his friend's removal to the day ward the next day, and his slow, recuperative rehabilitation to optimal energies.

Outwardly though, the Stephen façade of extreme shyness and social anxiety translated into an imperturbably defensive cool remained unchanged. Only able to relax in selective company, Stephen, who was naturally introspective, remained publicly on edge. Mental illness, as the subtext to his life, seems to have found its genetic marker in his mother, who had her first serious breakdown in 1960, after the family had been forced to leave their Govan home and relocate to an intensely depressing dockside Glasgow tenement. Felicitously relieved two years later by John Stephen buying them a house in Neilston, Renfrewshire, on the strength of his business growth, his mother continued to have periodic breakdowns every year, and to be medicated for the same manic cycle characterised by her son, with hyperactive peaks followed by catastrophic free-falls into inert solid-walled depression. A sense of loyalty and family bonding played an important part in Stephen's life, and extended particularly on his part to his young sister Rae, who throughout her school years had been the recipient of designer dresses sent her by her older brother from London exquisitely packed in layers of tissue and intended as gifts to celebrate occasions like her school qualifying dance, and her first year dance, events that recognised the transition between preparatory and secondary school stages. John Stephen also took on the solicitous role of organising and paying for Rae's summer holidays in Italy and France, and of a memorable teenage one in his house in Brighton, where Rae partied with boys often wearing John Stephen clothes, picked up from his East Street shop, as a Mod fashion statement. Rae, as an extension of her close family relationship with her brother, started working for the John Stephen Organisation when she was seventeen, as an office worker in his Queenslie Industrial Estate factory, before graduating to various posts in his shop in Hope Street, Glasgow, and finally to managing his girls' shop in Argyle Arcade.

Stephen, like most individuated outsiders, had by the age of thirty succeeded in creating a second family of his own, a self-created one in which Bill Franks and Frank Merkell were the key players, offering the continuous psychological support and domestic back-up necessary to help maintain the vulnerable and significantly impractical Stephen in a life singularly focused on accelerated work to the detriment of health or any form of recreation. If the 1960s was necessarily a decade of precipitous burn-out amongst its heroic pioneers, something manifested in the dangerously reckless ante and correspondingly early deaths of individuals like Joe Meek, Brian Epstein, Joe Orton, Brian Jones, Jimi Hendrix, Janis Joplin and Jim Morrison, then John Stephen, while surviving the decade, must also be counted amongst its casualties. Stephen, in the formation of his singularly inventive fashion empire, lived his times so intensely full-on, through the expression of his work, that his health unsurprisingly imploded from the sheer momentum of overreach. A persistent menu of cigarettes, alcohol, general lack of sleep, unprecedented chapters of unnerving early success, and the scorching burn-up of his neural circuitry, all contributed in part to his early cancer of the neck, and the residual side-effects of primitive radiotherapy that were to adversely impair his trachea for the rest of his life. But in 1966, for the key Carnaby Street players, time appeared temporarily to stand still, having an optimistic generation believe it was living in a permanent exclusion zone, a self-created euphoric space-time discontinuous with any other epoch in history. To its direct participants, the 1960s were a big-screen colour-soaked movie experience, hedonistic, self-referential, and totally modern in creating an ethos without apparent recourse to the past, and one that appeared too vital to ever end. But there was a political downside too, to the hedonistic thermal on which John Stephen and the pop generation surfed, and that was the social underclass, made apparent to British viewers by documentaries like *Cathy Come Home*, as the brutally realistic story of a homeless mother, and globally too by the tensions triggered by the US President Lyndon Johnson's decision to dispatch large numbers of combat troops to the legally contested Vietnam War. With the overwhelming superiority of US firepower partially strangulated by guerrilla attacks and amphibious operations, and with the US retaliating by the use of chemical defoliants like Agent Orange, the American intervention met with consolidated resistance on the part of active protestors. Vietnam was the mushrooming penumbra that infected sixties' optimism and dented the hope maintained particularly by the generational hippies of visionary idealism replacing active technomilitary ideologies. While the UK refused adamantly to offer military support to the US war effort, and elected simply to set up the creation of the British Advisory Mission (BRIAM), London was still the arena of solidly voiced opposition to the war, a protest involving regular clashes with mounted police on the part of the vociferous anti-war contingent, that included Mick Jagger amongst its consolidated numbers one memorable stone-throwing day outside the American Embassy in Grosvenor Square.

Lost in the immediacy of his creations, John Stephen remained outwardly little effected by the political climate, other than where it touched on fashion. The Mod ethic was in the course of mutating, but the look persisted, defined in the crowd by the more rigorous style aficionados who continued to inspire and be inspired by John Stephen. Stephen's Carnaby Street prowess in 1966 was additionally supported by the success of his line in the US, where low-rise hipsters, bright floral-print shirts with high white collars and cuffs, Dutch Boy caps in cloth, suede, or smooth leather with braided half-bands, brilliant extra-wide paisley and polka-dot ties, double-breasted 4–6 button sport or suit coats, and bulky-knit turtleneck poor boy sweaters proved the highlights of the fashion moment. The cover of *Life* magazine's May issue showed four young Brian Jones look-alikes standing in front of the high-rise Chicago skyline, dressed in cutaway teal corduroy jackets, chessboard-patterned check trousers and shirts with long spear-pointed button-down collars. Stephen's fitted or shaped look jackets, characterised by slightly broader shoulders, a definite waist suppression, and with very deep side vents with a flair at the bottom of the jacket were particularly popular amongst a Mod-look converted American youth looking to create their own sense of cool.

But the frenetic energies of the pilled-up Mod ethos to which John Stephen was inextricably tied by the Ferrari speed of his own chemistry was starting to be invaded by the bohemian lifestyle of hippie culture, with its muted, passive energies, period revival clothes, LSD-induced altered states, and orientation to psychedelic rock as the sonic interpreter of substance-hallucinated psychic landscapes. In defiant opposition to hippie-inflected culture, an intransigent Mod splinter-group mutated into hard Mods, or gang Mods, and while they retained the basic elements of ticket dress – three-button suits, Fred Perry and Ben Sherman shirts, Sta-Prest trousers and Levi's jeans – they mixed them with working class accessories such as braces, and cherry-red Dr Marten boots, and got their hair cropped short in the skinhead style. These were hard factionists determined to transcend the Faces, and resist the concession to bohemianism, with its soft-focus foppish clothes and pot and acid culture, and reinstate Mod values hardwired to speed and individually sharp dressing with attitude.

The gap, too, between Carnaby Street and the King's Road, as the two dominant thoroughfares of innovative, gender-flexi fashion, were beginning to widen under tensions created by the inerasable distinctions of class. Barry Fantoni pointed to the fundamental dichotomy between the two epicentres of action as a discerning aesthetic backed by money. 'Carnaby Street customers are,' he wrote, '(to use an unfashionable expression) working class. While they think nothing of spending a week's wages on a complete outfit, the class that shop on the King's Road will spend that sort of money on a shirt.' It was a constant that the press were continuously to remind John Stephen of his own working class background, and invasive entrepreneurial impudence in challenging the traditional methods of fashion. Stephen's Soho was considered déclassé by the Chelsea set, a dodgy side of town in which the underworld congregated, selling sex, drugs, and fashion for gay men. It was also cheap by comparison, in that Stephen's rapid turnover was reliant on affordable prices, whereas King's Road mark-ups and rents were proportionately higher. As an overview of some of the prices being charged that year in the King's Road boutiques, we might consider that James Wedge and Pat Booth's Countdown at 137 King's Road sold clothes in a range between £2–£60 Ossie Clark's Quorum, at 52 Radnor Walk, on a quota of £3–£30, Susan Locke at 414 King's Road sold shirts at £3 and trouser suits at £20, while Unique at 56b King's Road, managed by Eric Shemilt, clothes between £3–£15, and Vanessa Frye, of Sloane Street, whose prices ranged between £2–£35. Chelsea was sniffy and made no countdowns on account of its origins, its men preferring to dress in Art Nouveau period revival, and its leggy girls for provocation, in mini-skirts that looked according to *What's On In London* 'like scarves that have slipped down a bit.' Girls had also taken to wearing pop art nail transfers, with white nails decorated with black transfers, or vice versa, and the King's Road crowd hung out in the Chelsea Drugstore, a throwback to Stephen's seminal Carnaby Street Drugstore, originally a chemist, with a highly stylized chrome-and-neon soda fountain upstairs, and in the 1970s the site to Vivienne Westwood and Malcolm McClaren's punky SEX boutique. The oscillating tension between Soho and the King's Road as the two epicentres of rivalry in fashion extended also to hip places at which to be seen. Soho had the Trattoria Terrazza, which looked out on to Romilly Street, with its sophisticated Italian cuisine, and its hothouse basement Positano Room impacted with wickedly effervescent bright young things, whereas the King's Road boasted Alvaro Maccioni's Alvaro's, a magnet to pop bohemians and faux-aristocrats, and so driven by accelerated patronage that, as the ultimate gesture of restaurant cool, its phone number was ex-directory. And Soho, as Stephen's affronting clothes fortress, excelled in nightclubs like the riffish The Bag o'Nails, that played live music by the residential John Mayall Blues Band, and most famously as the epitome of hipster pursuit, the Ad Lib Club, reached by a tiny lift in an alleyway behind Leicester Square, with mirrored walls and the dinner-jacketed DJ's turntables concealed inside a piano, the clubs speakers resounding like hangar noise into the murky blue Soho dawn. But Faces were losing out on originality as the Chelsea look adopted a hybrid mixture of exaggerated dandification and Eastern bazaar, in the attempt to challenge Stephen's equally colourful but more minimal modernistic line. As a fashion marker Mod was still there, in the likes of its modified look promoted by the likes of the Small Faces, whose street-gutsy soul-charged No 1 hit single, *All Or Nothing*, that year placed Mod back on the map as a fiercely recombinant energy. Late to the Mod scene, but quickly taking on the role of Carnaby Street style elitists, with their white shoes purchased from Toppers, their imposing television screen-shaped black glasses, their ultra-low slung hipsters, inexhaustible repertoire of button down collar shirts in every pattern created by John Stephen and Lord John, and with their girlie exaggeration of Mod hairdos, cockney accents and chippy street edge, the Small Faces came to represent style legends for all aspiring teenage fashion aficionados, as well as a distinct class identification with the affordable Carnaby Street signature.

John Stephen as style guru to the male look in the early sixties remained caught in the middle of the transitional phase between Mod and hippie, unwilling to desert Mod sartorial values, but at the same time impelled commercially to design for the dedicated follower of fashion. Stephen, no matter his individual preferences, continued in the role of style magnate to the constantly mutating updated fashion of mid-sixties, unapologetically swinging London, a city at the time so saturated by the radical changes brokered by its uncompromising youth, that it was to remain for the rest of the decade the outright cultural marker upfront of both Europe and America.

7

HAVE YOU SEEN YOUR MOTHER BABY STANDING IN THE SHADOWS?

It is rumoured, although the facts are variable, that LSD was introduced into Britain by Michael Hollingshead, a young employee at the British Cultural Exchange, who had experimented with the mind-altering substance on a cultural visit to LA. Hollingshead had been advised by Aldous Huxley, the author of *The Doors of Perception of Heaven and Hell*, a known recreational user, and the author of the futuristic allegory *Brave New World*, to contact a Harvard researcher who was prosetylising for psilocybin, called Timothy Leary. After experimenting with the drug together, Leary suggested Hollingshead visited London with 2,000 trips of acid, purchased and imported legally from a government laboratory in Prague, with the affirmed mission to turn London on to the intensely hallucinated states that the drug provided. Hollingshead, with the financial backing of an ex-Etonian impresario called Desmond O'Brien, implemented the plan, and based the London office of the World Psychedelic Centre at 21 Pont Street, Chelsea, just off the King's Road thoroughfare, with its two upmarket John Stephen shops, competing with the John Michael shop, as well as Michael Rainey's newly opened, distinctly foppish and elitist Hung On You. The apartment, as the projected basis of recreational acid experimentation, with a mission to proselytise Britain, was an Art Deco Belgravia affair, incorporating sounds from John Cage, Ravi Shankar, Soriabin and the bossa nova, while images of mandalas, yantras, Hindu gods and the Buddha were visuals posted on the ceiling. The apartment was also stocked with multiple copies of the Leary/Alpert/Metzner *The Psychedelic Experience; A Manual based on the Tibetan Book of the Dead*, 200 issues of the *Psychedelic Review* ed. Drs Weil and Metzner, and 200 copies of *The Psychedelic Reader*, edited by Gunther Weil. That LSD was quickly to replace speed as the drug that left an indelible signature on the collective psyche, was to have a profound and permanently altering effect on fashion, the playful elements and tropically drenched colours associated with acid finding their equivalents in the loud tones, exaggerated swirls, revamped military tunics and free-floating hectic mandala patterns that began to enter fashion post-1966.

Despite the new pandemic for second-hand clothes, period revival, military tunics and psychedelically saturated kaftans, Stephen and his by now sensationally mediatised street, was still the nub of the 1960s look, and Stephen, as its originator, more personally in touch with what kids on the street wanted to wear than any other contemporary designer. In a defining song of the period, *London Boys*, Marc Bolan had expressed the enduring Mod interest in serendipitous thrift, in the lines, 'Do you remember/Going to Petticoat Lane/With all the conceptions/Moving in your brain'; the conception of rooting for home-made glamour on the street conforming to the very ethic from which Carnaby Street had evolved. Mods understand-ably resented the upmarket King's Road intrusion on their look, and the attempt to reclassify it through the hybrid of expensive materials and period revival embellishments that obscured the dynamic of its essentially simplistic modern line. For Mods, their look was necessarily sharp, clean, detailed but not fussy, directly original and stand out, and strictly Western, as opposed to the Eastern influences that came rather superficially to permeate sixties fashion under the inspirational tutelage of LSD.

If in 1967 the generation John Stephen had dressed had either grown up or were starting to desert him on account of his concessions to a more popular market, and the fact that Carnaby Street was no longer patronised by a coterie of committed Faces, largely known to each other on the Mod circuit, then the change in the type of customer was gradual but significant. With unstoppable enthusiasm for his line Stephen created another first by putting men into brightly coloured satin shirts, with high, long pointed collars, puffed sleeves and three or four button cuffs, the sensual fabric carrying the sheen of slippery fish on the racks, and coming in fruity, sumptuous colours like imperial purple, dark blue, glowering vermilion, bottle green, oily black and champagne. The dandification of the male, through the popularity of the satin shirt, a fabric previously concealed in its use on men in the context of jacket linings and the backs to waistcoats, was another inspired fashion first for John Stephen. For most Mod-influenced teenagers, there was still only

one way forward, and that was the fashion moment, invariably originating from Stephen's premises and then copied in rapid-fire movements across town by the chains. Stephen, as evidenced by a photo of the pop balladeers the Merseybeats, in *Big Beat Magazine*, pictured modelling his new designs, was also experimenting with light blue denim shirts with lace-up front and cuffs, and as a mark of daring sexual provocation, low-rise hipsters with a white lace-up front. Denim shirts with three-button polo-necked collars, as a total remake of the shirt, also featured prominently in his stock, and were accepted in some social circles, if worn with a jacket, as a permissible substitute for a tie.

Stephen's loud blazers in orange, blue and white pyjama stripes were from the first endemically popular amongst Mods, and his association with pop further enforced, when Mick Avory, the drummer with the Kinks, was seen on *Top of the Pops*, wearing a white Russian-styled satin shirt with peasant trimming and a round collar, as one of his designs. The BBC switchboard was jammed literally for hours after the Kinks' performance, with callers anxious to trace the shirt's provenance, before being directed to John Stephen's stores to buy the same, highly popularised shirt. Stephen also widened his leisurewear range by designing lambs-wool blazers with concealed pockets under the deep side vents for additional stylistic elegance, in the effort to beat the ubiquitous style-killer – crumpled pockets: a personal obsession with Stephen, who used his own pockets as a mini-office. He fought shy, however, of the endemic introduction of revamped military tunics into popular fashion, the jackets often lifted from Royal Engineers' surplus stock, and worn subversively by youth, as a political statement on the part of a pacifist generation who considered that war was a wholly unjustified offensive. That military costumes purchased second-hand were popularised by the likes of outlets like I Was Lord Kitchener's Valet, and Granny Takes A Trip, as essential street wear, was all part of the confused political incentives of the time. 1967 became stylistically the year of the braided military tunic, when the Beatles wore customised band uniforms on the front of their Peter Blake designed *Sergeant Pepper's Lonely Hearts Club Band* album sleeve, an upended piece of innovative British psychedelia that musically projected the ludic sensory appeal and visually surrealistic aspects of acid experimentation on to freakily studio-manipulated layered pop; the album's staggering commercial popularity placing the Beatles at the inspired apogee of their sixties' success.

Male sixties fashion was at its most resourcefully eclectic as Mod turned bohemian, and the journalist Ray Connolly, interviewing Mick Jagger in his

John's Children wear John Stephen kaftans as pretty boys in paisley and stripes.

fourth-floor Marylebone flat, reported that Jagger was wearing at the time, 'puce pants with clown's cravat to match, and a cosmic shirt with stars and moons and other celestial objects printed on it. Round his waist is a sequinned tasselled belt which be bought locally in the King's Road. He bought his socks at Marks & Spencer.' Jagger's clothes were largely an improvised mixture of cross-town choices, extending from John Stephen's constantly refreshed lines, to another favourite, Stephen's ex-colleague Michael Fish in Clifford Street, who was selling double-breasted printed corduroy furnishing fabric suits in psychedelic yellow, orange and red stripes. Jagger also, according to mood, favoured expensive bespoke threads from Rupert Lycett-Green's Blades at 25 Dover Street, or the more quirkily advantageous revamps issuing from the likes of Michael Rainey's Hung On You boutique, and Nigel Waymouth's Granny Takes A Trip, as Chelsea apparel, the one situated off the King's Road at 22 Cale Street, the other direct on the thoroughfare at 488 King's Road. Using Brian Jones' light-sealed hash-musty apartment at 1 Courtfield Road, Chelsea, as a basis for recreational LSD experimentation, Jagger had by now joined company with the likes of gallery owner Robert Fraser, Michael Rainey of Hung On You, where he purchased suits, the arch fashionista Christopher Gibbs, who specialised in antiques, the aristocrat Stash Klossowki, and the ufologist John Michell, whose recently-published book *The Flying Saucer Mystery* was linked symbiotically to the mystic visions and configurative psychic landscapes documented by acid. Jagger, who still filtered leisure time into making periodic forays on Stephen's chain of Carnaby Street shops, became at the time, and as an offshoot of acid pharmacology, saturated in popular occult books, purchased from Watkins Bookshop in Cecil Court, and Atlantis, just slightly north of Watkins, in the post-Virginia Woolf literary-stuffy precinct of Bloomsbury. Jagger's superficial occult reading extended to Eliphas Levi, Aleister Crowley, as resurgent avatar to druggy neophytes, and of course to the cult novel Mikhail Bulgakov's *The Master And Margarita*, reputably the inspiration for *Sympathy For The Devil*, a

fiction in which the devil comes in person to Stalinist Moscow and leaves a trail of physical and psychological debris. But the neuronal actions of LSD on serotonergic and other monoaminergic neural pathways in the brain was beginning through an epidemic of abuse to find its signature in fashion, with a West/East interface, the explanatory power of the drug directing some of its recreational users towards an almost Herman Hesse-inflected preoccupation with quasi-Tibetan, Vedanta and Mahayana Buddhism. The world of multi-patterned kaftans, worn by both sexes that year in the fumingly hot London summer, was a fashion eschewed by Mods, who saw it as a deviation from the

look, and as a spurious concession to highjacking cultures in which they had little or no interest. While the basis of dress from 1967–69 was unisex fashion, incorporating the sloppy ethnic line of the hippies, John Stephen resisted the trend towards chaotic sartorial jamboree by maintaining a Mod subtext to his collections, finding a balance between his largely indigenous Mod ethic and commercial update, at a time when British youth were spending a phenomenal upwards of £2 billion a year on clothes. Stephen, unlike his more opportunistic contemporaries in Carnaby Street, continued to emphasise a sophisticated line in suits and casual wear that was strictly modernistic, rather than diffused into the a-linear fragmentation and uncoordinated layering of hippie influenced fashion.

Carnaby Street, or more specifically by this time John Stephen's street, had by the mid-sixties become a major tourist attraction, the place additionally popularised by postcards, showing either a zoom-shot telescoping into the street, with its dominant John Stephen, Lord John, Lady Jane, Toppers and Ravel shop signs, or the contrived snapshot of a unisex couple posed under the street sign in their ubiquitously identifiable clothes, as a colour block concentrate affirming that London was the core city of a liberated youth devoted to clothes and music in that order. Not that the place was spared lacerating criticism for its apparent downgrading and sell-out of modernistic principles. Nik Cohn, as a discerning critic, was sceptical of John Stephen's accelerated momentum and the hawkier aspects of the street's unabating commercial hoopla. 'Salesmen grabbed you and cajoled you like pimps,' Cohn recalled, a few years after the street's imploding demise. 'Coloured streamers were festooned above the pavements and the clothes were like showgirl lipsticks: flaming orange, cherry red, candyfloss pink.' John Stephen's shops were also the colourful locale for several movies and TV collaborations, including a Liberace special filmed in the Teen Store, and a visit from the pop star Petula Clark, who performed a short set at The Man's Shop, having recently topped the charts with a torchy rendition of *This Is My Song*, excerpted from the movie *A Countess From Hong Kong*, starring Sophia Loren and Marlon Brando. But whatever the need in Stephen's case to aggrandise a decade of unremittingly inventive design, that had transformed a sterile backwater into a torrential human river, and made his personal image into the extended physical topology of the place, Stephen was confronted by the fact that the place itself now exceeded the importance of the clothes. Opportunists had saturated Carnaby Street with kitsch, like John Paul who fronted I Was Lord Kitchener's Valet, a shop that on the success of selling racks of second-hand Victoriana to rock stars and their epigoni at the top end of Portobello Road, had for singularly commercial reasons moved into both Carnaby Street and Wardour Street, Soho, to increase its revivalist hold on fashion. The eccentric Portobello flagship shop had received a mainline injection of endorsement through the patronage of John Lennon and Mick Jagger; Jagger having bought a red Grenadier Guardsman drummer's jacket there for an appearance on *Ready Steady Go!* when the Stones had closed the show by performing their sitar-driven, quirkily idiosyncratic Eastern-flavoured chart-topper *Paint It Black*, a song that perfectly fused the darker aspects of Western pop with intimations of Eastern music derived from the likes of Ravi Shankar. As a consequence of Jagger wearing the scarlet military tunic for a TV appearance, the shop had a line of hundreds of people wanting to buy the same garment the next morning, and had sold out of its entire stock by lunchtime. Unfortunately, Lord Kitchener's Valet, as a commercial enterprise, severely undermined Stephen's aesthetic, by promoting the sort of opportunistic tack that quickly branded the street as a centre for gimmicky patriotic bin-ends, further encouraging Mods to desert its milieu. Robert Orbach, who had worked for John Stephen in sales, and subsequently joined the staff of I Was Lord Kitchener's Valet, has described the shop's peculiar interior and eccentric milieu as one destined to be remembered for its spec-tacular transience. 'We painted all the windows black, so people were curious. By then we were selling Union Jack shirts and target T-shirts. We started buying plastic jewellery, cheap rings made in Birmingham. Little shirtmakers made the Union Jack shirts; we had seamstresses all over the place. It started like that – it was fun, it was simple.'

As a further disruption of Stephen's tailored line, and a deliberate incursion on the smart Chelsea set, the spoof deconstructionists I Was Lord Kitchener's Valet took over Kleptomania on the King's Road in 1967, a stra-tegically resourceful outlet that proved so commercially successful that there were rope barriers down the centre of the shop directing customers towards the cashiers. Lord Kitchener's was strictly a revivalist shop, selling second-hand clothes, and picking up on perverse nostalgia for empire, with most of their military jackets sourced ironically from John Stephen's old employers, Moss Bros in King Street, Covent Garden. They sold racks of braided tunics, of the type made flamboyantly popular by Jimi Hendrix, boas, tatty fox stoles, second-hand fur coats, pith helmets, Victorian dresses, psychedeli-cally painted furniture and general novelty memorabilia, and were at the heart of fragmenting the look into the dispersal of period eccentricity and decorated faux military pastiche. Mods didn't do acid, as the drug associ-ated with these largely unstructured lines, seeing LSD as a subversion of their

I Was Lord Kitchener's Valet, owner Ian Fisk stands among ruffs worn with military tunics that seriously undermined the military. The place was a favourite of Jimi Hendrix's.

individual control freakery, nor were they sympathetic to a foppishness that was at variance with their clean line personifying structured form. Mods too had little sympathy with facial hair, the beards and moustaches made popular by the Beatles circa the psychedelic fall-out of their mega-impacting *Sergeant Pepper's Lonely Hearts Club Band*, and their flirtation via George Harrison's immersion in Hinduism for Westerners, with the teachings of the Maharishi Mahesh Yogi: something triggered by the band's incongruously attending the Maharishi's exorbitant designer meditation for rich westerners tutorial at the Park Lane Hotel on 24 August 1967.

The neurobiological link between acid and intangible, but intensely coloured and detailed parapsychological experience of the nature considered religio-mystical by the drug's proponents like Timothy Leary, was starting to seriously infect pop culture in 1967, like a collective pharmaceutical rainbow come up behind the eyes, by inner journeyers, observing the chemical progress of microdots purchased from Soho dealers trafficking LSD, speed and hash in the Ham's Yard, Piccadilly Circus district of Soho. That the drug found a busy illegal commerce only ten minutes away from Carnaby Street, in a manner similar to speed directed at Mod consumption in the same precinct, was another significant pointer to the clash in cultures between hippie-bohemianism and resilient Mod.

And for all the qualitative class war between Stephen's optimal but downgrade Soho and the privileged King's Road bohos, John Stephen still retained the look, even when his line was temporarily submerged by the need to accommodate aspects of raffish hippie dress. Somehow Mods wouldn't recant on the look, and John Stephen continued to offer tailored suits, pastel shirts, ties, and an edgy line of trousers and knitwear, despite the necessary compromises made to accommodate the extremes of psychedelic fashion, to his devoted following. If Soho was still the look, and continuously forward-presenting under Stephen's precisional eye, then Chelsea and particularly Michael Rainey's Hung On You, that had the patronage of Michael Caine, Terence Stamp, David Bailey and Vidal Sassoon, was all about vintage colours, period revivals, wine-red flared Edwardian jackets, worn to match the right drink – campari and soda at Le Reve restaurant, or at Dolly's discotheque in Jermyn Street, or equally topically at Robert Fraser's fashionable art gallery on Duke Street. None of these places were on John Stephen's personal map of preferences, his sociable evenings being spent with his creative team, over coffee and drinks at his customised Jermyn Street flat, close to his operational Soho zone, and other personalised landmarks in his life like the Trattoria Terrazza, the Ivy and Tiberio's in Mayfair, L'Etoile and the White Tower in

Models stripping in the windows of I Was Lord Kitchener's Valet brought lunchtime crowds, and the attention of the Metropolitan Police, to Piccadilly.

Bloomsbury, when the occasion called. Meanwhile, serious Chelsea opposition and a consolidated poster advertising campaign came from the artists Michael English and Nigel Waymouth, otherwise known as Hapsash and the Coloured Coat, who in decorating the interior of Michael Rainey's Hung On You boutique, employed the rich velvet drapes and delusional mirror-tricks for the shop's interior décor, originally led by Myles Anthony's configurative shop designs done for John Stephen's plethoric chain of twenty-two London stores. Like Stephen, Rainey had no formal training as a designer, and was a gifted dilettante dependent on the assistance of skilled cutters for his creations, and like Stephen impeccable about his own sense of personal dress. The aristocratic Jane Ormsby Gore, who married Rainey, remembers that in their peculiar style of assemblage for Hung On You, they were initially influenced by portraits of the poet, Lord Byron, as infamous romantic lothario. 'For those shirts with frilly fronts and big sleeves. And literature, Spencer's *Fairie Queen*, the romantic mood. Michael would find beautiful materials, all made in London's East End, by proper old fashioned tailors. I suppose the Stones and Beatles would come in and say, 'We want four of those ...'

Rainey who had begun at 22 Cale Street, with a big jardinière mirrored feature in the middle of the shop, went upmarket to his detriment, by taking over a larger shop at 430 King's Road, just past the turn at World's End, which included an unattractive staircase going down to the downstairs showroom, with each banister painted a different colour, as an expression of low-budget improvisation. Unlike John Stephen, who on taking over 5 Carnaby Street, and with Bill Franks' assistance, put up a canary yellow façade himself in the course of a weekend to cut costs in making the shop personally attractive in a monochrome street, Rainey relied less on spontaneous resources than social networking. He applied his wife's aristocratic connections, as the daughter of Lord Harlech, to attract customers to the shop's unremitting psychedelic interior, where the two assistants, Jay and Bo, sat on a chaise longue in the window, smoking joints, and climbing down laconically to serve customers. Lacking Stephen's fiercely inventive imagination, Rainey relied instead on reworking vintage clothes, and tapered guardsman's trousers with a red stripe down the side, relined dragoon coats and military bandsman's jackets, as the very themes to which Stephen as a modernist was so antipathetic. While Rainey's use of military costumes was iconoclastic, in that the sixties as a predominantly pacifist generation, emancipated from conscription, tended to revile the military, there was something of the inauthentic about his work as a decorator of existing costume, rather than as the creator of original lines. In addition, he sold quilted, high-buttoned Mao jackets called 'The

Christmas lights in Carnaby Street were a major attraction and contributed to the street's endemic popularity.

Great Leap Forward,' and as a pointer to Mao's popularity that year with students, placed a giant blow-up of him swimming the Yangtse on one of his walls. Tall, and modelling his good looks and hairdo on Brian Jones, and the equally deep-fringed members of the Byrds, as blond, sunglassed pop star stereotypes, Rainey who dressed in Sherwood green suits, also sold Liberty print, mandarin collar ruffled shirts, afghan robes, and suits the colour of Neopolitan ice cream in white, pink, pistachio-green and cream, colours imparting a teasy summer feel to the near-edible pastel fabrics, worn with floral chiffon shirts. Hung On You, as a cult shop, developed a reputation as a druggy elitist ecosphere for the popocracy, hippie, decadent, subversive and smacking of all the agglomerated strains of King's Road chic and cool that could be brokered into a single psychedelically-decorated space in 1967. Trevor Myles remembers too, the extreme prankster aspect of the shop's milieu, remembering how, and unforgettably, 'The first time I went to Hung On You there was this guy prostrate on the pavement outside, with blood pouring from his mouth. A concerned crowd gathered around him. Suddenly he leapt up and ran back into the shop cackling. It was one of the assistants who had used blood capsules as a prank on the passers by.'

Defending his originality, and more importantly his undisputed role in creating the sixties look, Stephen was quoted that year as saying, 'Carnaby Street is my creation. In a way I feel about it how Michaelangelo felt about the beautiful statues he had created.' And even if the analogy, like John Lennon's overstated messianic claims for the Beatles' significance in popularity, appears exaggerated, there is an element of truth in Stephen's claim to have singularly created a new masculine look, as far-reaching as Michaelangelo's sculptural aesthetic, only he had achieved it through the ephemeral expression of clothes, rather than the durable form of marble. And it's the essential disposability of clothes, and the fact that they are consigned to the moment, and as quickly deleted, that undermines the durability of all fashion, there being in the process of time little that ever survives outside of museum archives of an original line. For all the clothes he created in conjunction with his cutter, and Stephen unfortunately destroyed his drawings, little remains, other than a small number of clothes owned by the Victoria and Albert Museum, those in private collections, and the occasional shirt put on a 1960s rack by a dealer with a selective eye for retro.

If fashion is a direct indicator of the collective mood of a generation in a particular moment, then John Stephen and his contemporaries were in 1967, close to attempting to give shape to the conflicting cocktail of political, social, subjective, artistic and prevalent drug issues motivating their times. A decade's impacted momentum of youth learning to express themselves and their cultural preferences through the individual statement of dress, had by now accelerated to an apogee of exaggerated excess. Rock and roll and Carnaby Street, and increasingly the King's Road, fed off each other in a symbiotic union of synchronistic energies. Soho itself, following Stephen's lead, became the intense localised site of hyperactive production, with Stephen having basement factories in Carnaby Street, and the young designer Gerald McCann, who was harnessed to supplying Vanessa Denza and Woollands' 21 Shop, as well Roger Nelson, Jean Muir, Rosalind Yehuda and Foale & Tuffin, having four separate factories functioning in Brewer Street and Poland Street, for demands that ran to 350 in a single style. Of the indomitable role played by British fashion of the period, McCann recalls, 'We had the music, didn't we, so that set the stage, and then we gave it form. We produced the clothes that epitomised the look. It was so much fun though because everyone got on so well.'

If Soho retained an explosive work dynamic dominated by John Stephen's new designs, as simultaneous with the age, then the King's Road in Christopher Gibbs' assessment was in danger of becoming 'a parade of stoned harlequins,' looking to purchase figure-hugging laced suede jerkins with the outline of a purple eagle on the back, from Hung On You, or the floral puff-sleeved shirts made popular by Cream from Deborah & Claire, an exclusive Chelsea boutique in Beauchamp Place. Or there was putatively the best cutter of his generation, Ossie Clark at Quorum, who had benefited from the chance discovery of rolls of unused sharkskin in a warehouse at Chelsea Wharf, and had subsequently worked the skins into fitted jackets, modelled on the style of black leather Rocker jackets, to be worn with culottes and skirts cut to a longer length to challenge the ubiquitous popularity of the King's Road micro-mini as the exploited profile for elongatedly curvy pins. Clark's diary entry at the time records the propitious discovery of snakeskin as a novelty fabric. 'Jill Bennett finding the first snakeskin was no accident in the dark cavernous warehouse. Dickensian. "What's that?" I asked, touching the gentlest touch to the skin of a 26" python lain rolled 20 years. Sprang back to life and opened before me. "How much?" I asked, but matter-of-fact, hiding my enthusiasm. "Let's see, er, I can do that for thirty bob a foot," glad to get shot. It was so wide I made it into a suit and Linda Keith modelled it.' In London fashion, all barriers between what pop stars wore, and their image-hungry fans, were dissolved, as the two factors tended to shop at much the same recognised outlets, each learning to refresh their clothes inspiration from the other. Of the endemic confusion as to who was who, in terms of identity, Christopher Gibbs, recalls that 'everyone started dressing like Gram Parsons or Mick Jagger. It actually became quite difficult to suss out who was a pop star and who wasn't.' And in terms of dress the two formed a seamless unity tagged by the same Carnaby Street and King's Road labels. Robert Fraser, the owner of London's most pioneering pop art gallery on Duke Street, who wore both John Stephen Custom Built as well as upmarket threads from Blades, noted, 'Right now, London has something that New York used to have: everybody wants to be there. There's no place else. Paris is calcified. There's an indefinable thing about London that makes people want to go there.' And the incredulous reporter from *Time* magazine, addressing the apparent dissolution of class values in London, and the insurgent shopaholic upbeat drive of its youth to spend on clothes, reported on the following King's Road scene as a cameo of London life in 1967. 'Saturday afternoon in Chelsea. Up from Sloane Square tube station swarm the guys and dollies, girls in miniskirts, (three to six inches above the knee) or bell-bottom trousers. The morning has been spent raking amongst the Edwardian bric-a-brac, dusty candelabra, and other antiques in the stalls on Portobello Road. Now, as if by a common instinct, the whole flock homes in on King's Road, site of such boutiques as Bazaar, and Granny Takes a Trip, as well as Hung On You, the kinkiest (wildest) men's shop, which features a '30s look: George Raft lapels, Bogart fedoras, Al Capone boutonnieres. The sport of the day is mainly sauntering, not shopping, but as Cathy McGowan explains, "it's a very serious business. The point is to show off your close gear, and you have to do it in the proper style." Cathy, with Mick Jagger, 21, lead vocalist for the Rolling Stones, stops in at the Guys and Dolls coffeehouse, where a pretty blonde teenager, her yellow and black PVC miniskirt hiked high over patterned stockings, perches staring at a copy of *French Vogue*. Mick leans over her. She beams: "Luv," he says, "you've got it upside down."'

A photo captioned Carnaby Street Dandy, London, 16 April 1967, published in the *Manchester Daily Express*, shows a fashionable teenager wearing a bowler hat and fur coat over a double-breasted jacket standing in the rain-glossed street outside John Stephen's His Clothes. The street signs of Donis, His Clothes, with the gutted level above displaying an 'Acquired' sign from the agents Meadow Schama, and Lord John, dominating the still unpedestrianised street, and the anonymous window-shoppers throwing their heads back incredulously in the expectation they were sighting a celebrity, perfectly captures the moody atmospherics of a walled-in street, that despite its concentration of shoppers, was still partly residential, empty, or undeveloped on its derelict top floors. The radical dichotomy between the past,

Warren Beatty, Faye Dunaway and The Bonnie and Clyde look fed into John Stephen's love of custom built suits.

typified by two or three unfashionable floors utilised as workrooms, and the quizzically industrious foot-traffic in the street below, intently scrutinising John Stephen's colourfully vitaminised windows, is acute: the patina of an austere past rubbed into the brick facades as the enduring signature of a previously unrelieved poverty.

Something of a distinct reaction to the hippie predilection for unstructured and unco-ordinated dress, occurred as a direct result of the film smash that year, *Bonnie and Clyde*, a movie that John Stephen was quick to use as a fashion basis to his advantage, the clothes accent in the film wardrobe being on wide-lapelled double-breasted gangster-style suits for men, variations of which he had been marketing for years, and berets, silk shirts and the reintroduction of maxi-length skirts for girls. One of the sixties' most visually eloquent, volatile and controversial crime/gangster movies, combining comedy, terror, love at desperation point, and unrestrained violence, the film starring Warren Beatty as Clyde Barrow, and the emergent talent Faye Dunaway as Bonnie Parker, exemplified many of the characteristics of experimental film-making pulled from the French Nouvelle Vague movement, so appreciated by Mods, and was originally intended to be directed by Jean-Luc Godard, or François Truffaut, who declined and made the sensational *Farenheit 451* instead, finally falling to the counter-culture exponent Arthur Penn. The film's sympathetic revolutionary characters, Clyde was the leader, and Bonnie a Myrna Loy fan, who wrote poetry, appealed not only to anti-authority American youth protesting against the Vietnam war, the corrupt social order, and the US government's role in these issues, but likewise to their British counterparts, who while not directly affected by military involvement in Vietnam, were nonetheless vehement in their denunciation of an unwarranted and putatively illegal war. For John Stephen, always aware of the influence of film on fashion, the Depression-era wardrobe, designed by Theodora Van Runkle, with an admitted passion for thirties clothes, injected new ideas into his arrogantly-styled sartorial line for 1967, with suits turning thirties', chalk-striped and gangsterish in their imposingly threatening cut, and with the hemline falling on skirts to a midi-look, no matter the continuous overriding popularity of the mini. *Bonnie and Clyde* precipitated one of the most far-reaching effects on fashion ever perpetrated by a movie, and grey fedoras, double-breasted suits in mohair and flannel, co-respondent shoes, splashy kipper ties, cloche hats and berets and maxi-skirts began to proliferate, not only in John Stephen's personalised adaptations of the style, but in all the flourishing Carnaby Street windows. The epidemic also engendered an immediate demand for American cars; posters were produced and the whole accoutrements of the gangster era went on sale: a club opened called the Speakeasy, in deference to the film, and a band called The Saint Valentine's Day Massacre tried unsuccessfully to piggyback its way into the charts on the strength of the movie's contagious epidemic. And if Theodora Van Runkle's acclaimed period revivals became through the filtering of hip designers, standard street-wear, then her influences were five years behind Stephen's busy, constantly mutating update of double-breasted jackets and suits for men's fashions.

With the Beatles electing to wear customised kaftans as a sign of their topically capricious flirtation with LSD-informed Eastern mysticism, and so too members of the newly formed Simon Napier-Bell managed John's Children, who as a late addition to London's Mod music scene scored a hit with *Desdemona*, John Stephen, in tune with the times, took up the colourful art of designing kaftans in the floral, paisley, hallucinated whorls and galactic starburst spirals that were coded into the visual vocabulary of LSD. In a publicity photograph of the period, two of the teenage members of John's Children, namely John Hewlett and Chris Tounson, both sporting typical tiered, lacquered Mod hairdos, were posed up against a brick wall in nearby Foubert's Place, as representative models of John Stephen's new addition to unisex. Designed in brightly coloured cottons or tricels, the pattern inhibited the need to accessorize, and Stephen used bold fabrics, storming red, blue and black paisley and mandala shapes on white cotton backgrounds, or lilac stripes, combined with a yellow, black and white pattern. To simplify the traditional design Stephen had the garment fall to a few inches above the knee, so that the effect was like a mini-dress for men, worn over white or pastel-coloured hipsters. The kaftan issuing from Stephen's assiduous workrooms was still another and more extreme move towards the seamless androgynous template on which he had based his origins, the dominating and gender-bending notion that men's and women's fashion should be fluently interchangeable. The kaftan came close to completing the ideal, in that it was the closest he got as a fashion statement to putting men into dresses, while still retaining a pronounced element of masculinity in the design. And as a variant means of appeasing Mods, as an update to the look Stephen created white leather hip-length windbreakers, with long button-down collars like a shirt, buttoned patch pockets, and a button-fastening at the waist, as a revision of the original denim jean jacket, the accessorised details fitting with the conception of the new Mod dandy, as opposed to the steady recession of original Faces from the publicity-drenched street.

Although Stephen, as an original, appeared indifferent to the lines of other designers, his American counterpart Rudi Gernreich was busy attempting contemporaneously to popularise unisex in New York, but without the prevailing social tensions that promoted Stephen's stimulus to create an entirely new form of masculinity. The unstoppably flamboyant Gernreich, in contrast to Stephen's impecunious one-room start in Soho's Beak Street, had in 1963 opened a Seventh Avenue showroom in New York, where he exhibited his popular designs for Harmon knitwear, and his own more expensive line of experimental clothes. Unlike Stephen, who stuck a needle into the mainline fashion needs of essentially working-class teenagers, and inveigled them into the unprecedented concept of democratising clothes, Gernreich, in the attempt to have male dress emerge from the aesthetic exile into which it had been consigned since the late 19th century, aimed at the high-end of the financial market and its top buyers. Gernreich like Stephen, conceived of interchangeable clothes for men and women, such as floor-length kaftans, or white knit bell-bottomed trousers worn with black and white midriff-tops, while his racily innovative and scandalously modern creations for women extended to see-through blouses, chiffon T-shirt dresses, mini-dresses inset with clear vinyl stripes, and the thong bathing suit, cut sensationally high to expose the buttocks. But no matter the temerity informing his design aesthetic, what Gernreich lacked, that Stephen had in abundance, was the sizzling cutting-edge of a music complementary to fashion, created by new London garage teenage desperados. Stephen too, had the edge on his contemporary, by being able in his capacity as designer to infiltrate and learn from the needs of a generation living on the fault-line of fashion as it was being created. His strength was derived in part through his direct contact with the milieu responsible for creating the look. He was in touch on a daily basis with the impacting bustle and furore of the Soho fabric shops, and Carnaby Street itself, furred by the insignia of persistent London rain, and pollution, or soaked lemon in a peculiar aching sunlight common to the 1960s as an epoch less saturated by the dense blanket of hydrocarbon emissions that envelops it today. New York lacked those credible, punkish constituents that made London's Soho and the King's Road the vasodilated arteries of a fashion epoch powered by surges of rebelliously youthful hormones promoting the inimitable look. America imported the Stephen look, through his outlets in large departmental stores, copied it, or came to Carnaby Street to buy, or in the case of musicians like the Walker Brothers and Jimi Hendrix, actually based themselves there, for the impetus of immersion in the hectic paces of metamorphic fashion and equally transgressive music.

Granny Takes A Trip was for Chelsea aristos, Carnaby Street for Mods.

Meanwhile, John Stephen and John Michael as the initial pioneers for

men's fashion on the King's Road held their stylishly individual own as the street underwent continuous transmogrifying facelifts, as rag trade opportunists set up ephemerally-based, luridly-painted psychedelic fascias, before quickly disappearing. Forbidden Fruit, Mr Freedom, Gloryhole, Dandie Fashions, Just Men, Through the Looking Glass, Mitsukika, Mexicana, Ad Hoc, Hem and Fringe, Just Looking, Skin, Clobber and Blast Off were just some of the short-lived outlets that set up shop between 1966/67, along the persistent fashionista shuffle of the King's Road thoroughfare. One of the more enduring landmarks of the late sixties' King's Road boutiques were the Nigel Waymouth owned Granny Takes A Trip, operating under a slogan above the door: 'One should either be a work of art or wear a work of art.' The faux-Wildean proviso introducing the shop indicated the degree of affectation and exaggerated pretension that had entered fashion, not via John Stephen, but through revivalists substituting decoration for original ideas, and burying Stephen's look in layered frothy excess. Waymouth's predilections had always been for personally collecting vintage and, perceiving a commercial market for his serendipitous finds, he decided to retail his collection through a fashionable King's Road outlet. 'We used to go down to Church Street Market and Portobello Road, collecting these old clothes, and we thought that it might be a good idea to open a shop with all these things. I got the name when one night I sat down and I thought, well, Granny clothes, acid trips, it's obvious: Granny Takes A Trip, that's funny, let's do it. We used to change the windows every three months. We had black windows, a car coming out (that was about eighteen months after we started) ... we did everything. The whole point was just to keep it change, change, change. We used to stay up all night and do it so that people would wake up the next day and discover a different shopfront. We started off exclusively with old clothes; rather nice beaded dresses, blazers, all that camp nonsense. That was fun.' Waymouth had gone a step beyond Stephen in not separating men's and women's clothes, but simply placing the two together on the rack. Waymouth remembers, 'Our customers were debs, gays, pop people, and both sexes. It was completely androgynous, we had only one changing room and the clothes were mixed on the rail.' The shop's purple interior was complemented by low lighting, the vintage clothing supplemented by a range of John Pearse's satin and floral shirts, with 4- or 6-inch pointed collars that took collar elongation to the maximum tailoring ante generated by the weird euphoria and visual distortion that was the chemical print-out of LSD-induced psychedelia. Stock comprised an undifferentiated mix of flapper dresses, Charleston dresses, Chicago gangster suits, floral ties, wine-gum coloured velveteen trousers, gold-rimmed sunglasses made popular by the likes of John Lennon and members of the Jimi Hendrix Experience, plastic mini-skirts, feather boas and a mosaic of faux antiques and eccentric empire memorabilia. The shop definitely had an intimidating quality that Waymouth recalls. 'It was not a friendly shop. We were spearheading a movement, not consciously in a political way, but certainly style-wise. We were trying to break away. We weren't following designer traditions. The shop was part of that, trying to establish a look for people of the underground culture.'

If the consumer habit for new clothes hot on the racks at Biba or John Stephen's stores kept spiking up an increased mania amongst the young to purchase the look, then both Hulanicki and Stephen led the way through creating fashion firsts that were proportionate to teenage income. The thing about Barbara Hulanicki's Biba, which had the highest turnover per square foot of any shop anywhere, was that like John Stephen, she specialised in highly-affordable limited runs that provoked instant purchase on the part of dedicated fashionistas intent on updating their look each week. To see was to have, with one perception leading spontaneously to the next, in terms of the impetus to buy in order to outrival competitors for the look. If Carnaby Street had become the central site for camera crews, home-movie buffs doing celebrity spotting, TV interviews, and John Stephen continuously harassed by an invasive media anxious to have him predict fashion tips for the coming season, then the street was also in danger of overdosing on its own insurgent popularity. Stephen outwardly retained his immutably youthful looks, despite the pressure on his nerves, his attitude switching between ruthless pursuit of business interests, and the natural kindness that was integral to his personality.

What had boosted Stephen's continually escalating turnover in 1966–67, was the spin-off from the impacting cover article in *Time*, April 1966, with its racy, raised beta-endorphin tone and concentrated focus on London, and in particular Carnaby Street, as the indomitable epitome of cool. London was written up as a capital in which the popocracy set the rules in defiance of convention, and in which youth had succeeded in subverting tradition, not through violence, but through the hedonistic shape-shifting contagion of music, street drugs, partying, and the adoption of Stephen's look as the vehicle of antagonistically ageist expression. As a result Stephen found his shops overrun by inquisitive American tourists, all wishing to participate in the look, and buy into Carnaby Street quite literally as an integral expression of England. A John Stephen carrier became the new hip password to Americans attempting by long-haul flights to overcome the culture gap that had opened

John Stephen singularly created Carnaby Street. His rivals all came after 1964 and were second-wave in the street's history.

across the Atlantic. The credited author of the *Time* encomium, 'You Can Walk Across It On Grass,' Piri Halasz, rejuvenated a directionless Carnaby Street, by an overkill of emphasis on a sexually-liberated, panda-eyed, mini-skirted capital, in which louche playboy aristocrats dressed in plum velvet Regency clubbed at Annabel's, the Scotch Of St James' and Sibylla's, while in the lower echelons of society, a wired, defiant youth recreated their work identities as wannabes every Saturday afternoon, by dressing like pop stars in Carnaby Street clothes.

In pop terms, London in 1967 was transformed not only by the pharmacological experimentation of the Beatles' LSD soundtrack, *Sgt Pepper*, but by the meteoric emergence on the scene of the virtuoso guitar maestro, and suitably exotically dressed Jimi Hendrix, whose use of feedback and distortion was to singularly reinvent the guitar as sonic interpreter of the LSD-saturated times. The Seattle-born Hendrix, with his Afro-penumbra of permed hair, and left-handed guitar figures given detonative pedal, completely cut free from the sound of London's prevalent beat merchants, by improvising chords gunned with the wah-wah ferocity of an attacking rattle-snake. The Jimi Hendrix Experience, a trio including the stick-thin Noel Redding on bass and Mitch Mitchell on drums, free associated their psychedelic costumes, cutting aspects of the look with revamped braided military tunics purchased from Lord Kitchener's Valet, worn with purple satin shirts with puffed sleeves purchased from John Stephen, and a variety of mismatched period dress picked up from the likes of Granny Takes A Trip. The Jimi Hendrix Experience, more than any other band of the period, personified the interface between colour-soaked fashion and the hallucinogenic substances helping fuel their creative energies. Wearing ruffled floral shirts, decorated military jackets, loops of ethnic beads, vermilion hipsters, snakeskin boots, wire-rimmed octagonal glasses, and a variety of pimpy hats, the Experience represented a druggy, foppish, dandified androgyny, as an image congruous with the quirky, skewed, idiosyncratic, riff-distorted, stratospheric blast of their shatteringly bandit music. The trio, perceived as altered state outlaws, fried on LSD, wore reconstructed clothes that expressed the unstructured fashion of the times, in the way their music also explored the outer reaches of consciousness in its turbulent mixture of blues tooled into fuzz-box distorted supersonic rock. Hendrix's tropically coloured flamboyant fashion statement was seen by Mod purists as still another derivation from the look, a hectic cocktail of period revival that was decidedly anti-modern in its reversion to retro, complete with the incorporation of vintage granny specs, rather than the cool European attitude conveyed by dark shades.

Mods were starting in 1967 to do a vanishing trick from mainstream fashion, with even their spearhead London bands like The Who and the Small Faces growing their hair longer, even if they retained the original tiered structure of the Mod cut, with the ears exposed and the front curtain shaped to meet the cheek and chin. The Small Faces, led by Steve Marriott's intensely soulful vocal chutzpah, quickly graduated from being exemplars of the look into full-blown psychedelic dress, as a pointer to changes in their music and in the times. The prominence of Barbara Hulanicki's Biba had succeeded by 1967 in stimulating girls into a corresponding obsession with clothes and buying as their male counterparts, as contagiously fast to meet the latest nuance of style. With Hulanicki looking to the past for style inspiration, John Stephen found himself isolated by his adherence to modernism, as the forward presentation of fashion, as Hulanicki joined the list of period revivalists, eager to recreate recognisable design tropes at the expense of the creatively new. But unlike John Stephen, who invariably prosecuted for theft, Hulanicki who had periodically to go outside the shop to wipe nose marks off the window with a damp cloth, as a mark of the shop's assiduous popularity, declared, 'when people are stealing, you're doing the right thing. It's when they stop stealing you have to worry.' Operating initially from 87 Abingdon Road, near Earl's Court, and later from 19/21 Church Street, Kensington, a shop that incorporated the first communal changing room, and in which the décor showed amalgamated traces of art nouveau, art deco, and hints of Tsarist Russia, Hulanicki by sheer devotional invention outpaced John Stephen's Carnaby street outlets for girls in terms of creating an egalitarian niche that concentrated strictly on the feminine look. Hulanicki gave girls back the advantage they had lost to John Stephen's Mod male clientele, rejuvenating their diminished profile after years of losing the initiative to a reinvented masculinity. Hulanicki chose broody deep autumnal colours for her racks: maroon, puce, plum, crimson, purple, black, brown, bottle green and 5pm winter sky violet, alternating skirt lengths from micro to midi to maxi, turning girls into slinky recreations of 1920s flappers, stepping out into mid-1960s London sunlight, believing with optimal conviction that they would never grow old. Slithery gowns in glowing satins, feathered boas, lingerie heaped on Victorian dressing tables, hats with black veils, floor-length raincoats and dusky suede boots with long zippers, all added to the recognisably vampish Biba look.

If Jimi Hendrix patronised John Stephen's colour-saturated shops for searchingly low-rise hipsters and the icy sheen of purple, champagne or lipstick red satin shirts, and Cathy McGowan as the face of her time predominantly wore Biba, then the dispersal of the look into a collage of period effects was further accentuated by the popularity of a stall run in the Chelsea Antiques Market by two ex-waiters, Adrian Emmerton and Vernon Lambert, who sold sailors' trousers dyed in outrageous colours to gays and pop stars, as well as lace shirts, overhauled demob suits and cavalier jackets in upholstery fabrics. Emmerton and Lambert's poppy drag was the exact sort of clothes favoured by the Chelsea-based Rolling Stones, in the run-up to releasing their one incursion into psychedelically-based rock, *Their Satanic Majesties Request*. The Stones' abandonment of the look was also the first druggy intimation of their superficial absorption of the more sensational aspects of the occult filtered through the likes of Kenneth Anger's endorsement of Aleister Crowley as the satanically lugubrious archetype best suited to the liberated times. The Stones, who only two years ago had on their American tour epitomised the John Stephen look, by wearing his clothes, were now, and especially through the exaggerated travesty of Brian Jones, the purveyors of a style that mixed hippie, regency, Chelsea Market, King's Road and Carnaby Street into uncompromising, gender-bending androgyny. Embellished with sparkling paste broaches, their clothes resembled amalgamated decoration, the John Stephen look persisting only in the style of colourful shirt or sharp fitted, double-breasted jacket, worn under a woman's fur coat, picked up at Chelsea Market or Granny Takes A Trip, as a token of inspired sexual anarchy. The Stones, too, were loosing the gritty London sound of rough trade in contact with the street that had so authenticated their early R&B, offensively lascivious attitude, a sound that like their clothes had come to be replaced with layered textures of studio engineering. By 1967, the Rolling Stones were more King's Road-affiliated, and less conspicuous on John Stephen's Soho patch, although Brian Jones remained a regular visitor to his shops, fussy with detail and almost invariably suggesting alterations to the clothes he chose. The emphasis in London's fashion parameters was changing, and while Stephen maintained a high profile in both Soho and the King's Road, Carnaby Street was considered more and more a downmarket locus for shopping tourists, while the King's Road was perceived as serious territory for bohemian fashionistas, who were also doing the new shape-shifting drugs like acid, rather than being zipped on pedestrian speed.

Probably no photograph better exemplifies the eclectic assemblage of clothes sources incorporated into rock star saturation of the look in 1967, as Michael Cooper's 11 January shot of the Rolling Stones grouped in monochrome Green Park, Mayfair, in the raw London cold, breath atomized into smoky contrails, bodies physically braced against the invasive damp. Michael

Cooper, who was to die of a heroin overdose in 1973, had been introduced to the Stones in 1964 by the entrepreneurial art dealer Robert Fraser, and his iconic street-edgy shots of the Stones in the flash-forward transitional phase of the mid-sixties, are amongst the most memorable of the period in framing the band's evolution from trashy R&B-inspired white copyists, to cocky extollers of self-penned hits that came packaged with an increasingly draggy fashion attitude. In a visibly glacial park shoot, under a sky clear as a blue diamond, only Charlie Watts, dressed in a dark blue double-breasted blazer, a French blue button-down collar shirt and arty scarlet and blue silk neck tie, his hair cut short in the Mod style, still maintains the clean-tailored John Stephen look. Keith Richards in period granny specs and a broad-brimmed woman's black felt hat, worn to complement Jones' white creation, with both guitarists revealing glitzy paste brooches, Richards draped in a white fur coat, and Jones wearing dandified striped trousers and a three-quarters length double-breasted jacket, together with his archly louche colleague, epitomises the whole revivalist's look, put together with optimal King's Road panache. Bill Wyman's cerise shirt, and ten-button double-breasted striped jacket, with a deep highwayman's collar, a cut introduced by John Stephen, and quickly hijacked by Sidney Brent's Take Six boutique, succeeds in the shoot in upstaging Jagger's collar turned-up black greatcoat, silver grey slacks and immaculate white shoes, worn with poutish style, as a partial footnote to the Stephen look modified by John Crittall's Dandie Fashions' King's Road boutique. And as a provocative footnote to the Stones' outrageous drag at the time, a diary entry by Ossie Clark provides considerable insight into their clothes' sources. 'When Brian Jones and Keith Richards took to wearing the silks and satins printed by Celia [Birtwhistle] and the skin-tight jewel coloured trousers from a stash of pre-war corset satin AP found, I made men's shirts with frills in chiffon, in crepe, with a one-sided collar, and a metallic leather jacket with blue snake.' Clark also mentioned Jagger coming to his Radnor Walk shop for stage costumes, and 'fitting his crotch in gold leather' for eye-catching attention on the revolving stage of *Top of the Pops*, and of first snorting cocaine on the Georgian mantlepiece in Jagger's riverside Queen Anne house at 48 Cheyne Walk in Chelsea.

Stephen's personal reaction to the degeneration of the look was to maintain unbreakable style, dressing in increasingly better-tailored suits, and to remain a Mod icon in his predominantly pastel shirts and dark patterned Jacques Fath ties. 'When my friend Eric Clapton got an Afro perm,' Pete Townshend remarked, 'I knew the Mod look was over.' It wasn't so much over as relegated to a subtext, with diehard Mods regrouping as an enduring cult, rather than being continuously newsworthy as London's fashion spearhead. In a London in which fifty fashion businesses were filing for bankruptcy each month, as symptomatic of saturation point, and in which the economy was starting to wobble towards its inevitable crash at the end of the decade, Stephen through his advisers maintained a securer financial hold than Biba, who despite their inordinate ambition and endemic popularity were black-holed by insufficient investment and an absence of the very systems that had saved the John Stephen Organisation from liquidation in 1965.

Something of the exiled status of gay men, criminalised for their sexual propensities in the sixties, and forced into a fugitive existence in the workplace, was dramatically highlighted in the suicides of two prominent figures in the music industry in 1967, the uncompromising and quirkily inventive producer, Joe Meek, and the inwardly tormented Beatles' manager, Brian Epstein, both of who as gay men killed themselves before being able to benefit from the law decriminalising homosexuality between consenting adults, passed through Parliament in the same year. A generation older than the Mods dressed by John Stephen, Meek, as an independent producer who had scored massively with the Tornados' smash, *Telstar,* and Johnny Leyton's overtly gay summer 1961 hit, *Johnny Remember Me*, was an inveterate cottager, drawn particularly to soliciting for sex in the toilets at Madras Place in Holloway, with his recognisable scarlet Sunbeam Rapier parked outside, and was kept under regular police surveillance. Joe Meek was, like John Stephen, from whom he bought white and ice-blue tab-collared shirts and knitted ties, a suit man, who never dressed casual, but whose signature look was invariably dark tailored suits, narrow ties, and with his Tony Curtis quiff gelled immovably into place. Innately paranoid, ostracised within the industry, and speed-addicted, as well as reliant on a cache of prescribed anti-depressants, Meek, who had already been prosecuted for cottaging in November 1965 and acquitted by a King's Cross magistrate, was due to face further charges, when on 3 February 1967, in a state of pilled-up pathological delusion, he shot his landlady Mrs Shenton, over an exaggerated conspiracy theory, that he associated with his homosexuality, before blowing his own head off over her body at the top of the stairs, as a last annihilative act of shattering. Police investigating the crime discovered twenty-four bottles in his flat containing barbiturates, amphetamines, dexadrine and purple hearts, as indicative of his dependency on personality-warping prescription drugs.

Meek's final offering to the recording world, through the now dated Tornados, and complete with ocean effects, indented percussion and alien keyboard sound, was the single, *Is That A Ship I Hear*, backed by the astonishing flip-side *Do You Come Here Often*, as an organ-drenched burlesque instrumental opening that dissolves into the recorded stringent camp repartee between two queens bitching in the toilet of a London gay club, arguably Peter Burton's Le Duce in D'Arblay Street, the Apollo or the 50/50. As a document of real speak, the exchange is extraordinary for the affected mannerisms and vicious rivalry of two alienated and competitive queens, running to the likes of killer dialogue, like, 'Wow! These two coming now. What do you think? Mmmmmmm. Mine's all right, but I don't like the look of yours.' The exit line of the pretended winner is, 'Cheerio. I'll see you down the Dilly,' to which the other replies with lacerating venom, 'Not if I see you first, you won't.' The searing loneliness of gay men, cut up as much by their own as by the consolidated intolerance of a conventionally straight society, was the one in which John Stephen lived in the sixties, at a confused time of emergence and coming out, as well as paranoid intrigue as to who was who, with queer politics often proving as inimical to their own as to the opposition. Eighteen days after Meek's suicide, Brian Epstein, an acquaintance of John Stephen's – the fugitive and taciturn Epstein found friendships unmanageable – was found dead of a barbiturate overdose, the drug used being Carbrital, in the locked bedroom of his Belgravia house, partly as a response to the Beatles having stopped touring and effectively dispensed with his crucial entrepreneurial role, but more directly as the knock-on effect to his lowered self-esteem of his hustler boyfriend, Diz Gillespie, having robbed him of money and valuable documents containing sensitive information. After going to his house in Kingsley Hill, for a projected weekend with a group of friends, Epstein had decided to drive back prematurely on Friday night to his London Chapel Street home. Over the next twenty-four hours he left a series of intermittently threatening and coercive emotionally strained messages on his friend Simon Napier Bell's answering-machine. They comprised bits of chopped-up emotion that were partly cajoling, searingly bitchy, booze-dissociated, but all of them compounded out of the core of solidified loneliness that locked Epstein into the tormented inner world he inhabited, in which his sexuality was the intolerable hang-up he attempted to dissolve in drink and drugs. It was rumoured too that Epstein in his recourse to rough trade, had paid for a Coldstream Guardsman that weekend, and that the affair had gone badly wrong, adding to his tendency at overwrought times to become careless about self-medication. Accident or not, the police discovered twenty-eight bottles of prescription medication in his bathroom, and Epstein, his bloodstream loaded with Carbrital, had taken the additional precaution of locking his bedroom door, as the final seal on his disquieting exit. Both Meek and Epstein personified the intense loneliness experienced by so many gay outlaws of the period, when guilt and a pervading sense of social and emotional exclusion often led to psychological extremes of behaviour like suicide when faced with seemingly irremediable situations.

And if Meek and Epstein's suicides weren't sufficient indicators of the often intolerable pariah status of gay men in mid-sixties Britain, then the brutal murder of the controversial playwright Joe Orton, beaten to death with nine hammer blows shattering his cranium by his competitively jealous partner Kenneth Halliwell, created a catastrophic triumvirate of gay celebrity suicides in 1967. Orton, like Meek, was a compulsive, sex-addicted Islington cottager, detailing his escalating chain of lugubrious underground conquests in his diaries, and although an occasional visitor to Stephen's Carnaby Street, was more often a John Michael customer. In a diary entry written a week before his death, Orton noted: 'Wandered round Lillywhites. I bought a blue vest in their sports department. Went to John Michael's in Leicester Sqaure. I bought a pair of blue jeans made of cotton. Kenneth bought a black shirt. I saw a pair of trousers made of white towelling but decided against buying them. The colour mainly.' Within two weeks of making his John Michael purchases, Orton was maniacally bludgeoned to death by Halliwell in a ferocious attack, who apart from a prescribed drug regime of Librium and Nembutal, had also been abusing the purple hearts he was taking for depression, accentuating the pathological aspects of his disturbed personality. After murdering Orton, Halliwell swallowed twenty-two Nembutal capsules with a glass of grapefruit juice, and was found naked, dead in the centre of the bedroom, the coroner's report stating that Halliwell died first of a barbiturate overdose.

The deaths of these three homosexual figures, all of them known to John Stephen, no matter how peripherally, were significant for the fact that each died for varying reasons attached to a criminalised sexuality, that Stephen was at immense pains to hide. Meek was named in the *Evening Standard* in 1963, after being prosecuted at King's Cross for alleged soliciting, Epstein had been arrested for persistently importuning in 1957 while he was a drama student, and Orton and Halliwell were imprisoned in 1962 for stealing and defacing library books, an unjustifiable sentence they attributed to the fact that they were known to the police as queers.

A blonde dancer with a rainy-day smudged eyeliner look, Jayne Harries, spotted on camera dancing to the Four Tops' chokingly anthemic *Dancing In The Shadow Of Love,* on *Top of the Pops*, wearing second-skin black velvet hipsters and a white silk frilled blouse was voted Miss Mod 1967, by a panel including Steve Marriott, as an affirmative reminder that the John Stephen look was still out there as a style dominant, despite the macaronic chaos of uncoordinated hippie dress. The presentation was sufficiently high profile to merit a ceremony at the London Hilton, on Park Lane, and came with the award of a clothes voucher from John Stephen, as well as the facility to permit Jayne Harries access to most of the major pop acts on tour, including the Small Faces, Cat Stevens and the Walker Brothers. Mod was still making a consolidated stand, no matter its subversion by psychedelia, with its musical firepower issuing from the exceptionally talented Geno Washington, Jimmy James and the Vagabonds, and the London-based the Foundations, who wrote the Long John Baldry hit *Let Their Heartache Begin*. Mods still convened at the Wardour Street Whisky a Go Go, for a weekly disco on Thursdays, featuring Motown, Stax, Bluebeat and Ska, as the musical equivalent of Mod DNA, at a time when psychedelic rock with its virtuoso rococo guitar figures threatened to supersede the white-boy-sings-black-R&B template to which Mods danced as the plasma on which their hyped-up nocturnal existence depended. And John Stephen, in the hope of restoring prestige and a semblance of sartorial gravity to a Carnaby Street beleaguered by voyeuristic tourists, launched the Beau Brummell award for the best dressed personality of the year, as a reminder that his interests were still with the showiest articulated components of the look. A moulded figure of the Regency dandy Beau Brummell, a 12in tall silver statuette, came with a voucher of £500 to the winner, for use in John Stephen shops, and was effectively decided by a Radio Luxembourg panel in collaboration with John Stephen and his managers.

Stephen too, despite the overriding popularity of his shops, continued out of habit to use strategically-placed advertisements in papers to supplement his considerable turnover as a fiercely resistant independent. An insidiously worded Mike McGrath ad in the *East London Advertiser* was aimed at making his clothes accessible through mail order to those who lived outside the fulminating square mile in which his industrious street dominated the precinct. 'No need to travel to London to get them,' the advertisement advised. 'Drop a letter in the post with your vital statistics to Stephen House in Carnaby Street W1 and you'll be wearing them within a week. For the go anywhere anytime male there's a fabulous beige blazer in lambswool smart, and no trouble with crumpled pocket flaps. The pockets are hidden under the deep side vents. It'll go with anything, and if you don't fancy beige as a colour, there's navy, wine or tobacco. Comes in stripes too, if you don't like plain gear.'

If Carnaby Street appeared exhausted of serious interest to the mainstream press in Britain, then the European underground, late to come to it, and anxious to perpetuate the street's cutting edge image, provided Stephen with a renewed and invigorated following. Substantial commentaries and photo-essays, with the main focus on John Stephen as 'King Of The Road,' appeared in *Die Zeit* (Germany, March 1966), *Sagno* (Italy, June 1966), *Oggi Illustrato* (Italy, August 1966), *Realités* (France, October 1966), *Triunfo* (Spain, November 1966), and *Zie* (Netherlands, July 1966), with *De Spiegel* (Netherlands, July 1966), running a special illustrated feature on contemporary London that included an alternative map of the city, focusing on Carnaby Street and the clubs and discotheques constellating Soho as its intransigent nucleus for dictating the times. There was in addition the Dutch fanzine *Carnaby News*, freely distributed from several new London-style boutiques in Amsterdam, the September 1967 issue featuring an exclusive interview with the unremittingly pressurised John Stephen on the continuity of the look.

Something of the radical re-routing of the youth zeitgeist in 1967, due in part to LSD-25 chemically piloting the flight-paths of its cultural thrust, was reflected in the changing look and musical direction of the London bands with which Mods identified. Synthesised psychedelics of the sort manufactured in the States by a one-time radar technician from Berkeley University, Augustus Owsley Stanley III, and better assimilated by the altogether more benign ethos of West Coast hippiedom, proved a more dangerous agent as a psychotropic introduced into London's grey climate and vigilantly policed clubs and aristo-druggy King's Road and Portobello milieu. In 1967, The Who in keeping with the times had allowed their seminal Mods-from-Shepherd's-Bush influenced hairdos to grow long, and had taken to wearing khatoun jackets over thrift and union jack shirts from the déclassé racks of extracurricular Carnaby Street opportunists. Participants in corrupting the Stephen look, they had released their acid-inflected epic single, *I Can See For Miles*, which despite its accelerative energies as a reminder of Mod speed, pointed more towards the marathon pop single experimentation of chaptered late-sixties psychedelic singles, than the compressed fast track of their more familiar snappy pop. The Small Faces too, had graduated from paradigms of the John Stephen look and Carnaby Street popocracy, into a degeneration of Mod, their newly long hairdos accompanied by striped or crushed velvet hipsters, decorative girlie scarves, unstructured blouses in the case of Marriott and Lane, and a general deconstruction of the look, carried into their more ponderous July 1967 single release, *Tin Soldier*, that smacked of defiant breaking with pop management in its lyrically reflective intro and cyclonic gutsy guitar-scherzo finale. The Action, as a prototypical Mod band, were also departing from their soul-influenced staple Mod template to create a druggier, layered texture, with a buried melody line and skewed trumpet right on the middle break of their *Shadows and Reflections* single, as an admission of the shape-shifting psychotropic chemical which was altering pop, and more importantly for John Stephen, the look that accompanied it.

The changing attitude of the times, begun with Stephen's temerity a decade earlier in transposing queer into straight, were synthesised into focus by his admirer and critic, Barry Fantoni, in reviewing the relatively genderless line of clothes, together with a progressively exhilarative palette of bold colours, men were permitted to wear in 1967. Commenting on Stephen's beginnings as the catalyst to reconfiguring masculine identity, and the gradual evolution of that look into mainstream currency, Fantoni wrote of the unstoppable momentum affecting the change from sexual outlaw to acceptance. Hostilty, he wrote, 'was back in the days when it was considered somewhat unmanly to take a proper interest in clothes, and the gay young men who began to make a regular pilgrimage to Carnaby Street were at first the only ones to appreciate what they were being offered. In those days you still wondered if a man in a pink shirt wasn't queer, and tight trousers round the crotch smacked a bit too much of uplift bras and all that. Who worries about that sort of thing now? That's what men are saying all over the world as John Stephen and Lord John (Mr. Warren Gold to his lawyers), export hipsters and thick corduroy outfits in wild colours like lavender or buttercup yellow, or bright scarlet, with broad fetishistic black leather belts, crazy wide Arthur English ties, and shirts with big floppy collars.' The escalation of exaggerated style wasn't an end of the look, so much as its dissolution into Chelsea period revival and a bohemi-anism encouraged by the fusion of dandy and ethnic hippie, and of the two it was only the bohemian-interested Stephen, in his continued propagation of a style he had singularly invented and continued to maintain as his own.

8

THERE'S NO-ONE KNOWS THE BUSINESS LIKE I DO

The John Stephen shirt look of the graduating sixties, heavy glowering satin, high-collared chemises in cerise, grape purple, ultramarine, tomato-red and ivory, the cool fabric imparting a lapidary quality to the wearer, and worn either with splashy kipper ties or paisley and polka-dot cravats, was very much the look adopted by the Syd Barrett-led Pink Floyd in 1967. Arguably the first British band to incorporate light shows into the stratospheric soundscapes of their residency at the UFO club, in the basement of 31 Tottenham Court Road, under the Berkeley Cinema, and opposite the Dominion Theatre, the band dressed to complement their improvised music. The early Pink Floyd, whose first groundbreaking psychedelic single, *Arnold Layne*, complete with ethereal space-probe keyboards, and rocket voyager guitar effects, and produced by Joe Boyd, co-founder with John Hopkins of the UFO club, personified in their choice of clothes, all the disparate components that comprised the over-crowded, colour-saturated and inevitable implosion of the look in 1967–68. Wearing tackily smudged black eyeliner and vermilion military tunics picked up at Lord Kitchener's Valet, with a rack of dandified John Stephen shirts, striped pants and dressy double-breasted frock coats, Barrett as much as Mick Jagger came to embody the overcompensated, mismatched excess of the look at the apogee of its late sixties popularity. With Granny Takes A Trip having a license outlet to sell clothes at the UFO, and Stephen's wildly over-popularised clothes barrio situated within walking distance of Tottenham Court Road, the UFO became the cult club for drugs, mostly acid, clothes influences and experimental music, with its residential band, the Cambridge art house purveyors of mind-stripping psychedelia, Pink Floyd, dressing to complement the hallucinated chemistry of their music.

In his memoir of the period, *White Bicycles – making music in the 1960s* – the independent record producer Joe Boyd, relives the whole lawless, LSD directed high sixties ethos of the arts experimental basement UFO club. The club's unequivocal accent incorporated an altered state cocktail of psychedelic music, Nigel Waymouth and Michael English designed 3-D posters in lividly assaulting colours, and rogue bohemian fashion sold in a merchandising outlet on the premises. 'My friend Nigel Waymouth was a partner in Granny Takes A Trip, King's Road's most extreme boutique,' Boyd writes, 'where they sold floral jackets and mattress ticking suits and shirts with collars that drooped to the nipples. Nigel had painted their shop window in a post-Beardsley acid dream style with the front end of a car protruding on to the pavement. I nominated him for the task of creating our first poster.'

The druggy UFO underground ecosphere, with Boyd substituting Soft Machine for Pink Floyd when their tenure expired, was, despite its subterranean West End location, more King's Road influenced than John Stephen's Soho, and marginally left-field of his fashion remit, with his continued resistance to uniforms and revamped Victoriana as a recycled expression of contemporary fashion. The essentially bohemian styles dominating the closure of the sixties, and at radical variance to the economic line favoured by Stephen and the diminished Mod look, were not only the product of psychoactive visualisation infiltrating fashion, but owed something of their foppish influence to film. The fusion of bohemian and hippie, perverse empire nostalgia and faux ethnic appropriation was discernible in two highly influential black-and-white productions for BBC television in 1966: the series *Adam Adamant Lives*, starring Gerald Harper as an Edwardian adventurer who had been cryopreserved in time and Juliet Harmer as Georgina Jones, a Mod fashionista who took up with him; and Jonathan Miller's hallucinated gothic production of Lewis Carroll's mid-Victorian children's fantasy *Alice in Wonderland*. Both productions were reliant on conflating period costume with modern in an almost seamless join of the two styles, and as a consequence Edwardian spats were reintroduced into late sixties bohemian fashion, as were dandified velvet Regency coats and waistcoats worn over ruffled shirts with absailing round and elongated collars that extended to 7in.

The John Stephen workrooms persisted tirelessly in their production of new styles, but something of their inspired designer's initial direction had gone in his effort to remain fiercely competitive, as well as attempt to modify bohemianism to his own impressively distinct style. 'I go mad with materials

John Stephen's white German shepherd dog Prince accompanied him everywhere, including board-meetings. His partner Bill Franks stands behind him.

I like,' was the John Stephen caption used to promote his discovery of a green floral patterned linen he had picked up in nearby Soho, and sketched six outfits in it to be made up immediately as samples. The two he liked best were put into production with a publicity shoot engaging models Stevie Holly and Jan Barber, a singer with the short-lived pop act Piccadilly Line. Stevie's two-piece with accompanying wide slacks came in green, pink or black, typifying Stephen's obsession with multiples, while Jan's culotte in the same pattern came in green, pink or yellow with a 4in-wide belt with frog fastening. In the same photo shoot Nigel English modelled a hip-length white leather windbreaker with a high button-down collar and buttoned patch pockets over a white Shetland sweater and white cotton slacks, as part of Stephen's new collection for men. The all-over-white theme carried sailor-boy connotations, as Stephen effectively transposed the long-collared shirt style popular at the time into a casual white leather jacket set off with black and white leather shoes available from nearby Topper's at 45 Carnaby Street.

Something of the existing social tensions between Mods and hippies, with hippies using the degenerative UFO club on Tottenham Court Road as their basement core of activity, their liberal intake of acid supplied by a German dealer known only as Manfred, is conveyed by Chris Rowley in his relating a potential clash at the UFO between the wired, asexual Mods as purveyors of speed, and the sensually motivated hippies as pot-smoking exponents of pacifist flower power. 'The Mods were standing there pilled up, chewing, looking around them, semi-freaked out. The girls, noting that this Mod group were hostile, almost lashing out at the hippies around them, descended on them semi-naked and began caressing them. These guys did not know what had hit them, but they soon calmed down and later on were seen to be holding flowers and talking to Manfred.' While friction between Mods and hippies was ideologically apparent, the pacifist ideals inherent in the idealistic lifestyle of hippies prevented the sort of antagonistic rivalry that had existed between Mods and Rockers, with hostilities spilling over into organised gang warfare. Mods, purely as an aesthetic issue, resented hippies adulterating their streamlined sartorial elegance, were suspicious of their advocacy of psychotropic substances like hash and LSD, and were equally critical of the psychedelic rock that evolved as the soundtrack to the drug's acute visual patterning. Mod, in line with John Stephen's aesthetic, was a narcissistic state that drew attention to itself through extreme individuality, was minimal, correct, uncopyable, and like Stephen's work application, the product of immense self-discipline. It was in every aspect of stylishness the opposite of the uncoordinated ethnic grunge worn by hippies, it was solitary as opposed to the communal instincts of flower power, its drug promoted speed and activity rather than passive lethargy, and its principle, nowhere better exemplified than in Stephen's life, was about the dynamic of doing. Although the fashion world remained polarised to Soho and the King's Road as its optimal resources, hippies made the large dilapidated and often disused buildings in the area of London's Ladbroke Grove, Westbourne Terrace and Portobello Road into their communal centre. The district quickly generated a nucleus of West Indian hash dealers, as well becoming home to the intransigent King Mob group of dissidents and urban guerrillas, their name being derived from an abbreviation of the graffito 'His Majesty King Mob' which had been scrawled on the walls of Newgate Prison when it was torched by insurgents during the Gordon Riots of 1780. The defiant, demonstratively gangsterish King Mob revolutionaries not only celebrated infamous hate-figures such as Jack the Ripper and the serial killer John Reginald Christie, and defaced Notting Hill facades with slashed graffiti slogans lifted from the visionary writings of William Blake, but also manufactured a drug called TMA or Paramythoxyamphetamine – a sort of psychedelic methedrin and precursor of Ecstasy that when shot up made everything go black and white and induced intensely discomforting chiliastic hallucinations.

In the face of anarchic turbulence beginning to infiltrate sixties culture, as the break-up of its earlier holistic grouping of fashion, music and a revisioned youthful ideology founded on the look as its identity, and liberated hedonism as its incentive to party, Stephen restructured the suit on a superb Mod line that deconstructed formal wear into a casual elegance that defined the basic principles of modernism, and as such could have been designed for the wardrobe of a Patrick Macnee and Diana Rigg *Avengers* shoot. A Stephen first that was based on classic Mod principles of incisively clean and precisely detailed styling, his leisure knitted suits, coming at a time when confected decoration predominated as the fashion signifier, was a lost opportunity for Mods to regain an endemic fashion ascendancy and to additionally reinvent the ubiquitous role the suit played in society. Designed in black, navy, white, red and aubergine, the wool top with matching trousers and a polo neck collar had seven bone buttons running down each side of the top, buttoned epaulettes and a matching belt with a circular bone buckle. Cut deliberately small, according to the Stephen bias for size zero amongst men, the suit was available only in 34, 36 and 38 to emphasise skinny and the futuristic accent the suit imparted. An inspired attempt on Stephen's part to reconfigure suit wear on an inventively androgynous line, that was practical, forward-tilted and space-times ahead of his derivative contemporaries, Stephen, in the attempt to popularise his own design, also imported an acrylic leisure suit in man-made fibre from Italy in beige, light blue and pale green, with a similar polo neck design also available in crew neck, with a wide leather belt and flared slacks. Stephen's design was altogether classier, imaginatively instructive, and incorrigibly unisex, and provided the wearer with comfort, acute attention to detail, and the sense of wearing something absolutely contemporaneous with the moment in which they were living. And customers to his main shop stepped out of the John Stephen Department Store at 33–34 Carnaby Street, Myles Antony-designed peacock-embellished carrier in hand, and headed up the agitated street, either north towards the Shakespeare's Head, and the imposingly fortressed Liberty, or south towards Beak Street with the dispersal of shoppers into the maze of alleys pointing towards Piccadilly Circus , with rent boys hanging out on the black railings outside Boots, and neons creating a crude red, blue and green edgy installation for inquisitive tourists. These were the same alleys through which Stephen would head for a take no prisoners lunchtime meeting, smouldering cheroot in hand, tie perfectly calibrated to emphasise its pattern, while his partner Bill Franks settled for a sandwich from a café in nearby Foubert's Place, and dealt with a tedious salesman from the tie manufacturers Michelson's, attempting to unload a dollop of mint green and Turkish Delight-coloured silk Jacques Fath ties into the ubiquitously busy The Man's Shop.

In contrast to Stephen's new look knitted suits, the windows of Gear in Carnaby Street were loud with printed cotton union jack shirts and jackets, while Lord Kitchener's Valet promoted red woollen Royal Engineers' jackets teamed with flared striped trousers, and Lord John windowed a fitted mid- and maxi-length dramatically belted denim-style overcoat with contrasting white topstitching, and Sidney Brent's Take Six black mohair suits to be worn with eight-button double-breasted long frock coats with tall highwayman collars offset with a purple tie for effect. On other parts of the fashionista map, and equally derivative in their styling, Rupert Lycett Green of Blades at the top end of Savile Row was showcasing slim-fitting clothes custom made from unusual fabrics, and as a centre-piece, a luxurious figured pale pink suit, made in France, with a matching cravat theatrically worn in place of a tie for upmarket sybaritic dandies.

Stephen, as the only true British original of his generation, the tireless instigator of a look endlessly hijacked and put through modified permutations not only by the chains but by piratical rivals in his street, stayed modernistic, his energies directed towards creating the new rather than parasitically feeding on modalities from the past. His enduring contemporary in modernism, Mary

Quant, had meanwhile created her populist Ginger Group label, aimed at a less wealthy clientele, but directed at a more discerning market than Barbara Hulanicki's contagiously popular and democratically-priced Biba.

As a more daring alternative to the modified revivalist camp of Lambert and Emmerton's Chelsea Antiques Market stall, obsessively fine-tuned London fashionistas in 1967 witnessed the opening of Kensington Market in a five-storey building on the south side of Kensington High Street, as a commercial venture aimed at renting out stalls to the upcoming bright young things who were at the heart of the underground's entrepreneurial spearhead of innovative fashion. As an interface between Chelsea and Notting Hill Gate, and with its stall-holders professing terminal ennui with John Stephen's Carnaby Street, as well as the foppishly maverick decadence of the King's Road, the market with its forty walk-in shops was intended as a challenging avant garde front to existing preconceptions of the look, including Stephen's demonstrative continuity as its cutting edge shaper of Mod. One of the lead stall owners was Cockell and Johnson, 126–127 Kensington Market, comprising the joint fashion thrust of Lloyd Johnson and Patrick Cockell, whose modest advertising stated their superior claim to the roomy patch with a winning stab at originality on the small-scale economics at which John Stephen had first pioneered fashion at Beak Street a decade earlier. The ad reads: 'It's not we're hustling super-salesman (far from it). It's just that all the clothes we sell are exclusive to us, designed by us to be just a little special and without hitting the price stratosphere. That includes velvet jackets, napoleon raincoats, gabardine trousers and a host of beautiful shirts in every colour and fabric. So come and look them over. You can be sure you won't find them elsewhere.' Their claim was authentic in the market milieu, but the surge of cultural energies stimulated by John Stephen that had given the teenage underclass an identity at the beginnings of the cataclysmically formative sixties, formed quite literally in the basements of his alley, had lost the firepower to impact with the same contagious pandemic. As talented as Lloyd Johnson was, in harness with the maverick designer Colin Bennett, who made tight velveteen trousers and leather clothes for the stall, the latter attracting gay clubbers wanting to inject oily black skins into their still ghettoized underworld scene, the impact was limited and absorbed into a chaotic androgyny shouting for attention. Bennett, who had something of John Stephen's ingenious flair for originality, had begun by cutting trousers at Colin Wild's Carnaby Cavern, before working for a year at Bona Clouts in Soho's Lexington Street, but altogether lacked Stephen's retailing chutzpah and his serial obsession with opening shops, preferring instead to design splashy one-offs for rock and pop

Barry Gibb of the Bee Gees dressed in dandified John Stephen clothes. He was given the John Stephen award for Best Dressed Man of the Year in 1966.

stars like Ronnie Wood, Rod Stewart and Long John Baldry, as well as making the grey satin frock-coated suits worn by Cream in their 'goodbye' publicity shoots, coinciding with their valedictory concert at the Royal Albert Hall on 26 November 1968. With Cockell and Johnson changing the name of their Kensington Market stall to Heavy Metal Kids, Bennett's designs went suitably weird, and like the King's Road advocates of decadent bohemianism, his creations dissolved all distinctions between stage and street wear. With the exterior of the stall comprising fake submarine panelling sprayed silver, and with a range of Kandinsky-coloured velvet suits in purple, hot pink, lipstick red, ultramarine and ochre, Heavy Metal Kids was at this stage of the evolution of sixties fashion still another distractive outlet for the attenuated popocracy, rather than instrumental to the reshaping of a generation that Stephen had undertaken a decade earlier, when his clothes had intrepidly defied all notions of what it was considered acceptable for men to wear.

The rapid-fire momentum of the sixties, rather like a kamikaze sighting its intended target but delaying before the impacting nose-diving free-fall, was one that was piloted by a collectively innovative youth zeitgeist, from excess to expiry, hedonistic sensation to inevitable burnt-out. It wasn't that John Stephen's prescient inventiveness was lost to the rock cognoscenti, it was more that his look had been remixed so often, and layered so transgressively, that it was submerged beneath a confection that diminished even the nightly floor-show at the Black Cap in Camden for camp, with few of its exhibitionistic exponents ever referencing Stephen as its traceable source. In the Rolling Stones' video shoot for their disdainfully delivered, snarlingly antagonistic No 1 hit single *Jumping Jack Flash*, the band chose to appear, as symptomatic of the times, in full makeup, brocaded blouses and velvet tops, with Keith Richards and Brian Jones wearing plastic-framed aviators, as synonymous with drag as the new expression of masculinity. And while John Stephen was a regular visitor both to Danny La Rue's glitzy Mayfair nightspot and Camden's Black Cap, the gay subtext to his clothes was always in the interests of masculinity, and his designs continued to resist the extravagant parodic camp that was the increasingly colourful accent promoted by his contemporaries. Jagger, as the spearhead of bisexual fashion, was now, amongst his assemblage of decorative headwear, wearing a brooched cloche hat and lipstick as a permanent fixture, while Jones and Richards wore a variety of headscarves and complementary women's hats, as a sign that the King's Road as the preferred Stones' precinct, rather than Stephen's Carnaby Street, was the epicentre of dandified cross-dressing that had taken over not only the stage, but revolutionised the street.

Still working at maximum pressure in the interests of his organisation, and never pursuing less than a tenacious twelve hours working day, six days a week, Stephen and his committee, comprising members of the Radio Luxembourg Club, voted a renowned John Stephen customer, Barry Gibb of the Bee Gees, best dressed personality of the year, for the first presentation of the John Stephen Fashion Award in 1968. It was a year in which the Bee Gees with their quixotic blend of rock and orchestral ballads had released two stratospherically successful albums, *Horizontal* and *Idea*, following on from mega-selling climactic singles like *To Love Somebody*, *Massachusetts* and *Words*. The silver Beau Brummell statuette was presented to Gibb by the diminutive Tsai Chin, who had starred in the movie *Virgin Soldiers*, on the first floor balcony of the John Stephen Department Store, overlooking a fan congested Carnaby Street, the intimidating maximum turn-out spilling all the way into Regent Street. The presentation, with John Stephen and Radio Luxembourg DJ Tony Prince also in attendance, had to be rushed at a frenetic pace on account of girls fainting in the street and having to receive medical assistance in adjacent boutiques. To receive the award, and dressed entirely in John Stephen clothes, Gibb wore a white shirt, tie, jacket and handkerchief, set off by cherry red velvet slacks and a matching waistcoat, as the epitome of the late-sixties pop dandy. With members of the Move, Family Dogg and the Tremeloes, all regular Stephen customers, available for interview on the balcony as an additional attraction to the ceremony, proceedings were broken up by the police, on account of fan hysteria, and the disappointed, demonstratively hyper crowds dispersed across the West End.

The Barry Gibb look, nurtured exclusively by John Stephen's shops, was an elegant sartorial one, with Gibb favouring three-piece woollen, velvet and mohair suits, eye-catching ties and a plethora of high-collared shirts in every available colour and fabric. Of his preferred mode of dressing, Gibb commented in conjunction with receiving the John Stephen Fashion Award that he kept 'to four colours most of the time – red, white, black or blue – makes it much simpler for me to interchange things I wear. Although I rarely put blue and black together, I have numerous suits in white mohair and red velvet and the jackets and slacks interchange quite effectively.' Barry Gibbs' aesthetic was a legitimate update of the look, rather than a departure from it, a dandification of the sharp line developed by Mods, and softened by period revivalist degeneration, but observantly there in its resistance to bohemian overkill, and in the careful selection of four colours as a basis from which to work. Barry Gibb, gay pop icon for his falsetto voice, was living at the time of the award in a palatial apartment in Eaton Square, to which John Stephen

Barry Gibb holding his award, a Beau Brummell statuette, presented by John Stephen on the right.

was a frequent visitor, personally supplying the pop celebrity with the clothes needed to keep his wardrobe in a state of transitional update commensurate with the look. Gibb, who spent an approximate £13,000 a year on clothes, and most of it with John Stephen, was a customer to be cultivated, and one who usually consulted Stephen's manager, John Crowley, as personal adviser to refreshing his prodigious personal wardrobe. Commenting on Gibbs' singularly obsessive propensity for clothes, Crowley, interviewed by the *London Express*, commented advantageously, 'you only have to show Barry one silk shirt, and if it takes his fancy he will order it in every available colour, which can be as many as thirty-six shirts, all with matching ties.' The same reporter, featuring John Stephen's phenomenal success as the hyperactively driven individual who was indubitably responsible for the look, additionally mentioned the fact that he had been given the keys to the city of Tampa, Florida, two years earlier, in recognition of his design achievements and wore the token proudly on a tie-tack. Attention was also drawn to his celebrity customers, like Judy Garland, Veronica Lake and Mama Cass of the Mamas and Papas, and to the fact that the histrionic diva Judy Garland had recently purchased a hat decorated with ostrich feathers from Tre Camp, an ostentatious millinery confection that she had sighted on one of Myles Antony's overtly bisexual display mannequins.

By the late sixties, and as the precursor of the wet-look plastic trousers adopted by punk in the mid-seventies, John Stephen had come up with still another memorably impacting design for a suit, so original in its modernistic styling that it stood out instantly as a first, conceived by the immediacy of his configurative imagination. Sleek, adventurous, streamlined, and instantaneously visually commanding, Stephen combined brown slacks made of cotton-backed polyurethane with a belted, high-fastening salt and pepper tweed jacket in brown and beige. By way of detail, the wet look of the slacks that flared slightly from the knee was continued in the jacket's shoulder yoke, belt and patch pockets. Filmic, urban and indomitably modern, the suit that picked up on aspects of the Avengers' wardrobe was an expression of Stephen's continuing Mod principles, a daring statement of making it new that superseded anything on the racks of his largely derivative Chelsea contemporaries. And for the less intrepid, the suit jacket could be teamed with tweed slacks that came in green, matching beige, brown and coffee, typifying the usual variety of Stephen colours attached to any of his original creations.

At the same time as Stephen was preoccupied with configuring ways of restructuring the suit, not just in terms of applied detail, but as a reinvented dynamic to accommodate the changing times, Tommy Nutter, who was trained in traditional tailoring in Savile Row, set up his innovative House of Nutter on the same prestigious street with backing from the Beatles' short-lived company Apple, a philanthropic arts-biased incentive that directed money into a chain of projects with some sort of creative basis. Nutter's highly original suits, worn by the likes of Mick Jagger, Eric Clapton and the Beatles, who are pictured wearing three of his suits on the Abbey Road record sleeve, brought boldness more than originality to his designs, and sensation rather than an imaginatively realised vision to his cut. 'Everybody was wearing a narrow suit at the end of the 1960s,' he recalled, 'so I just went wild with the lapels and cut them as wide as you possibly could – enormous – and it was terribly flared at the jacket. So that was my first look and it was different from anybody else.'

Nutter's highly inventive look, no matter how showy in its construct, like the whole neo-Edwardian revival that had saturated late-sixties men's fashion in Britain and the States, was considerably at variance with Stephen's look with its continued emphasis on modernism. Visited by *Disc* and *Music Echo*, who commented on the outstandingly attractive Stephen as 'slim, suave and still unaffected by it all,' Stephen was described as wearing a charcoal grey double-breasted suit, white shirt and gold tie with matching handkerchief, as synonymous with understated cool, and as nervously smoking Hamlet cigars. The journalist was visually stunned by the enormous colour range Stephen provided in shirts, knitwear and jackets, remarking on how if you wanted a blue shirt in a particular style, then Stephen's palette extended to at least six or ten variant shades of that blue, something that no other designer accommodated with such obsessive command of making a shirt or jumper collectible through the variety of its available shades. Stephen took the opportunity too to recapitulate on twelve years of continuously forward-thinking invention on his part, and of how through gritty, self-taught experience he felt he had come to practicalise and master his profession. 'Remember that I started in this business as a pioneer 12 years ago. I'd never had a shop or experience in manufacturing. I got machinists, but my girls were making a sweater one day and slacks the next, so you couldn't expect a consistently high standard of quality in such conditions. Now though, I'm twelve years older and there's no-one knows the business as well as I do.'

Mention too was made in the same feature of the high instance of shoplifting from his stores, with Stephen's assistant and manager John Crowley reported as having to go off with the unwelcome task of giving evidence at the adjoining Great Marlborough Street magistrates court. Crowley was quoted

Bright young things: Mick Jagger and Marianne Faithfull. Jagger, like Brian Jones, was a regular at John Stephen's boutiques.

as saying, 'It takes up half my day, dealing with all our shop-lifting cases. At first you feel soft and take pity, but after a time you simply harden.'

Stephen's always aesthetically-detailed creations continued in the form of svelte maxi-coats in black barathea with gilt buttons, and shirts in extra fine cotton with green, blue or rust thistle patterns. And as a perennial winner he reverted to gingham for a range of checked cotton shirts in bright pink, turquoise, green, yellow or red, worn with a matching silk-lined tie in the same material. And for his roster of committed fashionistas he supplied Dacron/cotton slacks dyed to match the shirt, although the pink gingham was modelled to advantage with a black cotton suit that had a velvet look without the pile that invariably marked. In the fashion shoot used to promote the shirt, again through the simple dissemination of black and white captioned photos sent out to magazines, model Bobby Rowe wore the shocking pink gingham shirt to effect with the black cotton suit and a black leather belt decorated with a gilt Victorian buckle purchased from Hope & Eleanor at the Chelsea Antique Market.

London though, through the mandatory experimentation with LSD by its dandified popocracy, gallerists, hipoissie and *jeunesse dorée*, all frothed into exaggerations of Stephen's beleaguered look, was starting to turn weird as the new chemical dangerously infiltrated a scene in which clothes as the complementary expression of the hallucinatory drug often represented significant markers to a Drugs Squad who approved of neither. There had already been the infamous Redlands bust in 1967, when Mick Jagger, Keith Richards and the gallery owner Robert Fraser had been respectively charged at Chichester Magistrates Court for possession of amphetamines on Jagger's part, Richards with complicity in allowing his property to be used for the consumption of cannabis, and Fraser for possession of heroin, with all three being jailed, although Jagger's sentence of three months, and Richards' of a year, partly for contempt of court, were both suspended on appeal as prejudicially disproportionate to the evidence, Jagger's amphetamines having been prescribed verbally by his doctor, and the case against Richards being wholly suppositional. The persistent police harassment of the Rolling Stones as renowned deviants, that led to two separate drug charges being brought against the conspicuously druggy Brian Jones, clearly had as much to do with their overtly decadent look as it did their lawless lifestyles. Extreme attention was paid by the press to the uncompromisingly peacock-style clothes worn by both Jagger and Richards for their initial court appearances, with Jagger choosing a bright green blazer and ruffled shirt worn with a striped tie, and Richards a gangsterish pinstripe suit on the first day, and a black silk suit with a white cravat on the second, their choice of clothes being seen as indicative of the high-profile image-mapping expected of them as Britain's defiantly a-moralistic bad boy bandit rock-libertines.

The advent of LSD into a British culture lacking a social context for its use, and as a legally prohibited substance that imparted an understandably edgy urban paranoia to the user on account of the offence, had by the late sixties infected fashion to an unprecedented degree in terms of the use of saturated primary colours, and op-art and helical mandala-shaped patterns on fabrics and was an instance of the drug finding its direct external correlate in fashion, unlike amphetamine that for Mods had stayed implicitly buried in the user's bloodstream and look. Something of the whole hallucinated aspects of the Granny Takes A Trip style of dressing, rather than John Stephen-conceived fashion, mixed like a violent happy-hour cocktail in a clash of unnaturally worked-up tones and textures, as an identification with psychotropic drugs and psychedelic music comes across in Nicola Lane's recollection of the times, as a partying art student with a restricted budget for clothes. 'My greatest aspiration was to dress entirely from Granny Takes A Trip, but I couldn't afford it, so I had to do with either borrowing friends' dresses from Granny, or somehow lashing something together. Granny's had little crushed velvet dresses in bottle green with medieval leg-of-mutton sleeves. But there was still a touch of naff about that and the real style was to have beautiful old clothes. Long black velvet dresses were very popular and I managed to buy one for 10/6. It had a fur collar, full-length, covered buttons, leg-of-mutton sleeves. I used to wear it over purple tights, with a belt. Nothing else. No bra, no panties. It was out to wear underwear. Men didn't really wear it either: you were very pleased if your man didn't wear underwear.' And as a sign of the demonstratively sexually liberated times, Dick Lawson recalls the explicit testosterone message generated by wearing sprayed-on hipsters. 'I wore extremely tight, light-coloured trousers with no underwear, and you knew, on the tube that somebody was always going to be offended. And I was intending to offend them.'

The bohemian hippy locus now centred in the Portobello district of Notting Hill Gate, a world increasingly distinct from John Stephen's Soho precinct by way of its ethnically-influenced dress, heavy drugs bias and communal ghettoization, was at the time the countercultural core of the emergent London underground. The district was cheap, run-down and littered with West Indian drug dealers, who also organised basement dances with live music, vegetarian food and copious supplies of beer and recreational drugs. A transient utopia to its young occupants, the milieu generated no

Dripping in baroque camp, but defiantly masculine, the shot defines Stephen's characteristic dualities.

designer, had its resident Lord Kitchener's Valet, but largely in its clothes' needs fed the local Biba and vintage clothes shops on Portobello Road and the nearby Kensington Market. A little intensely-coloured vignette of the times, when the Notting Hill underground appeared for a brief time to believe in the drug-hallucinated continuity of its generational hold on London, was supplied by Chris Rowley in his vivid recollection of the LSD rites attendant on Mike McInnerney's wedding celebrations in nearby Hyde Park. 'Sixty or seventy fey young people', McInnerney writes, 'mostly dressed in velvet, gathered around some bongo drummers and primitive guitarists. People were smoking grass, some had taken acid, there was a big cake ... The long sunset came on, the trippers nodded off under the trees. The wealthy got into their Rolls Royces, and Michael English went off to Portobello to put out the next poster and capture the atmosphere of trees, golden haze, an aura of decadence and mellowed out young people.'

The times were changing rapidly and Carnaby Street no longer reverberated with the irate fuel-injected surge of scooters navigating Soho's tortuous complex of alleys converging on John Stephen's landmark shops with their inimitably transgender Myles Antony window displays interchanging what was new for both sexes in John Stephen's inexhaustible shape-shifting design repertoire. The initial Mod teenagers on their hire-purchase, flag-flying Vespas and Lambrettas, who had dared to transcend their social status by adopting the look had dispersed from Stephen's street in disgust at its tourist attraction, and while Stephen had upgraded into owning a Department Store on Carnaby Street, the loss of his original core-following was significant in that their custom had provided a constant challenge to his creative stimulus.

Stephen was on creative overreach in the late sixties, with the dual thrust of designing for both sexes, and something of his unabating drive to keep ahead of his contemporaries was sketched out by Mike McGrath in a low-key publicity caption designed to promote a female suit, that in keeping with his edgy line was unapologetically modern. 'Some people read in bed, John Stephen puffs at tiny cigars and sketches on the back of envelopes. If the idea still looks reasonable in the morning he has samples made. And this two-way beige and blue suit in Persian suede is a sample that started life on the back of an envelope. Knowing *Charge of the Light Brigade* and the reissue of *Gone with the Wind* would keep people military-minded, he achieved the military look with a blue suede panel held with brass buttons. The panel is reversible to red suede if she has a mood to match and without the panel a belt can be added, the blue colour still supplying the contrast.'

The characteristic Stephen detail of a reversible as well as detachable blue/

red suede panel, suggested that he had lost none of his maverick instinct for killer detail, despite the fact that his alley had unanimously conceded street credibility to the touristic furore threatening to submerge his signature in popular, but image-discrediting attention. And to incrementally increase his sales, and as symptomatic of a move away from the exclusivity of his Carnaby Street shops, Stephen entered into a deal with Loggers New Wholesale Division, a menswear company contracted to wholesale Stephen's designs in shirts, slacks and underwear to retailers throughout the country, with Stephen's latest cotton hip slips for men coming in black, white, red or sky blue. And as a further indicator for the discerning fashionista, that Stephen hadn't as yet deserted his underlying principle of designing essentially gay clothes for straight men, he ran a line of see-through shirts, favoured by Barry Gibb of the Bee Gees, in fine white, navy, pink, beige, light blue, brown and black, with a stripe in a slightly heavier texture, the shirt never departing from his assured principle of imparting femininity to the look, without subtracting from its essential masculine appeal in terms of androgyny.

But, try as he did to maintain incorrigible integrity, Stephen couldn't help avoid in some ways endorsing the sensationalism that was now synonymous with Carnaby Street as a tourist sensation. Westminster Council had in 1967, by order of the Greater London Council, and in the interests of accommodating the unprecedented volume of foot traffic, pedestrianised the alley, putting an end finally to the ubiquitous scooter rafts that had territorialized the street with their Italian-style customised mode of transport. Stephen in 1968, approved of Christmas decorations for the street, comprising Fourteen pairs of illuminated legs in micro-minis with one pair suitably dressed in Union Jack panties, and despite defending the decorations as essentially subversive and unpatriotic, the display was nonetheless part of the inevitable concession on Stephen's part to the street's unstoppable commercial hoopla. Stephen's main custom was now drawn from the solid wedge of spectatorial tourists, all hoping somehow to manipulate time into reverse, and relive the era of the tiny cult shops that had through his flamboyant pop designs, succeeded in establishing the look. Interviewed towards the end of his life, in 2001, Stephen reflected on the street's late sixties implosion, and how populist imitators had contributed successively to the downgrading of his considerable reputation as pop svengali, to every bright young thing, wanting to turn a head in the crowd as inimitably drop-dead-gorgeous. 'We had shops in Australia, the States, Canada, Scandanavia, Italy and South Africa,' Stephen reflected in retrospect, 'it was really that big and the international scene was following us. But then we got all these people imitating what we were doing and, because they manufactured in cheaper materials, it all got given a bad name.'

As a style indicator for 1968, the American *GQ* magazine, despite expressing a measured caution about Stephen's initiation of the peacock male, nonetheless broke boundaries by advocating the use for evening or casual wear, shirts in terra cotta and fuchsia voile, gold cotton with mustard collar, cuffs and yoke, peach cotton with black-edged lace, and a sky-blue Dacron turtleneck shirt with embroidery on the front and a zipper in the back, all of the applied detail, new for the executive American male, having been partly lifted from Stephen's superb repertoire of audacious shirt designs over the previous eight years. And in line with the neo-Edwardian double-breasted jackets made popular by Stephen and his contemporaries, as part of the new dandified bohemianism, with four-button models, elongating to six- and finally eight-button fronts, the generally conservative black tie guide magazine, with its strict observance of protocol, featured a classic sixties Edwardian blue jacquard double-breasted jacket with black velvet trim on the lapels and pocket flap, blue velvet trousers, pink shirt and an oversized kipper tie. The velvet and brocade materials used for the coat were unsparingly opulent, fashioned not only in black, but also in brown, royal blue, ruby red and emerald green. Set against these surges of colour, were contrasting black facings decorating the lapels, as well as the flap pockets, with the buttons adding flare by appearing in contrasting colours especially on the white jacket aptly called 'The Swinger.' The trousers recommended to complement the jacket came in white wool, red silk or blue velvet, as a marker that American sophisticates could also cut it in a way of which their style-leading British counterparts would approve. And not wholly convinced of the appropriate-ness of bohemian dress, *GQ* added the following equivocal admonition: 'All that the peacock revolution does, really, is to stir men to dress as they please, not as some popular arbiter of men's fashions say they should. It's okay to refuse to wear a Nehru or turtleneck, and most of the results would look like hell on anyone over thirty.'

As the 1960s peaked in an apogee of androgynously-themed clothes for men, as the prophetic realisation of Stephen's starting-point in the fifties, that 'men should be able to wear anything that women do,' so Stephen's bipolar disorder became more pronounced. His initial periods of hyperactivity, symptomatised by accelerated enthusiasm, and manic overreach, were now tempered by corresponding lows, and the descent into submerged depres-sion, as burn-out began to set in, after twelve years of unremitting drive. For the protectively vigilant Bill Franks, who had grown accustomed over the years, to observing the onset of Stephen's periodic spiral into mania, the warning signs invariably started at home, with Stephen's fidgety compulsion to keep relentlessly shifting objects and reposition everything within his visual field. The extreme agitation was almost invariably the start of a process succeeded by Stephen's projection of momentous business schemes, and the uncontrollably rapid-fire torrent of creative ideas that could find no practical application. Sometimes unable to sleep for days on end, even when sedated, Stephen would voluntarily enter the Priory Clinic, as a refuge for two or three weeks at a time, with his eventual exhaustion giving way to deep submersible depression as his chemically-imbalanced mood of elation hit intolerable rock bottom. Finding the correct dose to maintain Stephen on lithium often eluded his doctors, as his oscillating mood swings increased in intensity. As the sixties drew to a turbulent closure, Stephen's manic episodes pitched between euphoric optimism and dumb irresponsive depression, as their alternating zenith and nadir, meant that he became increasingly dependent on his psychiatrist, Dr Dally, both for home visits and for urgent telephone consultations, to provide psychological reassurance if Stephen anticipated the onset of an attack.

Stephen's designs for men and women in 1968–69, continued with unabated originality and an audacious painterly use of colour, no matter the distressed air-pocketing of his mental state. Modifying the basic utility design of the flying jacket, he updated a unisex version of it that again pre-empted punk, with a hypnotic series of zips and fastenings for the waist and pocket, and made available in shock limo-colours like flame red, emerald green, ultramarine, beige and car-oil black. The jacket brought aviation wear onto the street with a reorganised geometry of zips that demanded attention by their conspicuous and surprising vertical and horizontal placements. Stephen too demonstrated a flair in his designs for women that is often overlooked, finding a consistent late-sixties seller in a suede vice-versa two tone, cut in malleably soft suede, in beige with a hunter green collar, pockets and belt that could be reversed, should the mood of the day dictate it, to hunter green as the dominant colour, with beige effects: a combination that also came in beige and yellow or honey and brown, the body of the suit being in any of these essentially leafy autumn colours.

Still with an eye to pushing androgyny to a seamless join, as the decade converged on an almost undifferentiated look for the sexes, Stephen looking to the romantic image of the dandy, as personified by both sexes, created stunningly embroidered white tricel peasant shirts, and matching blouse designs, with the attention-demanding blue and black motif on each, emphasised on

John Stephen's updates on the Russian peasant blouse were adopted as unisex.

the elbow of the sleeves, tapering to tight elongated three-button cuffs, as well as running down from the collar to the hem, the long-pointed extravagantly high-collared shirt, worn open on its three-button fastening. In the Carnaby Street photo shoot designed to spike up interest in one of John Stephen's outstanding later shirt creations, decorative but never burdened by *trompe-l'oeil* excess, London's leading young female impersonator Mr Pussy, alias Alan Amaby, and a personal friend of Mike McGrath's, was brought in to model a tapered midi dress employing an identical pattern, while the blonde Cindy Steeden wore a blouse matching the shirt, with both coming in white with a red and black or green and black motif to arrest the eye in an instantaneously enhanced detail-moment. Only John Stephen, with his gender-dissolving bias, would have conceived of promoting a shirt through a trio of wearers involving a man, Eric Juhasz, a drag queen Mr Pussy, and a dumb blonde Cindy Steeden, as an instance of unapologetically transgendering clothes through a triumvirate of wearers unified in giving the design appetent sexual appeal. With all items available from the John Stephen Department Store, 33–34 Carnaby Street, the shirt retailed at £8, the blouse at £5, and the midi dress at £7, with the man's shirt slightly flared in the sleeves and bottle-necked at the generous cuffs, by far the most commanding of the sexually ambidextrous designs.

John Stephen was now in competition with an opportunistic raft of transient King's Road fashion outlets that included the newly-opened Beatles' Apple Tailoring at 161 King's Road, a shop that together with the spectacular in Baker Street represented the retail division of Apple Merchandising. A launch party celebrating the opening of Apple Tailoring was staged at Club Dell'Aretusa in the King's Road, for the frothy velveteen-dressed popocracy, with John Lennon and his partner Yoko Ono, appearing in public together for the first time in the sunny ambience of late afternoon Chelsea. But the expensively manufactured clothes, smacking of repurposed designs lifted from contemporary sources, including Stephen, Michael Rainey, Ossie Clark and inevitably Nigel Waymouth's Granny Takes A Trip, failed to stand out as significantly individual, and the outlet dissolved within a year, submerged by pilfering shop staff, flagrant mismanagement, and symptomatic of the chaotic times, stoned accounting practices.

And while John Stephen was forced of financial necessity to abandon the idea of investment in the small shops that had consolidated his reputation, like His Clothes, Mod Male, Domino and Male West One, and to think in terms of expansionist stores, like the block-shaped John Stephen Department Store on Carnaby Street, the sixties as a decade were losing fizz, and with it the edgy linearity in clothes that had through Stephen's conception created the look. Even the sunlight filtered through the polluted West End appeared to be losing tone, the full-on euphoric Vitamin C orange of the light appearing dustier, and less concentrated in its magnitude, as it highlighted a generation journeying on bad LSD towards its inevitable event-horizon. The consolidated effects of hippy culture were to soften Stephen's line, converting even his incisive spear-pointed collars into round travesties of the kind sold by Granny Takes A Trip, and made fashionable by the likes of the London-based exponents of psychedelic rock, Cream and the Jimi Hendrix Experience, often worn with revamped flying jackets, and heavily brocaded military tunics. LSD as a drug, in its reverie-inducing capacity to slow down time in the user's space, and in the detailed chemical documentation of concentrated visual imagery it provided, effectively undid Stephen's line, replacing it in terms of fashion with patterns that appeared to imitate the drug's vocabulary of imagery. A little observed fact in the fundamental difference between Stephen, and say Michael Rainey or Nigel Waymouth, as his King's Road contemporaries, was that John Stephen never took LSD, or did recreational drugs, whereas both Rainey and Waymouth used their personal experimentation with substances, including acid, as the highly influential pointer sign-posting their taste in colourfully embellished clothes. Stephen's own elegant sobriety of dress, white shirts at a time of floral extravaganzas, suits at a time of Nehrus and velvet pantaloons, and short hair at a time of afro-perms fuzzed to the shoulders, kept him conspicuously an acid-free Mod, at a time when the poppier King's Road boutiques, shared drugs with their drop-in clientele, in a hothouse ethos of pot and druggy deliberation over purchases. Stephen's shops on the contrary were drug-free, and substances outlawed, and no matter the informal management in terms of customer relations, staff were nonetheless observant of the Stephen/Franks expectation of required protocol.

If the Rolling Stones had been major fashion-markers throughout the sixties in terms of influencing how men dressed, due to their gender-subversive attitude, then changes within the band's internal politics, as well as a deepening submersion in the shape-shifting promptings of LSD, were also symptomatic of the times and the accelerated warp on which the decade was burning out. The increasing alienation of the founder member Brian Jones, whose exaggerated transvestism, drug convictions, and opposing musical tangents had made him into a liability, was a contention that churned deeply in the band's disordered metabolism. Having played with the idea of psychedelic rock on *Their Satanic Majesties Request*, fired their sharp-dressing manager Andrew Loog Oldham, who like John Stephen suffered from bipolar disorder, abandoned touring, and returned to their lacerating R&B origins, with a No 1 hit single, *Jumping Jack Flash*, the Stones were anxious to separate themselves from the increasingly dysfunctional Jones. Almost as a commemorative Jones last-rites the band staged a musical variety show, directed by Michael Lindsay-Hogg, in the form of a burlesque Victorian big top called the Rolling Stones' Rock and Roll Circus.

Lined up on the 10 December 1968, for a projected apocalyptic bash in a television studio, in Stonebridge Park, Wembley, the Stones dressed as macaronic troubadours were joined by a power-pointed The Who, a chaotic the Dirty Mac (John Lennon, Eric Clapton, Mitch Mitchell and Keith Richards), Yoko Ono, Jethro Tull and Marianne Faithfull in the attempt through a literal and figurative circus to capture the delirious optimism of an era endgaming its way towards extinction. With the wardrobe credits given to John McKenna, the Stones dressed for the part, as circus harlequins in top hats, brocaded scarlet tunics, faux-Edwardian froth and cake makeup, and performing to an audience in a tent with railway stock, looked in a dazed state of whiteout sleeplessness in an epic extravaganza that continued for over eighteen hours. Almost no vestige of the John Stephen look remained in their flamboyant assemblage of stage clothes, with the dissipated Mandrax-dulled Brian Jones choosing to perform in a purple velvet suit, his long peroxided hair, Schiaperelli pink lipstick, and Swarvoski flashes of paste highlighting his state of analgesic confusion, as his dulled technique attempted to coax magic from his slide guitar playing. With Jagger in skin-fit damson hipsters, with a menacing broad leather belt, as an accentuation of skinny-rib androgyny, and Keith Richards wearing a black pirate patch, and resembling a one-eyed impresario, dressed in polka dots and a suede jerkin, the Stones had pushed sartorial melange into a parodic confusion of period mismatches that converged on chaos. With Jagger's look being groomed for the role of the sybaritic, reclusive rock star, he was in the process of playing in the Donald Cammell conceived, London-based movie *Performance*, involving the study of a gangster, a rock star, and a number of sexually-compliant women, his reinvention of masculinity for the part appeared to have reached an optimal point of transformation. It was an image that had moved a long way from John Stephen's initial modality of the look, in which predominantly innovative Italian influenced leisure-wear was updated by the advent of pop, in a way not so dissimilar to the Stones' starting point in inflecting black American blues music with infectious white pop hooks.

9

DON'T TURN AROUND

In the same way as Pete Townshend of The Who had been shocked into the realisation that Mod was finally over by seeing his compatriot Eric Clapton's devolution into a perm, supported by a choice of colour-soaked hippie clothes, so the Rolling Stones' Rock and Roll Circus was a public declaration of the look's final dispersal into undisciplined confectionised travesty. But ultimately Mod, defined by Stephen's look, no matter how it was relegated to a sixties subtext, was an unkillable phenomenon, maintained in part by his continued line, and a cult whose distinct fashion permutations always came back to the economic resources of modernism as a paradigm. In fact Mods, as stylists, rather like John Stephen, went conservative in the face of prolif-erating dandy bohemianism, regrouping as a constant to wear jackets that had off-centre six-inch or even smaller vents, patch pockets with horizontal flaps, and raised edging on the seams, and were an obvious throwback to the American Ivy League look that had preceded Stephen's recreation of it along European lines. Apart from John Stephen stock, the ubiquitously popular Squire Shop in Soho's Brewer Street became a centrepiece attraction to Mods who proved resistant to unstructured notions of hippie dress. The Squire Shop sold wing-tip Royal shoes in maroon and black French Cordovan horse leather with plain caps, American trousers with a one-inch cuff, and Careers Club shirts with soft roll button-down collars, in GI blue and white, with a pleated back and a button positioned at the rear of the collar to secure the roll. Harringtons, Italian cardigans in multiple colours, and trousers worn with clip-on scarlet braces flooded the Squire Shop racks, as Mods regrouped

with the self-assurance of a cult who having created the look in mainstream fashion, now went underground in order to maintain it. Integral Mods kept their hair short, and still went to John Stephen's shops for pastel shirts, custom-made suits, and the infallible stand-out cut of his wool and cotton trousers. With the Squire Shop run by John Simons, who together with Jeff Kwinter had set up the popular Brooks Brothers exec look the Ivy Shop on Richmond Hill Rise in 1964, stock catered for Mods who were into wearing rakishly angled trilby hats, three-quarter length crombies in suede, loafers and Gibsons, skinny ties and the obligatory button-down with a stylistically manipulated roll, part executive, part louche, but always incorrigibly modern in its look. Mod protocol demanded that you never undid the buttons on your button-down, and to do so was déclassé, tasteless and simply uncool: a violation of your John Stephen, Ben Sherman or Career's Club shirt.

The sixties as a persistently documented decade, including the locale of Carnaby Street as London's centre of gravity to acquisitive young tourists, had grown loud with self-destructing excess as the ethos imploded under its own drug-hazed momentum and arrogant belief in its own indestructible continuity. Stephen's clothes-based, frenetic alley had by 1969 become a slice of speculatively aggrandised real estate, its reputation for selling specific Carnaby Street merchandise, preceding the diminishing quality of its clothes, and his individual fall off as a designer effortlessly creating fashion firsts. Alfresco events including street musicians like the Happy Wanderers, the virtuoso busker Dan Partridge, and the recognisable chanting of members of Radha Krishna Temple, were matched by the novelty attraction of John Stephen's customised horse and black carriage, stamped with the gold Stephen logo that made a leisurely reconnaissance of the West End as a form of advertising, maintained by its elderly driver. The need to compete for attention, to be noticed in a street of livid, iconoclastically psychedelic colour, in which shop fronts had become pop art, extended to extremes of publicity like Warren Gold's PR having the dyed platinum-haired DJ Jimmy Savile, distributing free bags of money from an upstairs window, to promote the new Lord John shop. As a further exhibitionistic surge of PR Irvine Sellars for the opening of his shop Lady Jane's Birdcage, the third in his trio of Lady Jane outlets, had a girl in a black micro-bikini hoisted twenty feet above the street in a birdcage as an instance of spontaneous hoopla, part circus, part sensational defiance, and part pre-punk. Stephen's originally marginalised peacock alley, was also developing lucrative ventricles that extended deep into Carnaby Court, an L-shaped enclave of boutiques, with a concrete causeway making a right turn into Foubert's Place, with ten shops on the ground floor, and

The sixties saw the renaissance of the foppish dandy in ruffles, satin and velvet. John Stephen always got it right.

more above, and with a café reached by a wrought-iron spiral staircase. The Lord John Shop and the John Stephen Trouser Shop faced each other across the entrance to the arcade, in Carnaby Street proper, with fierce competition for the tenancies of both shops. Stephen's small shops like Tre Camp and Mod Male had been absorbed into the John Stephen Department Store, the original His Clothes had become His Clothes Her Clothes Their Records, as Stephen, like Warren Gold, started to think in the expansionist terms that would take him into Oxford Street within a year of the sixties terminating, and effectively kill the inimitable kudos to a label that had started as the gateway to the look; the coloured tag that coded modernism into the wearer, in the way a drug is metabolised by the user.

The radical makeover of the street, as a concession to its having become a luminous global centre for youth culture, was one that admitted the John Stephen Scottish Shop, Henry Moss' Pussy Galore, as a provocatively named girls' outlet, Tommy Roberts' Kleptomania, a serendipity store for Victoriana, uniforms, hippy bells and kaftans, that had started out in Kingly Street, before Roberts and his partner Charlie Simpson, had paid £18,000 to lease a lucrative high-end shop front on Carnaby Street. There was also the Carnaby Market, built on two floors in Beak Street, where twenty tiny boutiques competed for space and customers with the same entrepreneurial flair as the maverick first-timers in fashion with all their eclectic bravura pioneering for attention at the recently opened Kensington Market. If John Stephen's iconic success as an independent served as the template for the often ingenious Carnaby Market boutique owners, then it was ten years too late to be starting out, and Stephen's own expansionist politics within the street had disrupted the ideal of the small shop as a self-sufficient nucleus and factory on which he had founded his reputation. Stephen's Drugstore on the corner of Beak and Carnaby Street had been reconstructed as a department store, the walls forced out with the same necessary re-visioning that had transformed the seminal His Clothes into a dual shop, with a round counter for shirts and ties at the entrance, and customer traffic moving round it into sections of suits, jackets, trousers, leading in turn to a circular Her Clothes section.

As John Stephen looked out of his office window on the fourth floor of the Stephen fortress at 33–34 Carnaby Street, at the saturated rapid-fire density of crowds drawn to the street, no longer for the exclusive limited runs of his clothes, but for the international sensation preceding the place, he could feel in his burn-out a corresponding symptom of the decade's exhaustion. He could put himself into rehab, but he couldn't rehabilitate time: the accelerated changes of the fastest moving decade in history in terms of the continuous update of fashion, had made him rich, but also deprived him of the time in which to create, as his days became subsumed by admin and the incessant demands of the media on his time.

In 1968, worried about a persistent lump that had appeared on the left side of his neck, and wouldn't go away, Stephen was, after tests, diagnosed with cancer in its early stages, and treated at London's Royal Marsden Hospital, several times a week, with primitive radiotherapy aimed at burning off the lump. Made to sit inside a lead face-mask, surges of radiation were beamed on the cancer site with the residual effects of burnt skin scarring the site and spreading down into Stephen's hairline, the immediate disfigurement causing Stephen severe psychological distress. The nature of his illness was kept secret even from his family, with only Bill Franks and Frank Merkell sharing the knowledge, and Franks accompanying Stephen on his hospital visits to offer necessary emotional support. Characteristically, Stephen returned directly to work after each radiotherapy session, permitting no concessions in his ramped up business schedule on account of his illness. The diagnosis, personally shattering to Stephen, was in part a warning that the chronic overreach of his accelerated energies was seriously undermining his health, although little adjustment was made in his exhaustively overstrained lifestyle, and no form of relaxation programme ever entertained by way of therapy.

If the demise of the sixties in America is often signified by the infamous Altamont Speedway free concert, staged in a muddy wastelanded field in Livermore, California, on 9 December 1969, with the Rolling Stones presiding over satanic rock ceremonies, and at which a black youth Meredith Hunter was stabbed and clubbed to death by members of Hell's Angels, then the death of the sixties in Britain arguably finds its marker in the murder of Brian Jones, the seminal Rolling Stone, on 2 July 1969 at his Cotchford Farm home, a mile east of the tiny Sussex village of Hartfield. Jones, as the immeasurably arrogant, full-on, self-destructive, partying pretty boy, oversensitive and at variance with his band members, had come through his sexually ambiguous look to personify the image of sixties male androgyny. His death, or rather murder, putatively attributable to builders working on the renovation of his property, but equally to the possibility of a contract killing organised by the infrastructure of East End gofers who worked for the Stones as minders, and drivers, quickly entered into the domain of judicial disinformation. Jones, who had been fired from the Rolling Stones by a delegation of three, Jagger, Richards and Watts, descending on him at Cotchford on June 9, with an ultimatum to quit, cushioned by a pay off of £100,000, and the promise of an annuity of £20,000 a year for as long as the band existed, had been found dead at the bottom of his blue-tiled swimming pool, not the supposed casualty of a paroxysmic asthma attack, or a blackout caused by drug abuse, as was widely propagated by the press, but the victim of an undeniable homophobically motivated murder, whether premeditated or spontaneous. It was Jones, a regular and fastidious customer at the John Stephen shops in Carnaby Street, and particularly at John Stephen Custom Built, who far more than the rivalrously coquettish Jagger, had been consistent throughout the sixties, the paradigm for pushing the boundaries of what it was considered permissible for men to wear, a stage further. It was Brian Jones whose polka-dot, paisley and floral John Stephen shirts, tartan hipsters, white shoes and range of inspired suits, splashy ties and velvet blazers, who stood out as the clothes' detailist, who a generation, including Jagger, copied in their pursuit of the look. If the excessive use of alcohol and hard drugs had contributed towards the end of his short life, to Jones abandoning the look for exaggerated drag underpinned by grottoes of costume jewellery, then he was nonetheless one of the crucial markers describing sixties' men's clothes, and one of the most innovative dressers of his ubiquitously costume-changing generation.

Two days after Brian Jones' death, the Rolling Stones commemorated their estranged ex-band founder member, with a pre-booked free concert given in Hyde Park on 5 July 1969, with Jagger who had originally chosen a snakeskin suit made for the occasion by Ossie Clark, coming on stage in a Michael Fish white moiré over voile mini dress for men, worn over loose-fitting white trousers. The white chemise was based on traditional Greek military uniforms, and provoked outrage from a press intimidated by so flagrant a statement of cross-dressing androgyny. The look that had begun with John Stephen's pastel-coloured hipsters, and candy pink and peacock-blue denim button-downs in 1956, in Soho's Beak Street, as a re-evaluation of received notions of masculinity, had pursued a mutable trajectory for over a decade to culminate three miles west of Soho, in the size zero figure of a pouty Mick Jagger, electrifying the crowds in a ruffled dress, designed by the John Stephen trained Michael Fish, as the apogee of reconfigured masculinity.

The end of the sixties was still business as usual for a dynamically committed John Stephen, who even if his creative incentive appeared diminished, and his extraordinary originality as a designer and retailer partially used up, was still overseeing a lucrative expansionist business that would go public in 1972, before selling out to Raybeck in 1976, for what would prove the liquidation of the John Stephen signature. John Stephen, despite his first encounter with cancer, was an amazingly youthful thirty-two in 1969, old to the generation he dressed, still outwardly inscrutable about his personal life, still living in upmarket Jermyn Street, famous, but as yet too much absorbed into his times to have been credited with his part in having created the look.

An exhaustive and debilitating creative decade on Stephen's part, had been eaten up in a furore of high-octane energy work, in which there was no overlap, no allowance for any secondary pursuit in Stephen's singularly driven life. His days were spent pitching his creative energies to maximum potential into a Soho alley that was the physical extension of himself, with unnerving velocity, and with the metabolic burn of someone living a year in a month, a week in a day. There was no available time in his unremitting schedule to look back and evaluate his achievements, only the constant pressurised demands on himself to keep on reinventing the look, or go under. His personal frustration was that as a designer, there was nothing tangible to retrieve: whatever he created, whether it was a one-off shirt, cut from a provocatively unrepeatable remnant, was sold, dispersed and eventually discarded, as is the ephemeral legacy of fashion in which the original continues only in the form of a drawing or a photo.

By the late sixties, Stephen's promotions almost uniformly employed the Carnaby Street sign, as a brand name, with his campaign 'Shop where you see the John Stephen symbol of quality' headed by the recreation of the sign 'City of Westminster Carnaby Street W1,' almost as an admission that the street rather than Stephen's clothes were the sustainable selling point. A Mike McGrath press sheet at the time focused exclusively on Stephen's international sensation, with substantial merchandise exports to Melbourne and Sydney, as a result of magazine features, and with projected futures in China, Japan and South America. There were also optimistic plans for the opening of 150–200 Stephen boutiques worldwide, within the next three years, as optimal spin, aimed at reversing the truth of declining sales, at a time when Stephen had a complement of over 200 people in his employment. Even the iconic Beatles were by the time of their Abbey Road recording sessions in September 1969, in a state of dissolution, due to disruptive tensions between band members, as opposed to the regenerated Rolling Stones, busy gunning stadium decibels for dollars across America, with Mick Jagger wearing orange and black Ossie Clark Halloween creations, as his luciferian stage persona. London Mod bands like the Small Faces, the Dave Clark Five, the Action, the Creation and the original punkish Pretty Things, all of who had lifted their look from Stephen's shops, had mostly broken up, with members dispersed into other, more enduring bands. And while it was still paramount for rock stars to dress individually for the stage, the competitive edge focused on the look had lost intensity, and the exact height of a white collar worn on a lipstick-pink shirt, with double rows of grey square buttons, was no longer the focal point of a band achieving fashion credits for a TV appearance in which the clothes were largely purchasable at John Stephen shops. The competitive edge to sustain the look had gone with the defection of Mods from the street, and Stephen's wired assistants no longer ran competitively from small shop to small shop, trousers or jackets over their shoulders, anxious to make a sale that would increase their commission.

The blurring of definition brought about by the randomised, eclectic, collage-effect of late sixties' menswear, so too its popularisation by the chains, even D. H. Evans of Oxford Street had Juliet Glynn Smith design psychedelic posters in Jaffa orange, yellow and emerald mandala patterns, to promote their investment in the look, had resulted in an inevitable saturation level. Other stores were quick to cash in, with Peter Robinson's clothes democratised Top Shop, employing Twiggy as a model for a photo-shoot dressed in new synthetic fibres, and with the fashion-obsolete Oxford Street fortress Selfridges, under the ownership of Charles Clore, investing a million pounds in their updated Miss Selfridge, a floor of mirrors and breezily affordable skirts and sumptuous velvets, aimed specifically and with commercial temerity at young women under twenty-five, as its projected mass market.

By 1969, two out of three Mary Quant shops had closed, and the site of her seminal King's Road Bazaar sold for repurposed development. The utopian optimism that had culturally infused the sixties with an orange-tinged idealistic euphoria was showing erosion of parts, like a Boeing's circuitry, eaten systematically by uric acid molecularised from the cabin toilet. If John Stephen, like most of his contemporaries, lived partly in denial of the de-accelerating process of a decade that had begun to shatter through sheer excess, it was because he was caught up in a work momentum so integrated into the times that it was unstoppable. He was successful in ways that defied all previous conceptions of menswear design, and retailing, and in establishing the look had succeeded in breaking an entire system, and with it not only the inherent conservatism of men's clothes, but the arbitration of couture over seasonal collections. And in the process he had got rich. In a *Reveille* real-life rags-to-riches story called 'What Money Means To Me', Stephen spoke pragmatically of its function in his life. 'Often I have been asked what I enjoy most about the fortune I have made. Well, I do have a lot of clothes, but you would expect that. I do not need to worry about the rent of my West End flat, or the mortgage on my house in Brighton, or the six pounds of beef a day for Prince, my white alsatian. Yet at the same time, money no longer has the same meaning for me as when I was earning seven pounds a week and trying to scrape together a little capital for my first shop. Today, money is represented by a set of figures on a balance sheet. Those figures tell me if I can go on expanding, or whether I must cut back. For me, to be able to expand is more important than anything else. Having fun, going to parties, dining in expensive restaurants? Honestly, I do not have the time, unless it is in the interests of business. Most evenings I am in my boardroom office in Stephen House until nine or ten, or even later. But then it is what I like doing. Besides, I am in Carnaby Street, and just being there is pleasure in itself for me.'

Stephen also used the feature that finds him at his most basically utilitarian, as a means of recapitulating on the merits of colleagues like Frank Merkell and Myles Antony, both of who had excelled in their respective capacities in working for the Stephen organisation. With his emphasis placed on ideas and dynamic, irrespective of age, Stephen used the examples of Merkell and Antony, to endorse his thesis that within his business infrastructure, there was a place for individual talent to come through, and be given licence to pursue an energetic solo trajectory. 'Six years ago, Frank Merkell began with us as a shop assistant. In 1965 I put him in charge of a new line in mod women's wear we were embarking on in a Carnaby Street basement. It went very well under his management. Now he is responsible for all our women's wear outlets and is a director of the company. Frank is twenty-five. Another young man who has risen fast is Myles Antony who joined us five years ago as a window dresser. He was just eighteen, but you could see he had flair. Today he is my arts director, responsible for the interior designs, décor and display of all our shops. Seniority does not matter to me. Our wage scales are not graduated by age, as they generally are in the retail trade. Last summer we engaged a schoolboy as a temporary salesman on ten pounds a week plus commission. He was soon averaging twenty-two pounds a week – not bad for a sixteen-year old. He is now on our permanent staff, and will serve you if you go into Male West One – one of our Carnaby Street shops. His name is Laurence Whitcombe.'

Stephen remained full-on plugged into a source so explosive that he couldn't for direct involvement properly sight the idea of its eventual closure. Beginning in the fifties simply with Dutch-boy denim caps, see through black Aertex vests, leather posing pouches and crotch-impacting hipsters, he had fed an archetypal butch gay look into incipient Mod expectations of androgyny, and finally into mainstream assimilation as the international currency of accepted young menswear. The changes had happened so fast, so contagiously, by a generation moving at the speed of escape velocity towards shattering, that it seemed to the participants as though the sixties had no origins and no forseeable termination. It was the intensity of the times impacted like a flameout supernova, and John Stephen lived them to the full through the expression of his work as the clothes' detailist who never tired of reinventing the way men looked.

A survey by Westminster Council in 1968 revealed that an average of 15,000 pedestrians, and 2,000 cars past through Carnaby Street each day, with double and sometimes triple those figures at the weekends, a concentration that in its density of foot traffic, reflected entirely on Stephen's name for the street's focal attention and hyperactive commerce as a dollar earner. What had begun in 1958 with Stephen's The Man's Shop, as the solitary representative of transitional cutting edge fashion, attracting at most ten customers a day, in a downmarket bombed alley, with plague victims compressed beneath the foundations of a street engineered by Richard Tyler in 1686, had grown literally as the physical extension of John Stephen's creative dynamic and inspirational selling power, into London's busiest thoroughfare proportionate to space. The run-down, maverick, bisexually orientated qualities of a cult-boosted alley, initially dominated by teenage Mods in the early sixties, had been replaced by the commercial packaging of the precinct. There were now colourful window boxes of racy striped petunias, and geraniums, the ten lamp posts decorated with wrought-iron flowers, flags and the colourful bannering of shops, all ratified by the Carnaby Street Traders' Association, with Tom Salter of Gear as chairman, and John Stephen as secretary, accounting for the vertiginous commercial benefits to be realised by converting the street into the equivalent of a pedestrianised arcade for tourists. Old neighbourhood attractions remained viable in the form of George Grech's Cosmo Snacks, a local café unanimously popular with stars performing at the nearby London Palladium, in Argyll Street, and the Shakespeare's Head pub, where the landlord Barry Doherty was celebrated for the pub's homemade fare, including a cholesterol-elevating steak and kidney pie that was a favourite dish of John Stephen's.

John Stephen in his Jermyn Street apartment with Prince, and a rare instance of him not wearing a tie.

Carnaby Street was still unprecedentedly big business, as John Stephen intractably manoeuvred his silver Rolls Royce convertible KWS 55 through Soho's tortuous alleys on any late evening in 1969, in the direction of his Jermyn Street home – a distance he could have walked in fifteen minutes – only that the car like the street was also an important projection of himself. Soho was as usual a lowlife, lowlight arena of available girls, selling sex in spike heels and mini-skirts, spilling from Meard Street alleys into Wardour

and Brewer Street, restaurants, and clubs crowding on nightlife, bohemians, impoverished residents, pop stars, pimps, locals and tourists, all meshed into the common pursuit of recreational pleasure. And over on the Piccadilly marker, there were emaciated junkies redeeming heroin prescriptions from the 24-hour Boots pharmacy, and adjacent to it spotty rent boys talking indigenous polari on the black curved railings, below the flashy blue, red and green billboard neons. Outwardly, nothing appeared demonstratively to have changed, as one decade prepared seamlessly to dissolve into the gateway opened by another. But John Stephen had, distinct from his questionably declining sales figures, an instinctive hunch, as he sat waiting in his luminous shark grey Rolls for the lights to go green, an acutely insidious warning that had been growing on him for most of the year, that the epoch was over, and that the optimal time for clothes had peaked in 1967, and was falling, not in a dramatic free-fall, but as a measurable and irredeemable decline. He was exhausted, burnt-out, carried the discernible scars of radiotherapy, had made necessary concessions to his integrity as an independent by supplying Gary Elliott's suburban and provincial branches with his clothes, and on an unconscious level wanted out before the times turned against him. The gold St Christopher medallion on its gold chain that Bill Franks had bought him from Carrington's in Regent Street, soon after they had first met, and from which he was inseparable, was secure round his neck, as a token of unconditional love that had stayed with him for fifteen years, as an emotional pivot secure above his diaphragm. On his little finger was the thinly banded blue baguette diamond that his eyes were in the habit of returning to for the stone's blue scintillating catchlights. The sixties were breaking up around him like the electronic sequences of red and blue Piccadilly neon. His life to date had been one of obsessively inspired work consolidated by the continuous growth of the John Stephen organisation. His singular vision had driven the look at its most influential into the pop charts, attracted a regular cachet of celebrities to his shops, including Mick Jagger, Richard Burton and Judy Garland, and as importantly democratised clothes for a working class Mod contingent, before scoring a relatable success across America and Europe; but no matter his reputation, his personal satisfaction had come from the sustained rush of doing, rather than from any sense of reflective achievement. Metaphorically, he was leaving the epoch he had anticipated as a youth, worked with as his particular time, helped shape, grown rich in, and risked his health to the point of becoming one of its seriously damaged casualties. Like all sixties' luminaries, Stephen would slowly fade from celebrity status, as the seventies took over with a fashion bias conditioned by the exaggerated flairs and chemises associated with glam rock, and the ripped up, deconstructed line that came with Maclaren and Westwood's punk.

It was 9.30 on the surprisingly feminine gold watch he wore partially concealed by an immaculate white cuff, the usual time for his exhaustive fourteen-hour working day to end. His clothes were quietly, flawlessly elegant, a custom-made charcoal suit, a white shirt secured by diamond-studded cuff links, his indigo Jacques Fath silk tie given individual signature by a tie-pin, his shoes polished like the black glossed cellulose on a Jaguar in a display room, his hair inverterately maintained by professional grooming. It was his unalterable look, and the invariable image he had cultivated, no matter the endlessly resourceful shape-shifting fashion changes he had personally instigated over the past fifteen years, like a speeded up fashion movie. He knew from habit, that his partner Bill Franks was already back home in their repurposed Jermyn Street apartment, busy improvising some sort of simple late supper, at which he would pick, food being a substantially lower priority than work and drink and cigars in his repertoire of personal needs. He resisted food, as he resisted sleep, preferring always to sit up in the reverberant St James' night, evolving ideas into schemas, making sketches on the backs of invoices, writing memos to himself, or speed reading thrillers, before finally submitting to the acrid tasting green and white Nembutal capsules that would shut his mind down for the brief respite of three or four hours. He had been to Carrington's earlier in the day, at 130 Regent Street, a quick snappy cross-over from his pheromone-boosting alley into a sniffy, high-end moneyed façade, and picked up the diamond and gold cuff links he had asked to have made on the premises for Bill. The blue compact leather case was secure in his pocket – and what he liked about giving was the element of surprise – the suffused glow that would radiate across Bill's face as he found the leather box placed negligently on his chair. Prince, his white Alsatian, would be waiting for the key to turn in the lock, before surging to meet him in a blizzard of white fur, so demonstratively affectionate that the collisional impact of energies sometimes knocked him backwards by their eruptive furore. Home was that, and perhaps a call to check on his young sister Rae, his favourite in the family. It was 1969, and his optimal moment had peaked and almost gone. For reasons he didn't know, for these things just happen as part of an individual's particular destiny, he had set up in clothes at the right time in the right place, for a generation waiting to intersect with his liberally colourful designs. The timing was just right: five years too early, or five years too late, and he would have missed it. He had started with nothing, chanced it, lucked it, and relied for resources on the irrepressible self-conviction that he could and would succeed in establishing the look. It was behind him, but it was largely in every aspect of sixties popular culture his extraordinary and inimitable creation. As he parked the Rolls in St James' Jermyn Street, inexpertly and with difficulty as was his way, it had started to rain he knew, steadily for the night. There would be no let up now in the persistent big city downpour. Some things in London never changed.